GEORGINA CAMPBELL'S ireland

for garden
lovers

*Gentle Journeys through
Ireland's most beautiful
gardens with delightful
places to stay along the way*

Georgina Campbell & Marianne Heron

Georgina Campbell Guides

Georgina Campbell Guides
Epicure Press
PO Box 6173
Dublin 13

website: www.ireland-guide.com
email: info@ireland-guide.com
© Georgina Campbell Guides 2006,
in accordance with the Copyright Designs and Patent Act 1988

Publishing Editor: Georgina Campbell
Gardens Editor: Marianne Heron
Research Editor: Bob Nixon

The contents of this book are believed to be correct at the time of going to press. Nevertheless the publisher can accept no responsibility for errors or omissions or changes in the details given.

Front cover photograph: Ballyvolane House, Co Cork

BACK COVER PHOTOGRAPHS:

Top, left to right: Rathmichael Lodge, Co Dublin; Glin Castle, Co Limerick; Heywood Gardens, Co Laois; Grove Gardens, Co Meath; Ballyvolane House, Co Cork

Bottom, left to right: Mulvarra House, Co Carlow; Kilfane Glen & Waterfall, Co Kilkenny; Anne's Grove, Co Cork; Beech Hill House Hotel, Co Londonderry; Glenveagh Castle Gardens, Co Donegal

REGION INTRODUCTORY PAGES:
The Merrion Hotel, Dublin; Hunter's Hotel, Co Wicklow; Altamont Gardens, Co Carlow (courtesy of Carlow Tourism); Lisselan, Co Cork; Salthill Walled Gardens, Co Donegal; Rowallane, Co Down

Acknowledgments:
Thanks are due to the many people who have made this book possible, especially the gardeners themselves, without whom there would be no book; Marianne Heron for her gardens contributions and Bob Nixon, who compiled essential information; William Nixon for assessment and photographic assistance; Terre Ireland for use of additional photographs; and Brian Darling, of The Design Station, for his professionalism and patience.

Design & Artwork: The Design Station, Dublin
Printed and bound in Spain

First published 2006 by Georgina Campbell Guides Ltd.
ISBN 1-903164-14-1
    9 781903 164143

How to Use the Guide

THE IRELAND GARDEN 'ITINERARY'
The gardens selected for this guide tend to be grouped in clusters, with the heaviest concentration in the Dublin and East Coast/Midlands Areas. In order to facilitate the most convenient use of the guide for visitors planning an itinerary, we have arranged garden entries and their corresponding hospitality recommendations, as if taking an imaginary journey around Ireland, which is broadly clockwise (counties within each section are listed in anti-clockwise order, in order to lead neatly in to the following region):

DUBLIN is listed first, followed by **EAST COAST & MIDLANDS**, an anticlockwise arc of counties encircling Dublin (Meath, Louth, Monaghan, Cavan, Longford, Westmeath, Offaly, Laois, Kildare, Wicklow); next we move south to an anti-clockwise tour of the **SOUTH-EAST** (Wexford, Carlow, Kilkenny, Tipperary, Waterford); then to the **SOUTH-WEST** (Cork, Kerry). From here we move up to the **LOWER SHANNON** (Limerick, Clare), then to the **WEST** (Galway, Mayo, Roscommon), and into the **NORTH-WEST** (Leitrim, Sligo, Donegal). We finish our tour with the six counties in the **NORTH** (Londonderry, Antrim & Belfast, Down, Armagh, Tyrone & Fermanagh).

Location /Establishment name
- Within counties, the cities, towns and villages are arranged in alphabetical order with the exception of Dublin city, where postal codes are arranged in numerical order. (Even numbers are south of the River Liffey, and uneven numbers on the north, with the exception of Dublin 8 which straddles the river. Dublin 1 and 2 are most central; Dublin 1 is north of the Liffey, Dublin 2 is south of it.) Within each district, establishments are listed in alphabetical order.
- Entries are arranged alphabetically within location

Telephone numbers
- Codes are given for use within the Republic of Ireland / Northern Ireland. To call ROI from outside the jurisdiction, the code is +353, dropping the first digit (zero) from the local code.
- To call Northern Ireland from the ROI, replace the 028 code with 048.

Category(ies) of Entries
Recommendations - comprise of selected **GARDENS** (identifiable by the **green tinted pages**) and places which garden lovers will find most agreeable to **STAY & EAT**. These are usually conveniently close to selected gardens; **in some cases, these hotels or country houses also have important gardens**.

Admission Charges - approximate amounts charged are given where possible, but should only be taken as a rough guide; in most cases, the rate is €3-€6, with discounted rates given to groups, OAPs and children,

Garden Details - it is always wise to phone to check details (opening times, wheelchair access, toilet facilities, tea rooms), using the contact details given in each entry. Gardens, especially private gardens, may sometime be closed, for a variety of reasons; however, many private gardens are willing to open at any time by arrangement.

Further Information - available from Failte Ireland and Northern Ireland Tourist Board, and local tourist information offices. See also our listed Additional Information (page 255)

Address/contact details - includes an email address and website address if available (please phone/fax/email ahead for additional directions if required)
Maps are intended only for reference / planning itineraries: Ordnance Survey maps are recommended when travelling; available from Tourist Information offices

Prices & Opening Hours -
Please note that prices and opening hours are given as a guideline only, and may have changed; check before travelling or when making a reservation. Prices in the Republic of Ireland are given in Euro and those in Northern Ireland are in pounds Sterling.

Contents

Editor's Introduction   6

ENTRIES (By Area):
▸ DUBLIN: City and County   7
▸ EAST COAST & MIDLANDS: *Meath, Louth, Monaghan,*   35
  Cavan, Longford, Westmeath, Offaly, Laois, Kildare, Wicklow
▸ SOUTH-EAST: *Wexford, Carlow, Kilkenny, Tipperary, Waterford*   89
▸ SOUTH-WEST: *Cork, Kerry*   133
▸ LOWER SHANNON: *Limerick, Clare*   189
▸ WEST: *Galway, Mayo, Roscommon*   199
▸ NORTH-WEST: *Leitrim, Sligo, Donegal*   221
▸ NORTH: *Londonderry, Antrim & Belfast, Down, Armagh,*   233
  Tyrone, Fermanagh

PAGE REFERENCES BY COUNTY:
Dublin City & County   8
County Carlow   101
County Cavan   47
County Clare   194
Cork City   134
County Cork   147
County Donegal   224
County Galway   200
County Kerry   177
County Kildare   61
County Kilkenny   112
County Laois   57
County Leitrim   —
County Limerick   190
County Longford   48
County Louth   41
County Mayo   217
County Meath   36
County Monaghan   44
County Offaly   53
County Roscommon   215
County Sligo   222
County Tipperary   118
County Waterford   122
County Westmeath   49
County Wexford   90
County Wicklow   69

ENTRIES: NORTHERN IRELAND
County Antrim & Belfast City   241
County Armagh   —
County Down   249
County Fermanagh   —
County Londonderry   234
County Tyrone   —
Useful Contacts / Further Recommendations   255
INDEX   259

Garden Lovers' Ireland

Welcome to the first edition of Georgina Campbell's Ireland... for Garden Lovers. This book is the result of a unique partnership between an experienced garden writer, Marianne Heron, and our own team who have been travelling the length and breadth of Ireland in search of the most agreeable places to stay and the finest food on an annual basis for over two decades. Serious gardeners will, of course, find much to interest and inspire at the very special gardens selected here, but the casual visitor will also find them relaxing and rewarding - and, perhaps, feel the seeds of a real love of gardening beginning to take root. The Georgina Campbell's Ireland hospitality guides generally cover a wide range of categories, but we have always found that the long days of journeying have been eased by finding - and spending as much time as possible at - the kind of lovely leafy havens that we have selected for this book. Ireland, like much of the western world, is fast becoming an urban society leading the growing numbers of people living in the larger towns and cities to feel the need to escape from a world of concrete and (if you are lucky), small gardens and balconies, to another place - where space, serenity and natural beauty can recharge the body and soothe the soul.

We hope that this book will lead you to many wonderful places, and that you will enjoy reading and using it as much as we have enjoyed creating it - and, as everything to do with gardens is very much a work in progress, we welcome any comments you may wish to make that would help us to improve on it when preparing the next edition.

Georgina Campbell

Georgina Campbell, Editor

WITH its benign climate Ireland is a perfect paradise for plants. Add imagination, a dash of eccentricity and a rich underlay of history and you have a recipe for gardens that are as fascinating as they are diverse. Visiting Irish gardens is an adventure, there is no telling what lies beyond that tempting gate. It could be a lush subtropical jungle like Derreen in County Kerry, a romantic voyage round lakes and herbaceous borders like Altamont in County Carlow, or the riches of a passionate plant collector like the Dillon garden in Dublin.

Gardens can become the focus for a marvellous tour or a pleasant day out and I have tried to pick the most satisfying ones. One thing is certain you will come back with a store of memories glorious vistas, engaging owners, inspiring designs and maybe a special plant or two as a reminder. Happy visiting!

Marianne Heron

Marianne Heron, Gardens Editor

Dublin City
& County

Harrington Hall

Dublin 2
GUESTHOUSE

69/70 Harcourt Street Dublin 2 **Tel: 01 475 3497**
Email: harringtonhall@eircom.net Web: www.harringtonhall.com

Conveniently located close to St Stephen's Green and within comfortable walking distance of Trinity College, the National Concert Hall and the city's premier shopping areas, Henry King's fine family-run guesthouse was once the home of a former Lord Mayor of Dublin and has been sympathetically and elegantly refurbished, retaining many original features. Echoes of Georgian splendour remain in the ornamental ceilings and fireplaces of the well-proportioned ground and first floor rooms, which include a peaceful drawing room with an open turf fire. Beautiful relaxing bedrooms have sound-proofed windows, ceiling fans and lovely marbled bathrooms - and outstanding cooked breakfasts are another special feature. All round this is a welcoming alternative to a city-centre hotel, offering good value, handy to the Luas (tram), and with the huge advantage of free parking behind the building; luggage can be stored for guests arriving before check-in time (2pm). **Rooms 28** (2 junior suites, 6 superior, 3 shower only, 2 family rooms, all no smoking), Lift. B&B c. €87 pps, ss €20. Amex, Diners, MasterCard, Visa, Laser. **Directions:** Off southwest corner of St Stephen's Green (one way system approaches from Adelaide Road).

Number 31

Dublin 2
GUESTHOUSE

31 Leeson Close Lr Leeson Street Dublin 2
Tel: 01 676 5011
Email: number31@iol.ie Web: www.number31.ie

Formerly the home of leading architect Sam Stephenson, Noel and Deirdre Comer's hospitable 'oasis of tranquillity and greenery' just off St Stephen's Green makes a relaxing and interesting city centre base, with virtually everything within walking distance in fine weather. Public areas of the house are spacious and very comfortable, and fresh,

elegant bedrooms good bathrooms and nice little extras including complimentary bottled water as well as phones, TVs and tea/coffee trays. Breakfasts served at communal tables inside, and in the conservatory are not to be missed - freshly baked breads and delicious preserves, and lovely hot dishes like kippers or mushroom frittata cooked to order... Prices are moderate for central Dublin, and secure parking adds greatly to the attraction of a stay here. **Rooms 20** (all en suite & no smoking); B&B c. €75. Open all year. Amex, MasterCard, Visa. **Directions:** From St Stephen's Green onto Lr Baggot Street; turn right onto Pembroke Street, and left onto Leeson Street. Leeson Close is next left.

Dublin 2
HOTEL / RESTAURANTS

The Merrion Hotel
Upper Merrion Street Dublin 2
Tel: 01 603 0600 Fax: 01 603 0700
Email: info@merrionhotel.com Web: www.merrionhotel.com

Restaurant Patrick Guilbaud

Right in the heart of Georgian Dublin opposite the Government Buildings, the main house of this luxurious hotel comprises four meticulously restored Grade 1 listed townhouses built in the 1760s and now restored to their former glory; behind them, a contemporary garden wing has been added, overlooking two private period and formal landscaped gardens. Inside, Irish fabrics and antiques reflect the architecture and original interiors, with rococo plasterwork ceilings and classically proportioned windows - and the hotel has one of the most important private collections of 20th-century art. Public areas include three interconnecting drawing rooms (one is the cocktail bar with a log fire), with French windows giving access to the gardens. Elegant and gracious bedrooms have individually controlled air-conditioning, three telephones, personalised voice-mail with remote access, fax/modem, broadband and video conference facilities, also a mini-bar and safe (VCRs, DVDs, CD players and tea/coffee making facilities are available on request). Sumptuous Italian marble bathrooms with separate walk-in showers pamper guests to the extreme. The splendid leisure complex, The Tethra Spa, with classical mosaics, is almost Romanesque. Staff, under the excellent direction of General Manager Peter MacCann, are quite exemplary and courteous, suggesting standards of hospitality from a bygone era. There is a choice of two excellent dining options, at the hotel's **Cellar Restaurant** or city's premier restaurant, **Restaurant Patrick Guilbaud** (T: 01 676 4192; E: restaurantpatrickguilbaud@eircom.net; W: www.restaurantpatrickguilbaud.ie) which is also on site, although independently operated. Approached through a fine drawing room, where drinks are served, this restaurant is an airy, elegant room, enhanced by an outstanding collection of Irish art, and opens onto a terrace and the hotel's landscaped gardens, which make a delightful setting for drinks and al fresco dining in summer. Head chef Guillaume Lebrun has presided over this fine kitchen since the restaurant opened and is renowned for exceptional modern classic cuisine, based on the best Irish produce in season. Spa; swimming pool. Children welcome. No pets. Lift. Complimentary underground valet parking. **Rooms 143** (20 suites, 10 junior suites, 80 no-smoking, 5 for disabled). Room rate c. €370. **Cellar Restaurant:** L&D daily. Open all year. Amex, Diners, MasterCard, Visa, Laser. **Directions:** City centre, opposite Government Buildings.

Dublin 4
GUESTHOUSE

Aberdeen Lodge
53 Park Avenue Ballsbridge Dublin 4
Tel: 01 283 8155
Email: aberdeen@iol.ie   Web: www.halpinprivatehotels.com

Centrally located yet well away from the heavy traffic of nearby Merrion Road, this handsome period house in a pleasant leafy street offers all the advantages of an hotel at guesthouse prices. Elegantly furnished bedrooms and four-poster suites have air conditioning and all the little comforts expected by the discerning traveller, including a drawing room with comfortable chairs and plenty to read, and a secluded garden where guests can relax in fine weather. Staff are extremely pleasant and helpful (tea and biscuits offered on arrival), housekeeping is immaculate - and, although there is no restaurant, a Drawing Room menu offers light meals (and a wine list), and you can also look forward to a particularly good breakfast - including freshly baked breads, and delicious scrambled eggs with smoked salmon, kippers or buttermilk pancakes with maple syrup, as well as numerous variations on the traditional Irish breakfast.

The spa at a nearby sister property, Merrion Hall, is available for guests' use. Children welcome. No pets. **Rooms 17** (2 suites, 6 executive, 10 no smoking). 24 hr rooms service. B&B c. €75pps, ss €35. Residents' D about €19; all day menu also available; house wines c. €30. Open all year. Amex, Diners, MasterCard, Visa. **Directions:** Minutes from the city centre by DART; by car, take Merrion Road towards Sydney Parade DART station, then first left into Park Avenue.

Dublin 4
HOTEL / RESTAURANT

Four Seasons Hotel
Simmonscourt Road Ballsbridge Dublin 4
Tel: 01 6654000 Fax: 01 6654880
Web: www.fourseasons.com

Set in its own gardens on a three and a half acre section of the Royal Dublin Society's 42-acre show grounds, this luxurious hotel enjoys a magnificent site, allowing a sense of spaciousness while also being convenient to the city centre - the scale is generous throughout and there are views of the Wicklow Mountains or Dublin Bay from many bedrooms. Public areas are designed to impress, notably the foyer which is in the grand tradition, and the large Seasons Restaurant which overlooks a leafy courtyard; the original traditional cherrywood-panelled Lobby Bar was later joined by a second, larger bar called Ice, which provides a deliciously contemporary contrast. Accommodation is very luxurious and the air-conditioned rooms are designed to appeal equally to leisure and business guests: a choice of pillows (down and non-allergenic foam) is provided as standard, the large marble bathrooms have separate bath and shower and many other desirable features - and there's great emphasis on service, with twice daily housekeeping service, overnight laundry and dry cleaning, one hour pressing and complimentary overnight shoe shine: everything, in short, that the immaculate traveller requires. But the Spa in the lower level of the hotel is perhaps its most outstanding feature, offering a wide range of treatments and facilities - and a naturally lit 14m lap pool and adjacent jacuzzi pool, overlooking the outdoor sunken garden. **Rooms 259** (67 suites, 192 executive rooms, 4 floors no-smoking rooms, 12 rooms for disabled). Room rate from c, €275 (max. 2 guests); SC incl. **Seasons Restaurant:** B'fst, L & D served daily. Less formal dining is offered in **The Café**, open daily 11 am-midnight. Lifts. Valet parking. Open all year. Amex, Diners, MasterCard, Visa, Laser. **Directions:** Located on the RDS Grounds on corner of Merrion and Simmonscourt Roads.

Dublin 4   # Radisson SAS St Helen's Hotel
HOTEL / RESTAURANT   Stillorgan Road Dublin 4
Tel: 01 218 6000
Email: reservations.dublin@radissonsas.com   Web: www.radissonsas.com

Set in formal gardens just south of Dublin's city centre, with views across Dublin Bay to Howth Head, the fine 18th century house at the heart of this impressive modern hotel was once a private residence and, with careful restoration and imaginative modernisation, it makes a pleasing base for visits in the south Dublin area. Interesting public areas include the Orangerie Bar and a pillared ballroom with minstrels' gallery and grand piano, and bedrooms - in a modern four-storey block adjoining the main building - all have garden views (some of the best rooms also have balconies); rooms vary in size but all are comfortably furnished to a high standard in contemporary style, and have air conditioning. An informal Italian restaurant, **Talavera**, is in four interconnecting rooms in the lower ground floor - decorated in warm Mediterranean colours, it is atmospheric when candle-lit at night and one of the most popular restaurants in the area; head chef Giancarlo Anselmi specialises in authentic dishes from Tuscany and Basilicata, offering a balanced choice of dishes inspired by tradition and tailored to the modern palate - a fine antipasti buffet sets the tone for an enjoyable dining experience. *Lighter menus are also offered all day in the Orangerie Bar and Ballroom Lounge. Fitness centre; beauty salon. Garden; snooker. Children welcome. **Rooms 151** (25 suites, 70 no-smoking, 8 for disabled). Room rate from c. €155 (max. 3 guests). **Talavera Restaurant: Seats 110**. Air conditioning. Wheelchair accessible. D daily 6.30-10.30; Set D from c. €35 (early D from c.€25).Open all year. Amex, Diners, MasterCard, Visa, Laser. **Directions:** On N11, 3 miles south of the city centre.

The Dillon Garden

45 Sandford Road Ranelagh **Dublin 6**
Tel: 01 497 1308

GARDEN

Stunning garden with constantly evolving design, dramatic water feature and unusual plants

The Dillon Garden is deservedly one of the most revisited of Irish gardens. It isn't just the wonderful parade of plants unfolding through the seasons in this stunning garden that draws visitors back again and again. You simply have to keep on returning to see out what garden writer and plantswoman Helen and husband Val Dillon have done next. For this is an evolving garden, where new design ideas are introduced every year so that in the space of a decade almost every inch of the garden has been rethought.

One of the most daring changes of all involved replacing the verdant rectangle of lawn surrounded by exuberant borders in the back garden with a 30 foot long canal. Featuring a series of five shallow cascades, its edges paved in granite, the canal acts like a Baroque 'mirroir d'eaux', reflecting silvery light and establishing formality amid statuesque plants as vivid as a chorus line up. Blues and lilacs with frou frous of delphiniums, salvias and galega are offset by the glaucus foliage of *Melianthus major* and silvery *Salix exigua*, then face an opposing dance of carmines, pinks and scarlets.

It isn't just the structure of the garden that has altered, the way plants are used changes by the season. Tall plants and grasses have insinuated themselves into the scheme of things: choice salvias, Pseudopanax, the ginger lily *Hedychium forestii* (hardy yet as showy as any canna) and shimmering grasses like *Chionochola conspicua* have become the new stars of a collection featuring several thousand plants. Clashing effects also strike a new note with vivid magenta dahlias vying with coral salvias and pink fuchsias.

Helen removed the last area of grass in the garden from under a venerable apple tree. In its place stately *Helianthus* **'Lemon Queen'** heliopsis, inula, peusdopanax and paulownia now throw long legged shadows in a gravel garden.

Embarking on a new bed is one thing, revamping whole sections of an existing garden requires courage. The changes are part of Helen's search for a different approach to gardening,"What I want is mobility in the garden, it's very static when there are treasures that need to be kept in isolation, I've done that and I now have the guts to take things out, I'm always lecturing people on taking things out. And I have to shut my eyes and do it!"

Another dramatic transformation took place last autumn when the raised front garden, with beds of treasures like cherished celmesias, was swept away in favour of the calm green effect introduced by a grove of birches under planted with forms of ferns like *Polystichum setiferum* and *Onycium japonicum*.

Around the perimeter are a series of small gardens within a garden, and an enclosed area with raised scree beds is filled with plants requiring TLC, like the autumn snowdrop *Galanthus reginae-olgae*. Individual plants like the silver foliaged *Crataegus lanciata, Cestrum parqui* (stinky by day and perfumed by night to attract moths), *Strobilanthes atropupreus* behaving like a shrub, and *Desmodium elegans* catch the eye. But of course they may in time be replaced by something equally fascinating!

Open March & Jul-Aug, daily 2-6; Apr-Jun & Sep, Sun only 2-6. Not suitable for children or wheelchairs; no dogs; plant sales. Admission c. €5.

National Botanic Gardens

Glasnevin Dublin 9
Tel: 01 837 7596

GARDEN

Ireland's premier botanican and horticultural establishment - a rewarding and attractive place for gardeners and non-gardeners alike.

These extensive gardens on the north of Dublin city contain an important plant collection which includes approximately 20,000 species and cultivars. Features worth travelling for include include some stunning herbaceous displays, rose garden, rockery, vegetable garden, arboretum, extensive shrub borders and wall plants. The four ranges of glasshouses include the recently restored Victorian Curvilinear Range. There is a restaurant but it does not always match the standard of the gardens; just across from the main gate, **Addison Lodge** (01 837 3534) offers wholesome pub food and the lovely **Andersons Food Hall & Café** is nearby at The Rise, Glasnevin (Tel: 01 837 8394). Gardens open: Summer Mon-Sat 9-6, Sun 11-6; Winter Mon-Sat 10-4.30, Sun 11-4.30. Glasshouses are closed at earlier times, and at 12.45-2 each day unless otherwise posted. Guided tours (1 hour) available, c. €1.90. Times and other information posted in Education and Visitor Centre. Children welcome; no dogs; mostly wheelchair accessible. **Directions:** 3.5km north from centre of Dublin, off Botanic Road.

Airfield Gardens

Uppper Kilmacud Road Dundrum **Dublin 14**
Tel: 01 298 4301
Email: trust@airfield.ie Web: www.airfield.ie

GARDEN

Victorian garden with contemporary makeover and unusual plants.

In their day the late Misses Overend, Letitia (b.1880) and Naomi (b.1900) were a legend. There are lots of colourful recollections about the sisters from the way they gave lifts to local school children who were able to recite the registration numbers of their wonderful vintage cars, to their involvement with the St John's Ambulance Brigade.

Airfield, where the sisters ran a model farm with a herd of jersey cows, is their legacy to the city and was left in trust to the public. The gardens around the 1820s house now reflect both the old world charm of a long established garden and a bold new planting scheme very much in the pioneering spirit of the sisters.

In the walled garden at the heart of the estate, the contrast between the traditional cruciform layout of paths edged in precision clipped box and the blowsy newcomers - burly rudbeckias, *Salvia sclarea turkestana,* statuesque artichokes, *Maclea cordata* and a host of shimmering swaying grasses - is brilliant. Like happy champagne drunks, the plants refuse to behave primly and there is the odd surprise guest - banana palms and the glistening black berries of the Joe Pie-plant to liven things up even further. In the midst of all this exuberant display the rectangular sections laid out around a circle of hornbeam contain traditional rosaries planted with old roses like *R* **'Souvenir de St Annes *R* Comte de Chambord, 'Fantin Latour'** *R* **de Rescht,** an orchard with unusual fruits like medlars and mulberries, a knot garden of herbs, and a lily pond. The tea garden on the terrace looks out over a U shaped bed of yet more exotic planting with *Verbena bonariensis, Miscanthus sinensis* **'Zebrinus'** and *Ferna Osten.*

Guarded by an art deco gate twined with a wrought iron serpent, the yew walk with corseted Florencecourt yews has an exotic shrub border (the green catkins of *Itea ilicifolia* and the glory flower *Clerodendrum bungei* are particularly eye catching) and leads on to the soothing lawns where Wellingtonians sweep the grass with their skirts. On the far side of the walled garden, frost tender plants like aeoniums and tibuchina have their summer break outside the green house; there an inspirational garden packed with new grasses whispers to herbaceous plants,(sedums, Japanese anemones echiums and heleniums) around wood chip paths. And beyond are walks that invite exploration, past the orchard patrolled by speckled hens and geese, past the Garden Heaven Vegetable Garden, round the boundaries, through the flower meadow, or round the evocatively named Golden Path.

With a farm and car museum, paddocks with Thelwellesque ponies and a thoughtfully provided picnic area, there is a lot to see and do on family outings.

Open Tue-Sat, 10-5; Sun 11-5. Restaurant, gift shop, car museum and farm museum. Admission c.€4.

Glendale Gardens

14 Woodside Drive Rathfarnham Dublin 14
Tel: 01 490 5922
Email: mrc7@eircom.net

GARDEN

Inspirational suburban garden full of clever ideas.

There is nothing like a new bed as any gardener knows, and in Noelle Anne's garden there is bound to be some exciting new addition. Within this beautifully conceived plan there are five gardens within a third of an acre full of intriguing ideas.

A pergola swagged with creamy white *R* **'Alberic Barbier'**, ingeniously trained on chains, acts as the main lateral axis of the garden. Beneath this, contained by meticulously trimmed box, is a potager of salads and herb and beyond are three gardens within a garden. Designed by Dominic Murphy in brick and gravel, with a terracotta urn as a focal point, the Mediterranean garden has raised beds with all manner of tender silver leaved plants from eidelweiss to celmisias sheltering under a *Cornus* **'Eddies White Wonder'**. Frost tender plants in pots - like a protea and an agave spend their winters in the convenient shelter of Noelle Anne's Alpine house.

The 'see through' formal garden with low planting and a shimmering veil of *Stipa gigantea* and *Verbena bonariensis* allows a view through the garden from a sunset bench. In the formal area statue Edwina has silver plants *Brunnera* **'Jack Frost'** and *Artemesia* **'Powis Castle'** at her feet. And the stream garden, designed by Peter Boland of Vision Landscapes, offers a real 'wow factor' with water magically appearing to flow from a distant point under a bridge.

Elsewhere in the garden there is a fernery, a traditional garden featuring a herbaceous border in a symphony of pinks, and a pond garden frothing with alchemilla where a heron and angel's fishing rods lean over burbling water.

Open to groups by appointment, May-Sep. Not suitable for children; no dogs; wheelchair accessible. Teas by arrangement. Admission c. €5. **Directions:** *Turn off Milltown Road opposite the monumental arch.*

Burton Hall Gardens
Arena Road Sandyford Industrial Estate **Dublin 18**
Tel: 01 295 5888 / 086 2340068
Web: www.burtonhall.ie

GARDEN

Walled garden with a penstemon collection, fine herbaceous borders, vegetable garden and interesting plants for sale.

An oasis in the midst of a commercial hub, the fine old walled garden of 1731 Burton Hall has a new incarnation as a teaching garden and is part of the training and rehabilitation programme for Cluain Mhuire. There are lots of enjoyable things for visitors to learn there too: how to revive an ancient bay hedge, how to run a square foot vegetable garden and effective ways to ward off pests with companion planting.

Replanted from 1995 with begged and stolen plants (guaranteed to grow), the garden has matured beautifully. Yew, bay and beech hedges delineate different areas within the garden: an arboretum, a parterre, a fruit garden, and a central walk bordered with lavender, penstemons and *R* **'Perle d'Or'**. The vegetable garden is planted with unusual crops like physalis, pumpkins, Chinese mustard, purple podded peas and Pak Chow. Around the walls are glorious herbaceous borders with interesting plant associations Chephalia giganteum, eremurus with yellow thalictrum and Romneya coulteri, named after Romey and Coulter the two Irish men who discovered it. Burton Hall is also a place where children can marvel at the tallest of *tryffid*-like echiums, where strollers can sit on intriguing sculptured seats by James Carroll and see statuesque *Puja chilensis*, which grabbed the headlines as one of the first to flower in Ireland. Tempting plants propagated from the garden can also be purchased.

*Open Apr-Oct, Wed 2-6. Also groups by appointment. Supervised children welcome; guide dogs; wheelchair accessible; plants on sale; tea on request for groups. **Directions:** Just around the corner from Woodies in Sandyford Industrial Estate. Admission c.€5*

Fernhill Garden

Stepaside Sandyford **Dublin 18**
Tel: 01 295 4257
Email: dihb@eircom.net

GARDEN

Large historic garden planted Robinsonian style with many interesting features.

It is perfectly possible to forget the encroaching suburbs and to lose yourself to fantasy in this lovely oasis on the side of the Three Rock Mountain overlooking Dublin Bay. You might imagine yourself awaiting the arrival of the butler with afternoon tea at the end of the broad walk, as the Darley family did around the time the now giant Wellingtonias and Tsugas were planted there in 1860.

Equally you could be in the Himalayas marvelling at the spring display of rhododendrons in every shade from the towering cerise of *R. arboretum* to the yellow of *R. genestieranum* among the glades of the rocky hillside. Or pretend that you are following in the footsteps of plant explorer George Forrest when he discovered the rose red flowered *Camellia reticulata* in China in 1924.

The 40 acre estate has been owned by the Walker family since 1934, when RJ Walker began planting a magnificent collection of tender and exotic shrubs in the grounds laid out by the Darleys in the previous century.

A series of mysterious trails add to the sense of discovery as different areas create changes of mood. On entering, there is the old world charm of the kitchen garden, hedged in beech with a grid of paths running between herbaceous borders, espaliered fruit trees and vegetable beds. The stream garden, bright with candelabra primula in spring, leads on to an Edwardian rockery with a central pool feature and planted with bulbs, ericas and dwarf shrubs.

The route wanders on to a sheltered area where trilliums and hellebores have colonised beneath acers and camellias. Within the garden you can move from continent to continent courtesy of plants: in one minute you seem to be in an Australian forest amid woolly tree ferns, the next in China beside fragrant water lily like flowers of *Michelia doltsopa.* Magnolias provide some of the most unforgettable sights, like the huge flamingo pink flowers of *M. campellii,* borne on bare branches in early spring, or the ballerina like skirts of *M wilsonii* dancing in a grove on the hillside.

Open all year; Tue-Sat, 11-5, Sun 2-6. Supervised children welcome; no dogs; partial wheelchair access; plants for sale. **Directions:** *On the road to Enniskerry between Sandyford and Stepaside.*

Knockree

Glenamuck Road Carrickmines Dublin 18
Tel: 01 295 5884
Email: john@beatty.ie Web: www.dublingardens.com

GARDEN

Set amid granite rock formations, an informal one acre garden with splendid plants.

In the kind of conditions that would make lesser gardeners throw in the trowel, Shirley Beatty has turned the ice age formations of 'roche moutonné' to advantage. The rocky sheep like granite outcrops in her garden in the foothills of the Dublin Mountains have been used as features, here to hold pools, there as a natural container for a host of interesting plants.

The layout has several completely contrasting areas. There is the rock garden where a host of candelabra primula and a purple acer admire their watery reflections in a natural granite basin and choice plants colonise in the seams between the outcrops as though planted there by nature.

The path winds on past a greenhouse and vegetable garden, to the wild mountain view garden where heathers, rhododendrons and bulbs are sheltered by pine and larch. Around the house, with its cloak of clematis and roses, is a more traditional garden with island beds around a lawn and a shady area sheltering treasures like meconopsis and trilliums.

Hardy geraniums are particular favourites and visitors can make the acquaintance of **'Sue Crug'**, **'Mavis Simpson'** and **'Mrs Kendal Clarke'**. There are wonderful plant and colour combinations to be seen, and it is a good idea to bring a note book to take the names of desirable and unusual plants: who could resist a pink peony called **'Do Tell'**, statuesque cream edged *Symphytum uplandicum* or the huge white flowers of Clematis **'Carnaby'**?

Open to groups by appointment Mar-Jul. Supervised children welcome; no dogs; not suitable for wheelchairs; plant sales; tea by arrangement. Admission c. €5. **Directions:** *One third the way up the Glenamuck Road, between Brennanstown and Enniskerry roads.*

Ardgillan Castle & Demesne

Balbriggan Co Dublin
Tel: 01 849 2212

GARDEN

A 200 year old estate with a walled garden, potentilla collection and garden museum.

Corrupted from the Irish Ard Choill (high wood), Ardgillan was aptly named until the Rev Robert Tayleur paid labourers a penny a day to clear the land for his new home in 1737. The estate, with its Gothicised house situated in a 200 acre park above Barnageera Beach and views stretching to the Mournes, is now owned by Fingal Council and is open to the public.

The garden has the benefit of old bones combined with new ideas. The Council have restored the gardens near the house, adding a new rose garden planted with hybrid tea roses around a lily pond and climbing roses ingeniously grown over a pergola of chains. Manicured lawns, a herbaceous border, the beautifully restored glass house with peaches, nectarines and grapes all provide a traditional note. A national collection of potentillas with over 300 varieties has been planted in this area.

The reinterpreted walled garden is full of interest: there is a potager where unusual vegetables like garden huckleberries and physalis are contained by hedges of clipped box; a herb garden has been laid out around a central lavender bed, and there is a neatly labelled herbaceous and shrub garden and Four Seasons garden (two seasons actually, as it is planted with tulips in spring and dahlias in summer). The orchard area has fans of peaches and greengages and a collection of old Irish apple varieties dating as far back as Blood of the Vine (16th century) and Ballysattin (1820). The potting shed and bothy now house a gardening museum full of bygone horticultural technology, and new scree beds with Alpine displays have been created nearby. Walks in the grounds are recommended, offering the opportunity to discover the ice house and the quaintly names 'Lady's Stairs' leading to the beach.

Open all year, 10-6. Tea rooms & castle opening hours vary. Admission free. **Directions:** *Signposted from the main Dublin Belfast road at Balrothery.*

Carysfort Lodge

49 Carysfort Avenue **Blackrock** Co Dublin
Tel: 01 288 9273
Email: zakdillon@eircom.net

GARDEN

A secluded town garden full of happy plants.

This pretty 1890s lodge and its sunny, square back garden were rescued from a dreadful fate as the car park for a nearby pub. When the Dillons became its saviour the property was run down, there were a few old apple trees in the garden and the house had no electricity.

Now, 35 years later, the garden is an invitation to relax and enjoy the company of a happy congregation of plants and shrubs. It is also an inspiration for Siobhan's exquisitely embroidered flower pictures. The first thing the Dillons did was to plant shrubs and trees to blur the boundaries and give the garden structure. There is a *Chamaecyparis nootkatensis* **'Pendula'** (familiarly known as the Afghan tree), gleditsia, magnolia, a willow weeping obligingly over a gothic seat guarded by golden Florencecourt yews and a champion *Cornus controversa* **'Variagata'**, and a cherry tree is nearly invisible under swags of the Belvedere rose.

A deep herbaceous border stretches down the east, full of decorative plants, plumes of white willow herb, drifts of alstroemerias and campanulas, spires of veronicastrum and galega. Amid the cottagey profusion there are displays of hellebores and tulips in spring and, in summer, a *Crambe cordiflia* doing its spectacular thing. There's a peaceful green and white planted area with *Hydrangea* **'Annabelle'** and *Macleya cordata* at the bottom of the garden, while an L shaped box hedge holds back a crowd of alstroemerias and lilies near the house.

Open by appointment for groups only, May-Jul. Not suitable for children or wheelchairs; no dogs. Tea by arrangement.

Anna Nolan's Garden

12 Shanganagh Vale Cabinteely Co Dublin
Tel: 01 282 5207
Email: nolanjo@eircom.net Web: www.dublingardens.com

GARDEN

Plant collector's garden packed with treasures.

Anna Nolan caught the gardening bug in childhood from her grandmother. It has proved to be seriously incurable and her garden, which started out 27 years ago from unpromising grass and cypress trees, is a wonderful testament to her passion.

It is - quite simply- plant Heaven on Earth, with a wide collection of choice and unusual plants co-habiting in tightly planted, happy proximity. Anna is particularly interested in herbaceous plants - there isn't room to indulge in many shrubs and trees in a suburban garden. Her especial favourites are climbers and alpines but there are fascinating collections of all kinds of species from codonopsis to dwarf hostas.

The season starts with a flourish of hellebores followed by spring bulbs, and continues through the year into September, prolonged by late flowering monardas, lobelias, phlox and salvias. Anna gardens with colour as a strong theme, favouring stately and small plants with colour and form as a sub text. Many of her plants are grown from seed from various societies, others are found on trips to England-Crug garden in Wales is a particular favourite - and it would not be unusual for her to come back with 80 plants. The front garden is a symphony of reds, purple and blues in high summer with particularly striking *Astrantia* **'Cannaman'**, *Eryngiumx oliverianum*, *Sidalacia* **'Little Princess'**, *Acanthus* **'Carl Alexandriae'**, also herbaceous clematis **'Pangbourne Pink'** and **'Arabella'** - and there is a shady corner beside the greenhouse with a collection of ferns and treasures like *Arum candissimum*.

The real show stopper though is the sunken back garden where two water features tinkle beside the raised terrace around the house. Plants work together in colour groups - gold, rust and bronze cooled by *Stipa tenusssima*, or punchy reds crimsons and scarlets with *Crocosmia* **'Lucifer'** the brightest of them all. They also work in texture compositions such as sturdy veratrum combined with lacy selinum, architectural hosta and delicate tulbaghia. The walls of the house and a clever arbour with apertures which frame different views of the garden provide support of fascinating climbers: *Codonopsis convolvulacea*, with its wonder internal marking. *C* **'Innocence'** *Lapagerea rosea*, azure flowered *Tweedia oxypetalum*, *Lapagera rosea Passiflora* **'Innocence'**. At their feet are stone troughs with collections of Alpines and pots with collections of miniature hostas.

This is a garden where visitors proceed very slowly indeed, the better to admire the kind of plants that deserve celebrity status, *Salvia* **'Black and Blue'** for its stately habit and indigo flower, *Delphinium menszeii* with flowers like turquoise balls of crumbled tissue paper, *Brummeras* **'Jack Frost'** and **'Langtry'** for their exquisite leaf markings or *C aromatica* for her capricious deep purple petals. Gorgeous!

*Open Mar-Sep, groups of 10+ by appointment. Not suitable for children or wheelchairs. No dogs. Plant sales; tea by arrangement. Admission c. €5. **Directions:** Last left off the N11 before the Cabinteely turn off.*

Grasse Cottage

130 Rochestown Avenue
Dun Laoghaire Co Dublin
Tel: 01 285 2396

GARDEN

Plantsman's garden with paths winding through curvy borders packed with interest.

Dick Mallet's garden, created over 48 years, proves the point that passionate plants people have happy gardens. Appearing much bigger than half an acre, thanks to cleverly hidden boundaries and mysterious paths winding between a splendid collection of plants, the plan is given structure and year round interest by strategically planted shrubs and trees. Some, such as *Acer griseum*, *Betula jacquemontii* and *Prunus serrula* - Dick's particular favourites - have wonderful bark. Grasses, iris, salvias, old roses and herbaceous and viticella clematis are particularly well represented. *Clematis durandii* and *R. Belvedere* romp about, pheasant's eye grass glows gold in winter, *Salvia guarantica* is almost navy blue and gorgeous iris *I ensata* is a real show stopper. There are eye catching species: Brodiae, robust tar weed or Grindelia, choice *Eryngium x oliverianum* and *Catanachea caerulea* (romantically known as cupid's dart) plants proliferate merrily with *Geranium palmatum* and echiums self seeding around.

Dick loves to grow tender plants: The golden angle's trumpet *Brugmansia* **'Champagne'** flourishes in the greenhouse alongside curiosities like the marmalade bush *Streptosolen jamesonii*, and a wonderful collection of pelargoniums and streptocarpus. Other tender plants stay outside in pots and are lifted to shelter in winter, whilst cuttings and seed collection are also used as a strategy against frost casualties. Hidden within the garden are three ponds, a rose forest where the scent of old fashioned roses like *R d'amour* and *R* **'Fantin-Latour'** lingers, a vegetable garden - and a tropical corner, complete with a banana tree and cannas.

Open by appointment anytime. Not suitable for children or dogs; partial wheelchair access; plant sales. Admission c. €4. **Directions:** *On the right, just before the turn for Sallynoggin.*

Primrose Hill

Lucan Co Dublin
Tel: 01 628 0373

GARDEN

Herbaceous borders and a large collection of perennial plants

Primrose Hill is a most endearing garden and the way it is hidden away down a laneway in the middle of Lucan gives a pleasing sense of discovery. An avenue of beech trees with bulbs and cyclamen around their feet offers a suitably grand approach to a charming Regency House attributed to Gandon.

Behind it is a garden full of colourful plant characters, created by two generations of the Hall family, with many lovely old fashioned cultivars.

There are two distinct areas to the main part of the garden; an informal area in front of the house with large beds curving around lawns and gravel, and the former kitchen garden with a grid of paths, where herbaceous plants have taken over from the vegetables. There are seldom seen plants like handsome centurion, ondopardon auriculas and rosceas and the nut rose.

The plants seem to have active sex lives and among those that have interbred and produced hybrids special to Primrose Hill are Lobelia **'Pink Elephant'** and **'Spark'**. Snowdrop enthusiasts make a special pilgrimage to the garden in February to see one of the finest collections of galanthus in Ireland. There is also a developing arboretum covering five acres which shouldn't be missed, and a recently created foregarden at the entrance which gives visitors a taste of things to come.

Open daily in Feb & Jun-July, 2-6. Other times by appointment. Supervised children welcome, not suitable wheel chairs. Plants for sale. Admission c. €5. **Directions:** *Passing through village on main road from Dublin look out for Primrose Lane on left after the bridge.*

The Talbot Botanic Gardens

Malahide Castle
Malahide Co Dublin
Tel: 01 846 2456

GARDEN

Extensive gardens with large collection of southern hemisphere plants

Milo Talbot, 7th Baron Malahide was the last in a very long line of Talbots who had almost continuous connection with Malahide since they were first granted the lands in 1185. Between 1948 and his death in 1973, Milo Talbot enhanced the grounds of the castle, laying out 20 acres of gardens and introducing many rare trees and shrubs, especially species from Australasia which were his particular passion.

The castle, with its medieval great hall cloaked by a Gothic exterior, has a setting of sweeping lawns and fine old trees, among them cedars of Lebanon and a swooping boughed sessile oak under planted with cyclamen and snowdrops. Behind the castle a series of grassy rides are laid out and planted with a collection of trees and shrubs. Close inspection will be rewarded by the pleasing habits of lime loving specimens like *Stachyurus praecox* with its racemes of yellow green flowers, the violet coned *Abies spectabilis*, scented viburnums, Chilean holly with waxy red and yellow trumpets, and starry flowered olearias.

Hidden away in the four acres of walled garden is the holy of holies, which houses the most precious and tender species of the collection and is open only on Wednesday afternoons to guided groups. The most spectacular section is the luxuriant pond garden, while the Tresco Wall is a testament to Milo Talbots pioneering attempts to grow tender varieties such as the mimosa like pink flowered *Albizia julibrissin* and *Acacia pravissima* outdoors - and greenhouses shelter yet more tender specimens. An Australasian section of the garden has recently been created in honour of Milo Talbot.

Open May-Sep, 2-5; guided tour of walled garden Wed only, 2pm. Groups by appointment. Admission c. €4. Supervised children welcome; partial wheelchair access; no dogs; restaurant in castle.
Directions: *The castle and estate are on the Dublin side of Malahide.*

Malahide Area
COUNTRY HOUSE

Belcamp Hutchinson

Carrs Lane Malahide Road Balgriffin Dublin 17
Tel: 01 846 0843 Fax: 01 848 5703
Email: belcamhutchinson@eircom.net Web: www.belcamphutchinson.com

Dating back to 1786, this impressive house just outside Malahide (with its good restaurants and shopping) takes its name from its original owner, Francis Hely-Hutchinson, 3rd Earl of Donoughmore. It is set in large grounds, with interesting gardens, giving it a very away-from-it-all country atmosphere - yet Belcamp Hutchinson is only about half an hour from Dublin city centre (off peak) and 15 minutes to the airport. The present owners, Doreen Gleeson and Karl Waldburg, have renovated the house sensitively: high ceilinged, graciously proportioned rooms have retained many of their original features and are furnished and decorated in keeping with their age. Bedrooms are very comfortable, with thoughtfully appointed bathrooms and views over the gardens and countryside. Although its convenient location makes this an ideal place to stay on arrival or when leaving Ireland, a one-night stay won't do justice to this lovely and hospitable place and it would make a delightful base for visiting nearby gardens, including the Talbot Botanic Gardens at Malahide Castle, Ardgillan Castle at Balbriggan (see entries) and the National Botanic Gardens, at Glasnevin, Dublin 9. Walled garden; maze. Golf, equestrian, walking, garden visits, tennis, sailing nearby. Not suitable for children under 10. Pets welcome. **Rooms 8** (all with full bath & overbath shower). B&B c. €70 pps, no ss. Closed mid Dec-end Jan. MasterCard, Visa. **Directions:** From city centre, take Malahide Road; past Campions pub, 1st lane on left (sign on right pointing up lane).

21 Library Road

21 Library Road **Shankhill** Co Dublin
Tel: 01 282 4885

GARDEN

Medium sized suburban garden with an impressive collection of rare and tender plants.

Statuesque echiums and a profusion of unusual plants bursting over the garden wall signal the presence of a promising garden. But the real treat - a sumptuous feast for plant lovers- lies hidden behind Carmel Duignan's house. For here is a series of the most fascinating conversations going between rare southern hemisphere plants and unusual varieties of more familiar species. Plants talk colour to each other - the metallic blue tinge of *Acacia baileyiana purpurea* speaking in unison with Aconitum **'Stainless Steel'** and the silver of *Buddleja agosthera*. Unlikely bedfellows vie with each other to produce the most scintillating associations, the red black of *Aeonium* **'Swartkop'** smoulders against a lime green tansy. And choice solo numbers like *Prostanthera waterii* with trumpets that glow like pearls in the dusk or prolific golden *Tropeolum ciliatum* compete for notice.

On a lime rich sheltered site, the garden, started from a field 17 years ago, is laid out with a strong rectangular framework, the better to contain the glorious profusion of plants. Reds are marshalled to one side of the central lawn and blues to the other, with an arbour at the end as a the focal point. Paths burrow between the main herbaceous borders, punctuated by fountains of roses and clematis grown on pillars, and leafy side borders with unusual plants have inviting seating areas half way along this deeply satisfying voyage around the plant world. Fuschias, clematis and pseudopanax feature strongly in a collection which stretches all the way from *Salvia corugata*, with a black calyx and intensely blue flowers, discovered in Ecuador in the last 20 years to *Clematis* **'Princess Diana'** with droop headed pink bells who had her title changed just like HRH Princess of Wales.

Open May-Sep; groups of 10 by appt. Admission c.€4.50. Not suitable for wheelchairs, children or dogs.

Rathmichael Lodge

Ballybride Road **Shankhill** Co Dublin
Tel: 01 282 2203

GARDEN

Romantic garden, with herbaceous borders, roses, walks and pavilions.

Rathmichael Lodge is one of those gardens that wins an "oh!" of pleasure when they first burst into the field of vision. Like sex appeal it's a quality that is hard to pin down, but whatever it is Corinne and Richard Hewat's creation has it in spades.

It could be something to do with the allure of a half moon of herbaceous border packed with appealing plants and plant associations; it could be to do with the invitation to explore and find out what happens beyond a Gothic gate - and it could also be the desire to bury one's nose in one of the dozens of old fashioned roses, or simply the pleasure of sinking onto a strategically placed garden bench and drinking the whole scene in.

The garden is at its peak in June; Corrine loves roses and the garden is full of old fashioned ladies like **'Adelaide'**, **'Margaret Merrill'** and **'Mme Isaac Pereire'**. Cottagey plants, like foxglove and alchemilla mollis seed happily in corners and covetable varieties - violas, delphiniums, oriental poppies, thalictrum, hemerocallis - await admiration in the borders.

Festooned in wisteria and particularly exuberant climbing roses, the house forms a backdrop to this informal cottage style garden, and a terrace provides shelter for tender treasures in troughs and pots. Surprises waiting to be discovered include a Millennium Walk leading to a gazebo, a perfectly manicured tennis court and a pair of stone dogs wearing ivy collars.

Open to groups by appointment, mid May- mid Jul. Not suitable for wheelchairs; no dogs. **Directions:** *Turn off the N11 for Shankill at the Loughlinstown Roundabout, turn right at the garage and left down Ballybride Road, at Rathmichael Church. The house is the third on the right.*

COUNTY DUBLIN

Stillorgan
RESTAURANT

Beaufield Mews Restaurant & Gardens
Woodlands Avenue Stillorgan Co Dublin **Tel: 01 288 0375**
Email: beaumews@iol.ie Web: www.beaufieldmews.com

Dublin's oldest restaurant is located in a characterful 18th century coachhouse and stables - and, as the name implies, it is surrounded by beautiful mature gardens where guests can have an aperitif on the lawn before dinner, or take coffee afterwards, as the gardens are lit up by night. The effect in a built-up area is quite startling, as you are just a few hundred yards off one of Dublin's busiest roads and yet, with its mature trees, spacious surroundings and old-fashioned feeling in both the buildings and gardens, you could be forgiven for thinking you have been mysteriously transported to the country - there's even an antique shop, where guests are encouraged to have a browse before dining. This impression has been reinforced by recent changes - including the installation of a new 'Hayloft' bar and a new 'garden' look for the restaurant: atmosphere really is the trump card at this legendary restaurant and the cooking style and courteous service are in tune with the old-fashioned surroundings. A recently added outdoor patio area overlooks the gardens, which include an old walled hideaway and are open to the public at certain times in July and August. Not suitable for children after 6.30pm. **Seats 200** (private room, 60; outdoor seating, 20). D Tue-Sat, L Sun only. Closed Mon, bank hols, Good Fri. **Directions:** 4 miles from city centre, off Stillorgan dual carriageway.

*East Coast &
Midlands*

Rockfield House

Drumconrath Co Meath
Tel: 046 905 2135

GARDEN

Charming old walled garden with stream and a good collection of herbaceous plants

Rockfield House has a particularly peaceful setting, looking over parkland sloping down to the River Dee valley, and the walled garden mimics the landscape, folding around a central stream like a half open book around its binding.

The walls of the acre square garden probably date back to the late 18th century and, in its present incarnation, has been gardened for two generations, with some happy alterations. The place positively invites exploration in order to inspect the curious box gazebo at the centre, perhaps, or discover the source of tinkling water where the stream and miniature weir are hidden among swathes of hostas and *Primula florindae*. And who could resist taking a look inside the large greenhouse where peaches, apricots, grapes and nectarines are ripening... Deep borders run around the walls, packed with pleasing and unusual plants and interesting plant combinations, like golden hop combined with the deep crimson flower of *R* **'William Lobb'**. Vegetable gardens take advantage of the sunny side of the slope fitting seamlessly into the general scheme of things.

At the highest point of the garden there are deep shrub borders and, in the corner which catches the western light, there is an evening garden with golden plants and shrubs - and plants like *Salvia turkestana*, which love their sunny dry vantage point.

Open by appointment, to groups. Children welcome; partial wheelchair access; guide dogs only. Plant sales. Admission c. €5 . **Directions:** *Just after N52 Kells to Ardee Rd crosses with turn left at sign for McKeevers Mill. After one mile turn right house is on left.*

Grove Gardens
Fordstown **Kells** Co Meath
Tel: 046 943 4276

GARDEN

An informal garden on 6 acres with exotic animals and fowl, walks, roses and clematis.

This is a place with something for everyone, from preschool to retirement groups. Where else would you find a fairy ring, a magic tree, African Spotted Owls and a great collection of clematis and roses, all in the one spot? Pat Dillon has been gardening since he was a child which, combined with a farmer's knowledge, makes for green fingers and practical tips he is happy to share.

The garden flows informally into different areas, a cottage garden, sweeping lawns with beds of roses and shrubs skirted in box, a tranquil damp garden where rogersias, primulas and hostas flourish. In addition there is a gravel garden planted with roses, clematis and cheerful dahlias, and a vegetable garden guarded by a turkey who gets very upset at the mention of Christmas.

In the heart of the plan is a white and silver summerhouse garden where curtains of *R* **'Frances E. Lester'** hang from pergolas and *C* **'Paul Farges'** and *R* **'Francois Juranville'** have clambered up silver birches. Around the garden are eye-catching displays of clematis and roses, *C* **'Prince Charles'**, *C Arabella*, **'Etoile Violette'**, *R* **'Paul's Himalayan Musk'** and **'Felicité et Perpetue.'**

For the adventurous there are encounters with furry friends from lion rabbits to lemurs in areas adjacent to the garden, and walks with unexpected creatures like emus, leading to paddocks and to picnic spots. Altogether a great place for a family outing.

Open Mid Mar-Oct, 10-6 daily. Children welcome; wheelchair accessible. Teas. Admission c. €6.
Directions: *Signed half way between Kells and Athboy on the R164.*

Kilmessan
HOTEL

The Station House Hotel
Kilmessan Co Meath
Tel: 046 902 5239 Fax: 046 902 5588
Email: info@thestationhousehotel.com Web: www.thestationhousehotel.com

The Slattery family's unique establishment is an old railway junction, which was closed in 1963 and, twenty years later, all the various buildings were converted to a new use for the hotel. It is set in 12 acres of gardens, which are the hotel's greatest asset and supply all the fresh flowers; the bar overlooks a large patio (previously the platform) and this is a very pleasant place to sit on a warm summer's day when the roses are in bloom - especially, perhaps, as you sip an aperitif while taking your pick from their famous traditional Sunday lunch menu... The old engine and goods building have become a conference and banqueting suite - and the old signal box is now a romantic 2-room honeymoon suite. Children welcome. No pets. **Rooms 20** (1 suite, 1 executive, 20 no-smoking, 2 disabled). 24 hour room service. B&B c. €95, ss €25.

Restaurant Seats 90 (outdoor seating, 50). Reservations advised. Toilets wheelchair accessible. L & D daily except Sat. L Bar Menu also offered, Mon-Sat, 11-6. Amex, Diners, MasterCard, Visa, Laser.
Directions: From Dublin N3 to Dunshaughlin and follow signposts.

Navan
ACCOMODATION / B&B

Killyon House
Dublin Road Navan Co Meath
Tel: 046 907 1224 Fax: 046 907 2766
Email: info@killyonguesthouse.ie Web: www.killyonguesthouse.ie

You couldn't miss Michael and Sheila Fogarty's modern guesthouse, with its striking array of colourful flowers and hanging baskets - and its central location, just on the edge of Navan, makes it a convenient base for visiting any of the gardens in County Meath. The house is furnished with interesting antiques, and made comfortable by modern double-glazing which reduces traffic noise. The back of the house, which leads down to the banks of the Boyne, is unexpectedly tranquil, however, and the dining room overlooks the river, giving guests the added interest of spotting wildlife, sometimes including otters and stoats, along the bank from the window. The Fogartys are extremely hospitable hosts and nothing (even preparing a very early breakfast) is too much trouble. The house is very well run, rooms are all en-suite and comfortable, and there's also a separate guests' sitting room. Although they are too close to the restaurants of Navan to make evening meals a viable option, the Fogartys can advise on the best options, and they do a particularly good breakfast: an abundance of fresh fruits and juice, great breads, hot scones and home-made preserves as well as the traditional Irish Breakfast and variations, all based on the best quality ingredients, well cooked and hospitably served. Own parking (9). Children welcome. No pets. **Rooms 6** (all en-suite, 4 shower only, all no smoking). Room service (limited hours). B&B c. €40 pps, ss €10. Open all year except Christmas. MasterCard, Visa, Laser. **Directions:** On N3, opposite Ardboyne Hotel on River Boyne.

COUNTY MEATH

Loughcrew Historic Gardens
Loughcrew **Oldcastle** Co Meath
Tel: 049 854 1922

GARDEN

An insight into garden history, follies, big herbaceous borders and much more.

After a long and sometimes fateful history, a more serendipitous chapter has opened for Loughcrew. The original 17th century landscaped grounds, which were revived in the 19th century have been rescued again with help from the Great Gardens of Ireland. The restoration programme began in 1997, and work is ongoing. This is an intriguing place to take a walk through gardening and archaeological history. An avenue leads to the 6 acres of grounds, and to venerable survivors of the original plan: the great yew walk dating back to 1670, and a viewing mound.

Features include a long herbaceous border - long enough to rival Strokestown's record breaker - with planting designed by Daphne Shackleton, a hot border known as Hell Fire and a Grotesque border, with labels, for the curiosities of the plant world. Other curiosities include a huggy walk (wait till you see the trees) and a waterfall flowing from under the roots of a tree.

Reminders of the distant past lie in the Loughcrew passage tombs and cairns, a medieval motte or moot, and the ruins of a church dedicated to St Oliver Plunkett, born in the Plunkett castle which preceded three subsequent houses on the site. Said to have been the victim of a curse, the 1820s mansion burnt down three times in a century and, after the last fire in 1960, was abandonded. The Ionic portico has found a new incarnation, as the most dramatic of a number of follies in the grounds. Take stout shoes, and enjoy the walk to the Hill of the Witch and the Loughcrew Passage Tombs.

Open daily: mid Mar-Sep, 12.30-5; Oct-Mar,1-4. Supervised children welcome; partial wheelchair access; dogs on leads allowed. Admission c. €6. **Directions:** *4 miles from Oldcastle on the Mullingar Road.*

Beaulieu House & Garden

Barrow **Drogheda** Co Louth
Tel: 041 983 8557

GARDEN

Beautifully located three hundred year old walled garden with herbaceous borders, fruit and vegetables.

Beaulieu is a very special place, remarkable for its age, its history, and the fact that the same family have lived in the house ever since it was completed in 1667. The enclosed garden dates from a few decades later may have been designed by the Dutch artist Van der Hagen and - like the house - is walled in russet brick imported from Holland.

Both are very rare survivors indeed. Beaulieu, built in Carolinian style, is one of the earliest examples of an unfortified house in Ireland and the sudden sight of the building with its steeply pitched roof and moulded chimney stacks at the end of a short avenue makes an imposing introduction to the garden. The internal layout of the garden has changed over the years but, at the top end, there is a raised area similar to the Jacobean "terras" at Lismore Castle, where strollers could admire the view of the gleaming expanse of the Boyne estuary in safety. Now this area is the site of a double herbaceous border. with a wiggly path running between clumps of choice and unusual plants - perovskia, herbaceous clematis, crinum lilies, melianthus and sea lavender among them - and leading past a Victorian knot garden, to a diminutive gingerbread summer house.

The rest of garden is mainly given over to fruit and vegetables, with a golden border in the centre and a rockery tucked away near the rustic gardener's cottage.

By the entrance to the garden there is a hexagonal 19th conservatory, full of tender abutilons and pelargoniums. Outside the walls, you will find a curious wooden temple, a thatched summer house, duck ponds and an inviting riverside walk, which leads past a stand of ancient lime trees to Queensborough coastguard cottages - all waiting to be investigated.

*Open May-mid Sep, Mon - Fri 11-5. Not suitable for children; wheelchair accessible; no dogs. Plants for sale. **Directions:** Take the Termonfeckin Road from Drogheda, garden is at the right turn for Baltray.*

Listoke Gardens

Ballymakenny Road **Drogheda** Co Louth
Tel: 041 983 2265

GARDEN

6 acre Edwardian garden with walled garden, herbaceous borders and woodland walks.

Listoke is that happy combination of a mature but still evolving garden covering 6 acres. Twenty five years ago landscape gardener Patricia Barrow decided that she would put the Edwardian garden back to its original state and, as she says, it's not a smart garden but a very loved one.

At its heart is an acre and a half walled garden with a traditional grass tennis court overlooked by a garden room half hidden behind clouds of Japanese anemone blooms in late summer, and with mixed borders around its walls. Past a restored greenhouse and under overarching clouds of white roses is a new arboretum with paths mown in the grass. This is the setting for interesting trees like the Montezuma pine, and a snake bark maple sheltered by a leylandii hedge clipped every six weeks into neat submission, and fronted by a border of grasses, their cloudy shapes complementing the shape of the trees.

The golden rain of a laburnum walk has its flowering season prolonged by the cool blue flowers of *Solanum crispum* **'Glasnevin'** and is underplanted with *G* **'Johnston's Blue'** and daffodils. As any gardener will tell you there is nothing like a new bed, and Mrs Barrow has two deep curved borders with interesting herbaceous plants and bulbs, with apricot as the main accent colour in summer and blue and yellow in spring. There is galtonia, a black hollyhock, canna lilies, Knautia macedonica, low growing alstroemeria, shaggy Shasta daisies, the Shoo Fly plant, eremurus, and other lilies.

Elsewhere a curvaceous shrubbery path leads to a new wild garden, a traditional kitchen garden, and to a propagation area where excellent plants propagated from seed and from the garden are for sale. And the estate still has its woodland walks, through beech woods carpeted with bluebells and anemones.

Open Mar-Oct. evenings & weekends otherwise by appointment. Children welcome; dogs on leads allowed; wheelchair friendly. Plant sales; teas by arrangement. **Directions:** *Two miles from Drogheda on the Ballymakenny Road, the house is on the right.*

Knockabbey Castle & Gardens

Tallanstown Co Louth
Tel: 01 677 8816
Email: info@knockabbeycastle.com Web: www.knockabbeycastle.com

GARDEN

Victorian gardens with medieval fish ponds, herbaceous borders and visitor centre.

Also known as Thomastown Castle, the earliest part of the building dates back to 1399 and this tower house played a part in the strategic defence of the northwest corner of the Pale. A Georgian and later a Gothic wing were added, and the old tower was given a handsome Gothic doorway.

The "stew" or fish ponds (a medieval device to store fish for future consumption) in the grounds are thought to be even earlier, perhaps 11th century. The 30 acre demesne has may fine trees (the tulip tree in the small arboretum is one of the largest in Ireland), and other parts of the gardens within it date back to different periods. Some elements have been restored or reinterpreted with funding from the Great Gardens Restoration Scheme. Serious money has been spent totally rebuilding a vanished greenhouse and restoring an old teahouse beyond the ponds, once used as a soup kitchen.There is a video in the interpretative centre to explain it all, and a tree planted by Minister Dermot Ahern to attest to the importance of the project. An eye catching new double herbaceous border has been made below the castle terrace, with a classical urn at the end as a vista closer .

The view of a modern house built inside the walled garden strikes a jarring note beside the greenhouse and small Victorian garden. Walks lead off around the fish ponds to the teahouse and through the grounds. Although it doesn't have quite the same personality as a garden created by an individual gardener, this is an interesting place and makes a great outing for for a family visit.

*Open 10.30-5.30: May (Sat, Sun & bank hols), Jun-Aug (Tue-Sun & bank hols), Sep (Sat, Sun). Supervised children welcome; wheelchair accessible; no dogs. Visitor centre; tea by arrangement. Garden admission c. €6. **Directions:** From Dublin, exit M50 at Junction 5 to Ardee; at roundabout north of Ardee take Tallanstown road; 2km after Tallanstown the Castle is signposted.*

Carrickmaross
HOTEL / RESTAURANT

Nuremore Hotel
Carrickmacross Co Monaghan
Tel: 042 966 1438 Fax: 042 966 18543
Email: nuremore@eircom.net Web: www.nuremore.com

This fine owner-managed country hotel just south of Carrickmacross is set in a parkland estate, with its own 18-hole golf course, and serves the sporting, leisure and business requirements of a wide area very well - and would make a comfortable base when visiting gardens such as Lakeview Gardens at Mullagh, County Cavan, which is not far away. As you go over the little bridge ("Beware - ducks crossing") and the immaculately maintained hotel and golf club open up before you and, surrounded by well-maintained gardens, the hotel invariably gives a good impression on arrival - and this sense of care and maintenance is continued throughout. Spacious, comfortably arranged public areas and generous bedrooms with views over the gardens and lakes are regularly refurbished - and the country club has a full leisure centre and a wide range of related facilities , including a gymnasium and spa. But the best is yet to come: not only is **The Restaurant at Nuremore** well established as the leading restaurant in the area, but the head chef, Raymond McArdle, has earned a national reputation for the hotel, which is now on the must-visit destination list for discerning travellers in Ireland. Although not aspiring to fashionable decor, the restaurant is well-appointed in a fairly formal country house style, with generous white-clothed tables and a couple of steps dividing the window area and inner tables, allowing everybody to enjoy the view over golf course and woodland. Raymond sources ingredients meticulously, using local produce as much as possible in top rank daily set lunch and dinner menus, a separate vegetarian menu, a 'grown-up' children's menu, and an evening à la carte. The consistent excellence and innovativeness of the cooking is matched by good service and an extensive and well-organised wine list - and this is a restaurant offering outstanding value for money, especially at lunch time. Golf (18), fishing, walking, tennis; snooker. Children welcome. No pets. **Rooms 72**. B&B c.€130 pps, ss €50. **Restaurant: Seats 100** L Sun-Fri, D daily. Set L c. €25 (Set Sun L, €30); Set D c.€48 (Vegetarian Menu c.€25); Prestige Menu c. €80. SC discretionary. Restaurant closed L Sat. Hotel open all year. Amex, Diners, MasterCard, Visa, Laser. **Directions:** Just south of Carrickmacross, 55 miles from Dublin on N2 (accessed from by-pass).

Clones
COUNTRY HOUSE / GARDENS

Hilton Park
Clones Co Monaghan
Tel: 047 56007
Email: info@hiltonpark.ie

Once described as a "capsule of social history" in recognition of their collection of family portraits and memorabilia going back 250 years or more, Johnny and Lucy Madden's wonderful 18th century mansion is set in beautiful countryside, amidst 200 acres of woodland and farmland. With lakes, Pleasure Grounds - including a parterre, herbaceous border, herb garden and a Lovers' Walk to set the right tone - the house is magnificent in every sense and the experience of visiting it a rare treat. Johnny and Lucy are natural hosts and, as the house and its contents go back for so many generations, there is a strong feeling of being a privileged family guest as you wander through grandly-proportioned, beautifully furnished rooms. Four-posters and all the unselfconscious comforts that make for a very special country house stay are part of the charm, but as visitors from all over the world have found, it's the warmth of Johnny and Lucy's welcome that lends that extra magic. The gardens are also of particular interest - formal gardens have recently been restored to their former glory and Lucy, an enthusiastic organic gardener and excellent cook, supplies freshly harvested produce for meals in the house, while other ingredients are carefully sourced from trusted suppliers of organic and free-range products. Dinner for residents is served in a beautiful dining room overlooking the parterre and lake - and memorable breakfasts are taken downstairs in the lovely informal Green Room next morning. Not suitable for children under 8 (except babies under 1 year). Pets allowed by arrangement. Gardens, boating, fishing (own lake), walking, cycling. Golf nearby. * Self catering accommodation also available - details on inquiry. **Rooms 5** (all en-suite & no smoking). B&B c. €125 pps, ss C. €40 pps. Residents' D c. €55 Tue-Sat, 8pm (Fri 8.30); 24 hrs notice required; wine licence. Group bookings welcome. Gardens open by appointment. MasterCard, Visa. **Directions:** 3 miles south of Clones on Scotshouse road.

Monaghan
HOTEL / RESTAURANT

Castle Leslie
Glaslough Co Monaghan
Tel 047 88100
Email: info@castleleslie.com Web: www.castleleslie.com

Although it is not especially convenient to any of our recommended gardens, garden lovers are sure to relish a visit here. During the three centuries that this extraordinary place has been in the Leslie family it has changed remarkably little: once inside the massive front door (guarded by family dogs who snooze in beds flanking the stone steps) there is no reception desk, just a welcoming oak-panelled hall (and afternoon tea in the drawing room), and there are no phones, television sets or clocks in the rooms, although concessions to the 21st century have been made in the form of generous heating and plentiful hot water. The bedrooms are all different, with huge baths, wacky showers and outrageous toilets, reflecting both the family's eccentric history and the wonders of Victorian plumbing. In a charming reverse of circumstances, the family lives in the servants' wing, so guests can enjoy the magnificence of the castle to the full - it has all the original furniture and family portraits. The dining experience is central to Castle Leslie and it is all done in fine old style with pre-dinner drinks in the Drawing Room (or the Fountain Garden in summer), then dinner is served in several rooms including the original Dining Room, unchanged for over a century, by waitresses wearing Victorian uniforms. However, despite the obvious oddities of faded grandeur - tables with a slight list, chairs and sofas which have long since lost their stuffing - Noel McMeel, executive head chef since 2000, is essentially offering a restaurant dining experience rather than a country house dinner (and he has recently opened an impressive cookery school here as well). With formal gardens and a river, romantic walks, and pike fishing - boating and picnic lunches are available by arrangement - the Leslies see this as a wonderful refuge from the outside world for adults, so this is not a suitable place to bring children (although they are very welcome at the nearby Hunting Lodge & Castle Leslie Equestrian Centre). Pets allowed by arrangement. **Rooms 20** (3 suites; 5 ground floor, all no smoking) No lift. B&B c. €135pps, ss c. €35; 2-night bookings only at weekends. [Hunting Lodge: B&B c. €75 pps, ss €25 Restaurant: D daily, set D from c. €52. Licensed. * A Castle Leslie range of preserves and speciality foods is available from the castle and Brown Thomas, in Dublin. Amex, MasterCard, Visa, Laser. **Directions:** 10 minutes from Monaghan Town; Monaghan-Armagh road-Glaslough.

Lakeview Gardens

Mullagh Co Cavan
Tel: 046 924 2480
Email: jshack@indigo.ie Web: www.lakeviewgardens.net

GARDEN

A fabulous reincarnation of Edwardian style with stupendous herbaceous borders in the setting of an old walled garden.

The setting for the Shackleton's garden overlooking picturesque Lake Mullagh is a perfect endorsement for the curvaceous charm of Cavan's drumlin country. And the splendour of the garden, almost totally recreated starting from 1996, is a great testament to artist and garden designer Daphne and Jonathan Shackleton's skill, and to the capacity of herbaceous plants to become established and offer a breathtaking display in a short space of time.

Lakeview has wonderful old bones, parts of the house date back to 1660. But when the Shakletons began a phased move from the famous garden at Beech Park, Clonsilla, originally created by Jonathan's father, the late David Shackleton, very little of the garden remained bar a few apple trees shrubs and a pergola. Plants carefully transported from Beech Park were put in a holding area, an old pavery with a sundial terrace was restored and the main part of the garden ploughed before paths, yew hedges and borders were laid down.

At the heart of the design, a cruciform path runs between spectacular herbaceous borders, with sun catching gold plants in one direction and blues predominating in the other. Choice and unusual plants feature, eighty per cent derived from the collection at Beech Park, among the most handsome *Veratrum viride*, *Eryngium* **'Blue Wing'** *Kirengeshoma palmata*, *Anemone rivularis* and *Campanula Lactiflora* **'Russell Pritchard'**. A pause on a shady seat offers a vista back through massed hostas, ligularias and grasses, and a shrub walk leads to a top border with old roses that have treasure like celmesias at their feet and glimpses of water features ingeniously made from famine pots (used for soup for famine relief) and serried ranks of vegetables. A charming old stone-built barn shaded by an enormous magnolia houses the story of the garden's making, and nearby there is a huge bed of fascinating and tender plants which commands attention. Allow space in your car when visiting Lakeview, as there is also a small nursery offering unusual trees and shrubs for sale in summer.

Open May-Sep, groups 10+ by appointment.only. No dogs; partially wheelchair suitable. **Directions:** *Signed from Mullagh Lake on the R194 half way between Virginia and Moynalty.*

Longford
COUNTRY HOUSE

Viewmount House

Dublin Road Longford Co Longford
Tel: 043 41919 Fax: 043 42906
Email: info@viewmounthouse.com Web: www.viewmounthouse.com

James and Beryl Kearney's lovely 1750s Georgian house is just on the edge of Longford town, and not far from Strokestown Park. It was once owned by Lord Longford, and is set in four acres of beautiful wooded gardens which are designed as a series of themed rooms and under continuing development. It is a delightful house and has been sensitively restored with style, combining elements of grandeur with a human scale that makes guests feel very comfortable; it has old wooden floors, rugs, antique furniture and, most importantly, a great sense of hospitality which strikes the first-time visitor immediately on arrival in the hall, which has a welcoming open fire and warm red walls contrasting with a graceful white-painted staircase. Each room has its own character - there is an elegant period drawing room, and the six guest bedrooms all have their particular charm (one is especially large, but all are delightful); but perhaps the handsomest room of all is the unusual vaulted dining room, where an extensive breakfast menu is served. Some of the classic stone outbuildings have been converted to provide self-catering accommodation, and a restaurant is planned for the same area, in a room of great character overlooking a Japanese garden with water features. Children welcome. No pets. **Rooms 6** (1 suite, 3 bath & shower, 3 shower only, all no smoking). B&B c.€55, ss €10. *Self-catering also available - details on application. Amex, MasterCard, Visa. **Directions:** From Longford R393 to Ardagh. 7 miles, up sliproad to right following signs. Entrance 200m on right.

Tullynally Castle & Gardens

Castlepollard Co Westmeath
Tel 044 61159
Email thomaspakenham@eircom.net Web: www.tullynallycastle.com

GARDEN

The extensive pleasure grounds at Tullynally Castle, home of the Pakenham family since the 17th century, have seen whole chapters of garden history unfold. The earliest incarnation of the garden was in the Baroque manner with cascades, canals and trees marshalled into formal blocks. This was supplanted in the tide of enthusiasm for "improvements" by landscaping in the romantic style which included a serpentine waterway known as the "River Sham".

Further legacies of gardening history include Georgian greenhouses with intriguing fish scale glass, a grotto and a walled garden with a Victorian weeping pillar. Gardening enthusiasm continues in the present generation and Thomas and Valerie Pakenham have undertaken an ongoing programme of restoration aided by FAS workers. True to the theory that men and women tend to have different gardening styles Thomas Pakenham, author of Remarkable Trees and founder member of The Irish Tree Society, is passionate about trees. There is an arboretum with 43 different varieties of acer, magnolias and a handkerchief tree. Valerie, on the other hand, is involved with the restoration and replanting of borders. The distaff side of the gardens has a charming Victorian walled garden and a vegetable and flower garden with a patchwork hedge and a rose walk. Plants propagated from seed brought back by Thomas Pakenham from a plant hunting expedition to the Yunan have been used to create a Tibetan and Chinese garden.

Open weekends & bank hols in May; daily Jun-Aug 2-6. Supervised children welcome; partial wheelchair access; dogs on leads allowed. Castle open. Tearoom at weekends.

Ballinlough Castle

Clonmellon Co Westmeath
Tel: 046 33135

GARDEN

Very special restored Edwardian garden in an 18th century demesne.

Standing proudly on a hillside overlooking a lake, Ballinlough Castle looks for all the world like the illustration in a fairytale book and it has a story to match. Owned by the Catholic O'Reilly/Nugent family since it was first built in 16th century, it narrowly escaped demolition and the break up of the demesne two generations ago, before being rescued by Sir Hugh Nugent. In the 1990s his son Sir John and daughter in law Pepe Nugent undertook an ambitious restoration programme of both the Edwardian walled garden and the earlier landscaped grounds, aided by the Great Gardens of Ireland Restoration Scheme.

The three acre walled garden is influenced by Gertrude Jekyll's ideas on planting. In the main section there is a double herbaceous border of good old fashioned plants like campanula, astrantia and phlox, their colours shading from cool blues to hot reds with alchemilla, hardy geraniums and stachys frothing over the paths, a sunken garden area with a pool and traditional shrub borders around the walls. In the next section comes a magnolia walk, a rose garden of old fashioned roses, and flowering shrubs bordered in lavender. The fruit garden has been replanted with traditional apples, pears and plums, and more unusual medlars and mulberries.

The water garden, with its charming rustic bridge over an ornamental canal, the rockery and the lake - which was made, complete with a curious turf island, to give employment in Famine times - were also restored. It is well worth a walk around the lake, past the primulas, astilbes and rodgersia of the water garden, to the wooded Badger Bank for the enchanting view across the reed fringed lake to Ballinlough Castle with its 18th century additions, a happy example of heritage saved.

Open May-Sep:Tue-Thu & Sat, 11-6; Sun, 2-6. Supervised children welcome; partial wheelchair access; no dogs. Plant sales. Restaurant. **Directions:** *Signed from Clonmellon on the R52 from Kells to Mullingar.*

stock image

Belvedere House, Gardens & Park

Tullamore Road **Mullingar** Co Westmeath
Tel: 044 934 9060
Email: info@belvedere-house.ie Web: www.belvedere-house.ie

GARDEN

Historic 18th century house and park with a beautifully restored 2 acre walled garden.

With a Palladian villa, an idyllic location on Lough Ennel, a gem of a Victorian walled garden and Ireland's largest folly - a monument to the dark deeds of the 1st Earl of Belvedere - this historic 160 acre estate is fascinating.

The house, attributed to Richard Castle, was built in 1740 as a grandiose fishing lodge for Robert Rochfort, known as the 'Wicked Earl'. The soubriquet seems justified, for Rochfort locked up his young second wife Mary Molesworth in the family seat of Gaulstown for years on suspicion of an affair with his brother Arthur, and built the Gothic ruin known as the Jealous Wall partly as a fashionable statement but also to hide the view of Tudenham Park, home of another brother George. Rochfort also added two delightful follies to this chapter of gardening hisotry: the Gothic Arch and the octagonal Gazebo. The more benevolent Charles Brinsley Marlay, who inherited Belvedere in 1847, added the walled garden and the Italianate terracing in front of the house, and planted exotic trees in the park. He also had a habit of courting wealthy widows on the yew walk known as 'Widow's Walk'.

The exotic shrubs in the walled garden are a legacy of Himalayan mountaineer Charles Kenneth Howard Bury, who inherited in 1912 and created a celebrated garden there with his flamboyant companion Rex Beaumont.

The walled garden, which had gone into sad decline, as gardens will do, has now undergone a splendid reincarnation thanks to Westmeath County Council, funds from the Historic Gardens Restoration Scheme, and the hard work of garden staff over a four year restoration programme. Restoration plans were drawn up by Belinda Jupp and Terence Reeves Smith. After the garden walls had been repaired and conifers removed, the borders were replanted, old shrubs were identified and propagated.

The tour opens beside a restored greenhouse by Thomas Messenger, sheltering orchids and ferns. Beyond is a charming box edged potager with a rose arch of Kifsgate, espaliered fruit trees, soft fruits including monster blackberry **'Lough Ness'** and the decorative crab apple *Malus*. **'John Downie'** under planted with the Alpine strawberry **'Alexandria',** - Thompson and Morgan's **'Milkmaid'** nasturtium and sweet pea **'Matucana'**.

True to the original design, the garden is laid out with a grid of paths with magnificent shrub and herbaceous borders around the walls and a double herbaceous border along the central axis of the 2 acre garden, with golds predominating. In honour of Howard Bury there is a Himalayan theme with *Malus* **'Everest'**, hemerocallis, rhododendrons and meconopsis. There is a hot border, with monarda dahlias and cannas, Heliantus salicifolius and helenium and a wet border where ligularias and astilbes flourish. There is a delightful Rosarie full of old fashioned favourites like *R* **'Louise Odier'** and Irish cultivars **'Souvenir de St Anne's'** and **'Bloomfield Abundance'**, and a knot garden filled with different shades of hard geraniums from magenta **'Ann Folkard'** to mauve *G. clarkei*. It is truly a garden for all season starting in early spring with displays of crocus, hellebores and snowdrops. And the garden has given its name to two cultiavars, Rosa Belvedere and Fuchsia Belvedere, to be found in the plant sales section.

Open all year from 10 am. Children welcome; wheelchar accessible; dogs on leads allowed. Plants for sale; restaurant and gift shop. **Directions:** *Just outside Mullingar on the Tullamore Road. Well signed in area.*

Multyfarnham
COUNTRY HOUSE

Mornington House

Mornington Multyfarnham Co Westmeath
Tel: 044 72191 Fax: 044 72338
Email: stay@mornington.ie Web: www.mornington.ie

Warwick and Anne O'Hara's gracious Victorian house is surrounded by mature trees and is just a meadow's walk away from Lough Derravarragh where the mythical Children of Lir spent 300 years of their 900 year exile - and the lough is now occupied by a pleasing population of brown trout, pike, eels and other coarse fish. It has been the O'Hara family home since 1858 and is still furnished with much of the original furniture and family portraits and, although centrally heated, log fires remain an essential feature. Bedrooms are typical of this kind of country house – spacious and well-appointed, with old furniture (three have brass beds), but with comfortable modern mattresses. Anne cooks proper country breakfasts and country house dinners for residents, using fresh fruit and vegetables from the walled garden and local produce (Westmeath beef cooked in Guinness is a speciality), and Warwick does the honours front-of-house. There is a wealth of wildlife around the house, and there are archae-ological sites and gardens in counties Meath and Westmeath to visit nearby - this is a tranquil and restorative place for a short break. Pets allowed by arrangement. Garden, croquet; fishing. canoes,

boats & bicycles can be hired. Equestrian: trekking & a cross-country course nearby. Golf nearby. Not suitable for children under 12, except babies. **Rooms 5** (3 en-suite, 2 with private bathrooms, 2 shower only, all no smoking). B&B c. €70 pps, ss €20. Residents D €40, at 8pm (book by 2pm). Licensed. Short breaks offered. Closed Nov-Mar. **Directions:** From N4 / Mullingar bypass, take R394 for 5 miles, to Crookedwood. Left at Wood pub, then 1.5 miles to first junction. Go right; house is three quarters of a mile on the right.

Birr Castle Demesne

Birr Co Offaly **Tel: 0509 20336** / 21583
Email: mail@birrcastle.com
Web: www.birrcastle.com

GARDEN

Large demesne with important collection of trees, lake, walks, formal garden.

COUNTY OFFALY

It is possible to do a whistle stop tour of the world in this fascinating demesne surrounding majestic Birr Castle and embraced by the River Camcor. You can globe trot in minutes from Pakistan to New Zealand, and from Mexico to a glade that looks like the Yunnan region of China. In fact it is part of the Yunnan for all of the trees and shrubs are the realisation of a plant hunter's dream brought back from an expedition in '93 by Brendan, Lord Rosse and propagated at Birr. The 78 species, including birch, juniper, acers and cotoneasters, together with other recent introductions from around the world, are part of an exciting tradition of plant exploration at Birr .

There are many extraordinary things waiting to be discovered in the 130 acre grounds: the tallest box hedge in the world (due a vertigo defying shave), the Birr Zebra (a beech tree with amazing striped leaves), otters, nesting corncrakes, a hidden gravity driven water fountain amid a fernery, or an elephant foot tree. On the far side of the lake, children can try to catch a glimpse of Sweeney, who

lurks in the kind of native wild wood that existed in Ireland a millennium ago. Not far away is the 'Teatro Verde', an outdoor theatre of dramatic sculpture masks by Agnes Conway and with magical views of the castle. Nearby huge a *Magnolia kobus* so covered with white bracts they look like clouds come to earth.

Within the landscaped park are the fruits of three generations of distinguished gardeners spanning a century. The 5th Earl of Rosse made the terraces and began the formal gardens, the 6th Earl became a botanist, subscribing to and organising plant expeditions especially to China resulting in an important collection of trees and shrubs - you can follow the excellent Red Tree Trail around 50 Trees of Distinction. Together with his wife Anne (daughter of Leonard Messel, the owner of Nyman's Garden), Michael Rosse enhanced the gardens - Anne designed the Baroque Garden with a pleached hornbeam cloister, box parterres and delphinium border where the famous *Paeonia* **'Anne Rosse'** tree peony grows, its golden petals streaked with crimson..

The castle was remodelled in the 19th century but parts of it date back to 1620 when the lands were acquired by Sir Laurence Parsons - and his descendants still live there. Tradition is important in this family - specimens are still being propagated from seed brought back from the wild, and the gardens play their part as a field station for the Royal Botanic Gardens Edinburgh, in a propagations programme. The Baroque Garden and the terraces were restored recently, helped by funding from Great Gardens of Ireland Restoration Programme, and a new fountain was designed by the present Earl in the form of a Celtic Cross.

Open all year: Apr-Oct 9-6, Nov-Mar 10-5. Supervised children welcome; wheelchair accessible; dogs on leads allowed. Plants sales, gift shop; tea room; museum. **Directions:** *Entrance in Rosse Row in centre of Birr.*

Kinnitty
COUNTRY HOUSE

Ardmore House
The Walk Kinnitty Co Offaly
Tel: 0509 37009
Email: info@kinitty.net Web: www.kinnitty.net

Set back from the road in its own charming gardens, Christina Byrne's stone-built Victorian house offers old-fashioned comforts: brass beds, turf fires and home-made bread and preserves for breakfast. Bedrooms are deliberately left without amenities, in order to make a visit to Ardmore a real country house experience and encourage guests to spend less time in their rooms and mix with each other - tea is available downstairs at any time. All bedrooms are decorated to a high standard - one with jacuzzi bath - and a ground floor room is wheelchair friendly. Christina can provide you with maps and guides to walking in the area, and she offers a 4-day walking break, with 3 days' guided walking in Slieve Blooms, 1 day at Birr Castle Gardens and Clonmacnoise, and dinner in local restaurants, including Kinnitty Castle (where there's a traditional Irish night on Fridays), and Leap castle - Irelands most haunted castle. No evening meals are offered here, but there's a handy restaurant, The Glendine Bistro (Tel: 0509 37973), within walking distance in the village. Children welcome; pets allowed in some areas. **Rooms 5** (4 en-suite, 3 shower only, 1 with private bathroom, 1 disabled, all no smoking). B&B c.€35 pps, ss c.€15. Open all year. **No Credit Cards. Directions:** In village of Kinnitty, 9 miles from Birr (R440).

Heywood Gardens

Ballinakill Co Laois
Tel: 0502 33563
Email: heywoodgardens@opw.ie

GARDEN

Landscaped estate with formal gardens designed by Sir Edwin Lutyens

Representing two chapters of garden history, Ballinakill is an 18th century landscaped estate laid out in the romantic manner, with a rare gem - an architectural garden designed by Sir Edwin Lutyens (1869-1944) - at its heart. Created in 1906 for the Poe family, it is one of the few Lutyens gardens in Ireland (the other three are the War Memorial Garden, Islandbridge, The People's Garden Parnell Square and a private garden on Lambay island).

It has similar elements to Hestercombe Gardens, the best known of the gardens created by Lutyens, and is a beautiful exercise in structure with a sunken pool garden as the central feature. Here a romantic loggia overlooks the lily pond and fountain with circular terraces of planting originally planned by the other half of one of the greatest gardening partnerships ever, Gertrude Jekyll (1843-1932).

The whole is surrounded by a walk with ox eye windows, looking out over a panorama of seven counties, and approached by an alley of pleached limes. The other elements of the design are a cloister like terrace overlooking a chain of lakes, and a secret sundial garden hidden away by ramparts of yew. The earlier garden was commissioned by MF Trench who built the first phase of the now demolished Heywood (unusually named for his mother in law) in1773. These gardens with their Gothic follies, made partly from the ruins of Aghaboe Abbey, have been under restoration by the Board of Works who have been painstakingly unearthing their secrets.

Open all year round during daylight. Supervised children welcome; very limited wheelchair access; no dogs. **Directions:** *7 km south of Abbeyleix, off the R432 to Ballinakill.*

Durrow
HOTEL / RESTAURANT

Castle Durrow
Durrow Co Laois
Tel: 0502 36555 Fax: 0502 36559
Email: info@castledurrow.com Web: www.castledurrow.com

The restoration of this substantial 18th century country house and grounds has clearly been a labour of love for proprietors Peter and Shelly Stokes. It is an impressive building with some magnificent features, offering spacious, luxurious accommodation in high-ceilinged, individually decorated rooms and suites in the main house, with views over the surrounding parkland and countryside; some more contemporary but equally luxurious ground floor rooms are in a more recently renovated wing. Public rooms include a large drawing room/bar, where informal meals are available, and there is a lovely dining room with a pretty pastoral outlook at the back of the house. Major restoration work has been done in the grounds, including the old walled garden at the back which is progressing very well; there are interesting gardens to visit in the area too, as Emo Court and Heywood Gardens are both nearby. This is a pleasing place to stay, and to eat - **The Castle Restaurant** has earned a reputation which draws diners from a wide area. The dining room is gently contemporary, with beautiful tall windows over-looking the back garden; it is very pleasant at all times, whether enjoying the brightness and garden aspect in daylight or the romantic evening atmosphere, when generous tables are laid with crisp white linen, gleaming glasses and silver, and fresh flowers. David Rouse has been head chef since 2001, and the kitchen team do a good job; careful sourcing of all food is the policy - and the quality shows, especially as the walled garden is now supplying fresh produce, including herbs and salads. **Rooms 33** (all no smoking). B&B c.€100 pps, ss c. €40. 24 hr room service. Children welcome. Pets allowed by arrangement. Garden, walking, tennis, cycling, snooker. Golf, fishing, equestrian, garden visits all nearby. **Restaurant: Seats 65** (private room, 20; outdoor seating, 100). Reservations required. Toilets wheelchair accessible. D daily, 7-10. Bar meals also available, 12-7 daily. Set D €50; Bar L à la carte. Licensed. Closed 25-26 Dec, 31 Dec, 1 week in Jan. Amex, MasterCard, Visa, Laser, Switch. **Directions:** On main Dublin-Cork road, N8.

Mountrath
COUNTRY HOUSE

Roundwood House

Mountrath Co Laois
Tel: 0502 32120 Fax: 0502 32711
Email: roundwood@eircom.net Web: www.roundwoodhouse.com

This unspoilt early Georgian house lies secluded in mature woods of lime, beech and chestnut, at the foot of the Slieve Bloom mountains. A sense of history and an appreciation of genuine hospitality are all that is needed to make the most of a stay here – forget about co-ordinated decor and immaculate maintenance, just relax and share the immense pleasure and satisfaction that Frank and Rosemarie Kennan derive from the years of renovation work they have put into this wonderful property. Although unconventional in some ways, the house is extremely comfortable and well-heated (with central heating as well as log fires) and all the bathrooms have been recently renovated (all have full bath, some also with over-bath shower). Each bedrooms has its particular charm, although it might be wise to check if there is a convivial group staying, in which case the bedroom above the drawing room may not be the best option. The Kennans also have several attractively cottagey rooms in converted areas at the back of the house, and further outbuildings, The Coach House, The Forge and The Cottage, available for self-catering. Restoration is an ongoing process, and an extraordinary (and historically unique) barn is possibly the next stage; this enterprise defies description, but don't leave Roundwood without seeing it. Dinner is served at a communal table, and based on the best local and seasonal ingredients (notably locally reared beef and lamb); Rosemarie's food suits the house perfectly – good home cooking without unnecessary frills – and Frank is an excellent host. In the morning, a delicious, perfectly cooked breakfast will see you on your way - there is much of interest in the area, including numerous garden visits within easy striking distance. Garden, croquet, boules, walking - there is a mile long walk in the grounds and garden renovation is ongoing. Stabling available at the house; horse riding nearby. Golf nearby. Children welcome. Pets allowed in some areas. **Rooms 10** (all en-suite & 4 no-smoking). B&B c.€75 pps, ss €25. D €45, at 8pm (book by noon); non-residents welcome by reservation if there is room. Licensed. Dining room closed Sun & Mon except for resident guests. Closed 25 Dec & all Jan. Amex, Diners, MasterCard, Visa, Laser. **Directions:** On the left, 3 miles from Mountrath, on R440.

Gash Gardens

Castletown **Portlaoise** Co Laois
Tel: 057 873 2247
Email: gashgardens@eircom.net

GARDEN

A garden for plant enthusiasts to inspire those making new gardens.

Anyone needing the courage to start a garden from complete scratch could do no better than to visit Gash. It was started in 1986 by the late Noel Keenan in a field behind his farm, and what started as a walk to the river Nore became a fully fledged fantasy with contrasting areas covering four acres. The garden has now achieved remarkable maturity.

The star of the show is the Moon House Grotto, where a waterfall cascading from a mound of rocks, tumbles past a circular window into a lily pond. Around it gravel paths meander around raised beds with a wonderful collection of herbaceous and alpine plants, and past a whole variety of features, from a gazebo to a stream garden. Eyecatchers among the plant population include Persicaria virginana 'Painter's Palette', Ribes speciosum the fuchsia flowered currant and Veratrum nigrum producing its brown black flowers for the first time. A large collection of hardy geraniums features throughout the garden, personalities like 'Mrs Kendall Clark' and 'Bill Wallace' are bound to win friends.

Beyond a bridge over a stream - a great excuse to grow damp loving plants like gunneras and hostas - is a soothing garden with lawn winding around informal beds of mixed planting. Contrasting use of foliage helps to create year round interest with splashes of lime green or golden foliage, and hydrangeas like the velvety leafed lace cap H aspera and 'Annabelle' provide a late display.The hidden walkway to the river and the laburnum tunnel provide a sense of adventure.

There is something very special about a two generational garden. Mary Keenan has taken over her father's mantle, planting a new border of old fashioned roses like 'Baron Girod de l'Ain', and R chinensis 'Mutabilis', and beginning a collection of kniphofias and crocosmias with beauties like C 'Star of the East'and K 'Bees'Lemon'.

Open May-Sep, Mon - Sat, 10-5 (closed Sun unless by appointment). Supervised children welcome; not suitable for wheelchairs; no dogs. Plant sales. Admission c. €5. **Directions:** *Take the Mountrath-Castletown road, keep left through the village; the garden is half a mile on the left.*

Athy
COUNTRY HOUSE

Coursetown Country House

Stradbally Road Athy Co Kildare
Tel: 059 863 1101
Fax: 059 863 2740

Jim and Iris Fox's fine 200 year old house just off the Stradbally road is attached to a large arable farm. The house is welcoming, immaculately maintained and very comfortable, with some unusual attributes, including Jim's natural history library (where guests are welcome to browse) and extensive, well-tended gardens stocked with many interesting plants, including rare herbaceous plants, and old roses and apple trees. Bedrooms vary according to their position in the house, but all are thoughtfully furnished in a pleasantly homely country house style and have direct dial phones, tea/coffee facilities and hair dryers. Iris takes pride in ensuring that her guests have the comfort of the very best beds and bedding - and the attention to detail in the pristine shower rooms is equally high, with lots of lovely

towels and quality toiletries. (A bathroom is also available for anyone who prefers to have a good soak in a tub.) A ground floor room near the front door has been specially designed for wheelchair users, with everything completed to the same high standard as the rest of the house. Then there is breakfast - where the emphasis is on delicious healthy eating: fresh juices and fruit salad, poached seasonal fruit (plums from the garden, perhaps) pancakes, French toast with banana & maple syrup, Irish farmhouse cheeses, home-made bread and preserves are all offered - and the traditional cooked breakfast includes lovely rashers specially vacuum-packed for Iris by Shiel's butchers, in Abbeyleix. Not suitable for children under 12 (and older children must have their own room.) No smoking house. Pets allowed in some areas by arrangement. Garden. **Rooms 4** (all with en-suite shower, all no smoking, 1 for disabled). B&B c. €60 pps, ss €15. Closed mid Dec-early Jan. MasterCard, Visa. **Directions:** Just outside Athy, on R428. Turn off N78 at Athy, or N80 at Stradbally; well signposted.

Ballindoolin House & Garden
Carbury Nr. **Edenderry** Co Kildare
Tel: 046 973 1430
Email: sundial@iol.ie   Web: www.ballindoolin.com

GARDEN

Restored two acre walled garden, just as it would have been 100 years ago with woodland walks.

The gardens at Ballindoolin are a shining example of what can be achieved with buckets of imagination and hard work, plus some help from EU friends. When the Molony family inherited Ballindoolin estate in 1993 little remained in the large walled garden behind the 1821 house except for some venerable espaliered apple trees. Its restoration was carried out in 1997 with the help of the Great Gardens Restoration Scheme, to a design by Daphne Shackleton. A JCB was used to clear the jungle, uncovering a melon pit and original paths in the process, and the ground was ploughed before replanting began.

Now the garden looks much as it would have done in its heyday. There are 100 foot herbaceous borders with gold and white predominating, a lavender path running down the central axis of the garden, and a grid of paths delineating different areas for vegetables, fruit and new espaliered fruit trees, plus a curious whirling patterned parterre based on the original design.

Every bit as appealing are the woodland walks and displays of spring bulbs and flowering shrubs. There is a nature trail with curiosities like an iron age mound, and a lime kiln and the opportunity learn the Celtic lore of the trees which divided trees into chieftans and commons. There is a tour of the ground floor of the house and also a museum, a coffee shop and a gift shop - and you can rest assured that fruit from the garden makes the most delicious home made jam, which is on sale in the shop.

Open May-Jul Wed-Sun, 12-6. Children and wheelchairs welcome, plants for sale, teas; also house tours and museum. Entrance c. €6. House tours c. €5. **Directions:** *Turn off the N6 beyond Enfield. turning left at Moy Valley Centre for Carbury; turn right at T junction and follow signs.*

Williamstown Garden

Carbury Nr. **Edenderry** Co Kildare
Tel: 046 955 2971
Email: williamstownhse@eircom.net

GARDEN

Magical 18th century walled garden with ancient beech walk, herbaceous borders and much more.

If ever there is a place with an enchanted fairytale atmosphere it is the original 18th century beech walk at Williamstown. Seen through its twilit aisle of contorted branches a path, bordered with clouds of blue nepeta and leading to a blaze of scarlet plants, appears like a brilliant vision. This is the heart the old walled garden adjoining a Palladian house attributed to Nathaniel Clements, dating to 1760 and set in a 700 acre estate. Set within the old framework and ancient trees the garden was restored in 2000, its walls repaired, room like compartments created and borders reinstated.

The entrance to the garden leads through a charming 18th century potting yard to a garden of meditation laid out with a 'Path of Life'. With displays of hellebores, snowdrops, ivies and ferns, the play of sunlight through trees and the burble of a water tree fountain it's a place to soothe the senses. The double herbaceous border, which forms the axis of the garden, looks for all the world like an Edwardian watercolour. One of Gertrude Jekyll's favourite palettes, blues, white, silver and soft yellows - predominate with clumps of lemon *Primula florindae*, *Anthemis tinctoria*, krigishoma, agapanthus, tradescantia and tree paeonies. There is a vista to a sundial which marks one of the characteristic changes of mood, in one direction there is the gothic gloom of the beech tunnel, in the other is a bee border of cat mint and pink hardy geraniums. Beyond the sundial the double border continues in still paler shades to two clumps of gunnera marking the entrance to a hidden green area. Here extraordinary beech arches, fused 200 years ago, appear like Tolkeinesque monsters.

Other treats include an exquisite temple, its rounded Palladian arches echoed by the patterns of two meticulous box parterres each containing 1,000 plants, hot borders, a woodland spring garden, a model potager with cardoons, sunflowers fruit and vegetables with onions planted around circles of carrots to confuse the carrot fly. And, in a former deer park, grass paths lead among contented cattle through a young arboretum to inviting seats.

*Open late May-early Jul to adult groups of 15+ by appointment only. Not suitable for children; no dogs; wheelchair accessible; plant sales; teas by arrangement. Admission c. €5. **Directions:** On the N6 ,turn off at Moy Valley Centre; turn right for Carbury then right at T junction.*

Curragh
COUNTRY HOUSE

Martinstown House

The Curragh Co Kildare
Tel: 045 44 1269 Fax: 045 44 1208
Email: info@martinstownhouse.com Web: www.martinstownhouse.com

Just on the edge of the Curragh and conveniently located for visiting a number of County Kildare gardens including the famous Japanese Gardens at the National Stud, this delightful 200 year old house was built by the famous architect Decimus Burton who also designed the lodges in the Phoenix Park, Dublin, and is the only known domestic example of this 'Strawberry Hill' gothic architectural style in Ireland. It is on a farm, set in 170 acres of beautifully wooded land, with free range hens, sheep, cattle and horses, an old icehouse and a well-maintained walled kitchen garden that provides vegetables, fruit and flowers for the house in season. Meryl Long welcomes guests to this idyllic setting, aiming to offer them 'a way of life which I knew as a child (but with better bathrooms!), a warm welcome, real fires and good food.' It is

a lovely family house, with very nicely proportioned rooms - gracious but not too grand - open fires downstairs, and bedrooms that are all different, each with its own special character and very comfortably furnished, with fresh flowers. A stay here is sure to be enjoyable, with the help of a truly hospitable hostess who offers a delicious afternoon tea on arrival - and believes that holidays should be fun, full of interest and with an easy-going atmosphere. Golf and equestrian activities nearby. Croquet. Not suitable for children under 12. No pets. **Rooms 4** (3 en-suite, 1 with private bathroom, all no smoking). B&B from c. €90 pps, ss €20. Residents' D c. €45 (by arrangement - book the previous day. Closed mid Dec-early Jan. Amex, MasterCard, Visa. **Directions:** M7 south from Dublin, then M9 to Kilcullen exit. Turn right onto N78 (towards Athy) for 1 mile to crossroads, signposted Martinstown to the right; then follow the signs.

Maynooth
COUNTRY HOUSE / RESTAURANT

Moyglare Manor
Maynooth Co Kildare
Tel: 01 628 6351
Email: info@moyglaremanor.ie Web: www.moyglaremanor.ie

Only eighteen miles from Dublin and convenient to a number of very special gardens, Norah Devlin's classical Georgian manor is approached by a tree-lined avenue, allowing the arriving guest to appreciate this imposing stone built house to the full. Mrs Devlin's love of antiques is famous - gilt-framed mirrors and portraits are everywhere, shown to advantage against deep-shaded damask walls, and chairs and sofas of every pedigree ensure comfortable seating, even at the busiest times; no wonder a visit here is sometimes described as 'like being in an antique shop'. Spacious bedrooms and suites are also lavishly furnished in period style, some with four-poster or half tester beds, and all have well-appointed bathrooms. Dining in the traditionally appointed restaurant is always a treat: grand and romantic, it's a room with a sense of occasion; the house style is country house cooking, offering a nicely balanced combination of traditional favourites and sophisticated fare with an emphasis on seafood, and game in season - and a fine wine list to match. Not suitable for children under 12. No Pets. Garden; walking. Horse riding nearby. **Rooms 16** (1 suite, 4 executive, 2 disabled). B&B from c. €115 pps, ss about €25. Not suitable for children under 12. **Restaurant Seats 40** (private room, 25). L Sun-Fri 12.30-2; D daily 7-9. Set L c. €32. Set D c. €52, also à la carte. Licensed. Restaurant closed L Sat. Open all year except Christmas. **Directions:** From Dublin: N4 west; exit for Maynooth, keep right at church; after 2.5 miles, turn left at Moyglare crossroads, then next right.

Straffan
HOTEL / RESTAURANT

Barberstown Castle
Straffan Co Kildare
Tel: 01 628 8157 Fax: 01 627 7027
Email: barberstowncastle@ireland.com Web: www.barberstowncastle.ie

Steeped in history through three very different historical periods, Barberstown Castle has been occupied continuously for over 400 years and would make a comfortable and interesting base when visiting gardens in the area. It now includes the original keep in the middle section of the building, a more domestic Elizabethan house (16th century), a 'new' Victorian wing added in the 1830s by Hugh Barton (also associated with nearby Straffan House, now The K Club, with whom it shares golf and leisure facilities) and, most recently, a large new wing added by the current owner, Kenneth Healy, which is built in keeping with its age and style. Some of the individually decorated rooms and suites are in the oldest section, the Castle Keep, others are more recent, but most are stylish and spacious, and some have four-posters. Public areas include two drawing rooms and an elegant bar, and there are big log fires everywhere. Fine dining of character is offered in **The Castle Restaurant**, where head chef Bertrand Malabat, who joined the castle in 1999, presents a number of menus including a six-course Tasting Menu (served to complete parties only); the style is classic French with the occasional nod to international fashions, and the combination of good cooking and professional service should ensure an enjoyable experience. *Light meals are available in the Tea Rooms, 10am-7pm daily. Garden, walking. Children welcome. No pets. **Rooms 59** (16 junior suites, 17 premier rooms, 21 ground floor, 1 shower only, 3 disabled, all no smoking.) Lift. **Restaurant** not suitable for children under 12. Seats 110 (private room 24). Reservations advised. L daily 12.30-2.30, D 7.30-9.30 (Sun, 6-8); Set D c. €55; à la carte L&D also available. Open all year except Christmas. Amex, Diners, MasterCard, Visa. **Directions:** West N4 - turn for Straffan exit/ South N7 - Kill Exit.

Lodge Park Walled Gardens

Straffan Co Kildare
Tel: 01 628 8412
Email: garden@steam-museum.ie Web: www.steam-museum.ie

GARDEN

Deeply satisfying restored walled garden with garden rooms.

The spicy scent of clipped box, bees drowsy with heat, fruit ripening against sun warmed brick and herbaceous plants pampered into magnificence: Lodge Park has all the magic to be expected of a walled garden and more.

Originally dating back to the 18th century like the Palladian house, the present incarnation of the garden dates from the 1980s. A path between borders, their billowing plants and shrubs contained by box clipped into hedges and pyramids, offers a vista down one side of the garden and also access to a series of 'rooms', walled with beech hedges. Each one of these would make a pleasing garden in its own right and everyone has a favourite area. It might be the white and silver garden filled with phlox, lambs ears, nicotiniana and white agapanthus or the salad garden, with patterns made from the serried ranks of lollo rosso, lettuce, scarlet stemmed chard and chives, laid out among geometric brick paths.

It could be the handsome herbaceous border beside the tennis court, full of stately herbaceous plants like yellow centurion, erigerons, hollyhocks and pale sunflowers. And the scent within the canopy of the wrought iron rosarie made by Brendan Walsh is enough to make the senses swoon with the fragrance of old roses like **'Rambling Rector'** and **'Wedding Day'**. The working kitchen garden, screened by a sweet pea pergola and hedged in espaliered apple trees, filled with chard, asparagus, soft fruit and other treats, usually appeals to the non distaff side of the family.

There are plenty of other attractions too. Given the steam museum - with a collection of model engines and steam engines used for distilleries and breweries, and the Steaming Kettle Tea Rooms with sinful chocolate cake, and the gift shop - Lodge Park makes a good venue for a family outing.

*Open Jun-Aug, Wed-Sun 2-6; also May & Sep by appointment. Children welcome; no dogs; wheelchair accessible. Teas. Admission c. €5. **Directions:** Just outside Straffan. Turn off the N7 at Kill for Straffan.*

Ballymore Eustace
PUB / RESTAURANT

The Ballymore Inn
Ballymore Eustace Co Kildare
Tel: 045 864 585 Email: theballymoreinn@eircom.net

It's the fantastic food that draws people to the O'Sullivan family's pub and it's wise to book well ahead to get a taste of the wonderful things this fine country kitchen has to offer, especially at weekends. The building gives out a few hints about what's in store as you approach - the neatly painted exterior and clipped trees in tubs flanking the front bring a sense of anticipation; inside there's a large café dining area at the front and a bar for more casual dining towards the back - and unusual craft furniture, original artwork and striking fresh flowers and plants all add up to the kind of place where details count. Top quality ingredients are de rigeur here, so you will find Penny Lange's local organic vegetables, also beef, lamb, bacon, chicken and eggs that come only from recognised quality assured Irish farms, and Irish farmhouse cheese from Sheridans Cheesemongers in Dublin, who ensure that every cheese is correctly ripened before delivery. Immaculate sourcing, careful cooking and a relaxed ambience have proved a winning formula - so whether you want a full meal or a quick bite, what you will get here is quality and style. Crisp-based modern pizzas based on artisan products and baked in a special pizza oven are the house speciality, closely followed by great beef and fresh fish; just keep off the Ballymore Inn home fries -they're addictive. Children welcome. **Seats 50.** Air conditioning. Food served daily 12.30-9 (Sun to 7). Closed 25 Dec and Good Fri. Amex, Mastercard, Visa, Laser. Directions: From Blessington, talk Baltinglass road. After 1.5 miles, turn right to Ballymore Eustace.

Arklow
COUNTRY HOUSE

Plattenstown House

Coolgreaney Road Arklow Co Wicklow
Tel: 0402 37822 Fax: 0402 37822
Email: mcdpr@indigo.ie Web: www.wicklow.ie/farm/f-plattn.htm

About halfway between Dublin and Rosslare (each about an hour's drive away) and overlooking parkland, this quiet, peaceful place is set in 50 acres of land amidst its own lovely gardens close to the sea - and Margaret McDowell describes her period farmhouse well, as having "the soft charm typical of the mid-19th century houses built in scenic Wicklow". This is a charming base from which to visit gardens in County Wicklow and the nearer parts of Wexford, and the sea, riding stables and forest walks are all nearby. There's a traditional drawing room furnished with family antiques overlooking the front garden, a TV lounge available for guests' use and a lovely dining room where breakfast is served - and evening meals are also offered by arrangement. Bedrooms vary in size and outlook according to their position in the house and have interestingly different characters, but all are comfortably furnished. A lovely, peaceful place. Children welcome. No pets. **Rooms 4** (3 en-suite with shower only, 1 with private bathroom, all no smoking). B&B c. €42pps, no ss. Weekend / mid-week breaks - details on application. Closed Christmas-early Jan. MasterCard, Visa. **Directions:** Top of Arklow town, small roundabout, straight on to Coolgreaney Road. 5 km on left.

Ashford
FARMHOUSE

Ballyknocken House

Gleanealy Ashford Co Wicklow
Tel: 0404 44627 Fax: 0404 44696
Email: cfulvio@ballyknocken.com Web: www.ballynocken.com

Perfectly placed for garden visits, walking holidays in the Wicklow Hills, or simply touring the area, Catherine Fulvio's charming Victorian farmhouse provides comfort, cosiness, home-cooked food and hospitality. The farm has been in the Byrne family for three generations and they have welcomed guests for over thirty years - Catherine took over in 1999, and she has since refurbished the house throughout in old country style. A gently Victorian theme prevails: bedrooms have been charmingly done up, with antique furniture and very good beds - and pretty bathrooms, five of which have Victorian baths. The dining room, parlour and sitting room are in a similar style and her energetic quest for perfection also extends to the garden, where new fruit trees, roses and herbs have been planted, and a cookery school - which is in a renovated milking parlour in the grounds. Catherine cooks four course dinners for guests, based on local produce, including vegetables and herbs from the Ballyknocken farm (with wine list including some specially imported wines); the cooking style is modern and, influenced by her Italian husband Claudio, there's a Mediterranean flavour. All this, plus extensive breakfasts and a relaxing atmosphere ensure guests keep coming back for more. Self-catering accommodation is also available. Cookery school. **Rooms 7** (all en-suite & no smoking, 1 shower only). B&B c. €60, ss €35. Residents D Tue-Sat, c. €38 at 7.30. No D Sun or Mon. L for groups (8+) by arrangement. Licensed. Closed mid-Dec-mid Jan. MasterCard, Visa. **Directions:** From Dublin, turn right after Texaco garage in Ashford; after 3 miles, house on right.

Mount Usher

Ashford Co Wicklow
Tel: 0404 40205
Email: mount_usher.gardens@indigo.ie Web: www.mount-usher-gardens.com

GARDEN

Magnificent gardens in the Robinsonian manner with a river as the central feature.

Mount Usher is particularly blessed in a number of ways. Originally created by the Walpole family, the garden owes its character to one of those happy confluences of history: the garden took shape over a period when the enthusiasm for new plant introductions was at its peak, and the possession of exotic species brought back from plant hunting expeditions to the east and the southern hemisphere was a serendipitous form of showing off. At the same time ideas were influenced by William Robinson whose book 'The Wild Garden' rejected Victorian formality in favour of naturalistic planting of species assembled from all over the world. Then there is the bonus of being on the banks of the River Vartry, which runs swift, sparkling and shallow over a series of weirs. The combination of these elements makes for a veritable garden of Eden where, throughout 20 acres, visitors are treated to a series of glorious prospects and to a magnificent collection of trees, plants and shrubs in sylvan settings. It's a place to revisit in celebration of the changing seasons, with carpets of naturalised bulbs, snowdrops, crocus

daffodils, trilliums and 150 different species of rhododendrons and azaleas in spring, lilies - like the giant crinum and martagon - and Eucryphias 'the White Knights of August in summer, and the spectacular autumn colour of vivid scarlet Acers, bronze Liquid Ambers and saffron *Liriodendron tulipfera*.

Among Mount Usher's collection of over 5,000 trees and shrubs, there are three important collections: Nothofagus (the southern hemisphere beech), Eucalyptus, and Eucryphia - and also many rare and unusual plants like the Montezuma pine, *Gevuina avellana* and *Lapageria rosea*. Winding paths lead visitors on a voyage round the plant world, through varied groves and glades and back and forth to the river banks. A Maple walk, an azalea ride, an aromatic grove of Eucalyptus with a meadow of naturalised fritillarias nearby, and a secret fern walk are just some of the features. There are more intimate areas too - a herbaceous garden enclosed by tall beech hedges, a narrow river walk and a delightful stream garden where astilbes, hostas and candelabra primulas prosper. And, in a special touch, tribute is paid to the men who devoted a working lifetime to gardening at Mount Usher: George Burns, Charles Fox, Michael Giffeny and Miles Manning.

Open mid Mar- end Oct, 10.30-5. Supervised children and wheelchairs welcome; no dogs. Shop; tea rooms.

Clone House

Aughrim
COUNTRY HOUSE

Aughrim Co Wicklow **Tel: 0402 36121** Fax: 0402 36029
Email: stay@clonehouse.com Web: www.clonehouse.com

The oldest part of Jeff and Carla Watson's rambling country house in the lovely unspoilt south Wicklow countryside goes back to the 1600s, although it was largely rebuilt in 1805 after burning in the 1798 Rebellion. Today this elegantly furnished and hospitable house is full of comfort, providing a quiet and relaxing haven, away from the stresses of modern life. Open fires in every room are a particularly attractive feature - and thoughtful little touches abound, including fresh fruit and chocolates in each bedroom (some with four posters), as well as tea and coffee making facilities - and no television to intrude into this tranquil retreat. Landscaped gardens surround the house and are under continuous development; with lovely stonework in new pathways and walls echoing the old buildings beside the house, and many interesting features including ponds, the gardens are an attraction in themselves - although the natural countryside and mountain views would be difficult to upstage. Three guests' sitting rooms are comfortably furnished for relaxing in, and dinner is served in an elegant period dining room, also with an open fire. Carla, who is Italian, loves cooking and prepares traditional Tuscan dinners by arrangement - menus are changed daily, and Carla's food is simple and full of flavour - and different from other restaurants too, which adds to its appeal. A mainly Italian wine list complements the food well. This is a wonderful place to relax in beautiful, tranquil surroundings. * Short breaks are offered - details on application. Children welcome. No pets. Gym, weight room, sauna; table tennis; garden. Private parties (24). **Rooms 7** (5 en-suite, 2 private bathrooms, 4 shower only, all no smoking) B&B c. €90pps, ss €40 Dinner at 8pm by arrangement, c. €55. Licensed (BYO permitted, corkage €8). 10% SC on dinners. Open all year. MasterCard, Visa, Laser. **Directions:** Follow brown house signs from Aughrim or Woodenbridge.

Grangecon Café

Blessington

Kilbride Road Blessington Co Wicklow
Tel 045 857 892

Wholesome aromas will draw you into Jenny and Richard Street's smashing café, which retained its name when re-locating from the nearby village of Grangecon to the bustle of Blessington. Here, sensitive renovation has given an old building new life, with gentle modern decor and natural materials, but the fundamentals remain unchanged: the stated aim has always been "to provide you with a really good food stop", and this they do brilliantly. Everything on the menu is made on the premises, including the breads, pastries and ice cream; the ham hocks for the quiche lorraine are cooked here, the pork meat used in the sausage rolls is organic, fruit and vegetables come from Castleruddery organic farm, and all other ingredients are of the very best quality, many of them also organic and/or free range. The menu is understandably fairly brief, but the cooking is good, and flavours superb. This is not cheap food - how could it be when the ingredients are of such high quality – but it is extremely good value for money. **Seats 30.** Open Tue-Sat 9-5.30. Toilets wheelchair accessible. Closed Sun, Mon, Aug bank hol w/e & Christmas week. MasterCard, Visa, Laser. **Directions:** Centre of Blessington village, around the corner from Downshire House Hotel.

Hunting Brook Gardens

Lambs Hill **Blessington** Co Wicklow
Tel: 01 458 3972 / 087 2856601
Web: www.huntingbrook.com

GARDEN

Large garden with contemporary borders and wooded garden in mature woodland setting

One of the youngest open gardens, Hunting Brook has all the excitement of a fresh approach and new ideas. But the bones of the place are very old indeed - behind the house there is a ring fort dating back to the 7th century, and the namesake brook is part of a romantic landscaped demesne created in the 1830s.

Jimi Blake, former head gardener at Airfield, began gardening here in 2001, amid 15 acres of woods with beech, oak and larch. The area around his wooden house is now planted in a vibrant fusion of tropical and prairie style where tender plants like aloes and agaves rub shoulders with stately grasses like the rice paper grass Tetrapanx papyriferus and giant eryngiums like E pandanifolium. "I probably shouldn't be growing plants like this at 900 feet," says Jimi. So far so good though, and he is building up a national collection of miscanthus grasses amid particularly good late borders, and experimenting with plants propagated from species brought back from plant hunting expeditions to China, like Aralia echinotaulis.

A woodland garden is being developed near the ring fort with all manner of bulbs including trilliums 'Ladybird' and 'Empresss', shade loving plants like anemones and meconopsis, and rhizomes with exciting berries like the toad lilies and Diphyellia cymosa with vivid turquoise fruit. In between the two areas, acers and rhododendrons are being planted. At present five acres are open and the garden is still in the early stages of development, but it is an exciting place to see unusual plants and new planting styles - and Jimi runs excellent weekends courses.

* Nearby, **June Blake's Garden and Nursery** is a plantaholic's dream and the fact that it is just minutes away from her brother Jimi's garden at Hunting Brook creates a double attraction. June's half acre of young garden, set out around winding bark paths, mature beech trees and the terrible temptation of plants for sale, leads to many encounters with new and exciting plants especially perennials, shade loving plants and ornamental grasses. Many are propagated from seed from plant hunting expeditions and exchanges and June is on hand to tell you their stories and their habits. You won't go home empty handed. [Tel 01458 2500. Open 7 Mar-30 Sep, 12-5.30; closed Sun. Groups by appointment only. Wheelchair accessible.]

*Open Jun-Sep, several days each month, 12-5.30 (phone for dates), and other times by appointment. Children welcome; no dogs; not suitable for wheelchairs. Teas by arrangement. Plants for sale at Jimi's sister June Blake's nursery nearby. **Directions:** Just beyond Brittas, going south on the N81 Dublin-Blessington road; turn right at Tramway Antiques - the house is the second on the left.*

Chestnut Lodge

4 Sidmonton Square **Bray** Co Wicklow
Tel: 01 286 8623
Email: desbone@eircom.net

GARDEN

Inspirational small town garden packed with ideas and interesting plants

Chestnut Lodge is one of those gardens where visitors proceed at cocktail party pace for, like a good hostess Carol Bone, has an enviable gathering of plants and clever ideas guaranteed to entertain. All the features that you expect in a sizeable garden are concentrated in a small area: collections of ferns, a potager inspired by Villandry, a pond raided by herons, a clematis and wisteria arbour and an exuberant herbaceous border.

Fired with a love of gardening by her father, Carol Bone planned her garden so that it had hidden mysterious areas. With interesting foliage shrubs chosen with a flower arranger's eye, raised beds contained by sleepers, and gravelled paths as the backbone of the design, statuary, topiary and star plants provide the focal points. A pair of griffins guard the entrance to a secluded area with fatsia, ferns and other shade loving plants. In the main section, the old terracotta floor of the house became the new paved area bordered by the pond and a mixed border with choice shrubs and roses like David Austin's **'Pilgrim'**, and *Pittisporum* **'Irene Patterson'**. A potager edged in box and packed with serried ranks of vegetables and soft fruit was added to the garden to celebrate the Millennium.

Open mid May-Jul by appointment to groups + Wicklow Garden Festival. Not suitable for children, wheelchairs or dogs. Admission c. €5; tea available.

Graigueconna
Old Connaught Avenue **Bray** Co Wicklow
Tel: 01 282 2273
Email: rob.goodbody@eircom.net Web: www.dublingardens.com
GARDEN

Large old world garden with wonderful planting.

Some gardens are liable to take root in the memory and, thanks to the most magical planting effects, this is one of them. Graigueconna is proof of the point that gardens need time for that special symbiosis between gardener, plants and nature to evolve. Over thirty years ago Rosemary and John Brown restarted the garden begun two generations ago, growing choice plants from cuttings and seeds amid the mature bones of the original garden.

Beyond a sheltered stone terrace where Alpines flourish, two breathtaking borders face each other across a grass walk leading to the focal point of a bird bath with a froth of Alchemilla mollis at its feet. There are swags of species clematis and old fashioned roses rambling up through cordyline palms and all manner of handsome herbaceous plants and shrubs. There are wonderful examples of Rosemary Brown's painterly skill with plant compositions: shocking pink roses and geraniums with punchy purple clematis growing through, elsewhere the yellows and blues of athemis and eryngium complement each other.

The grass path down the herbaceous walk was once the site of a railway track, laid by an Alpine enthusiast in order to transport rocks down the garden the better to build a rock garden. A modified version of this remains, planted with southern hemisphere plants, shrubs, ferns and ground covers. It's a green and peaceful place, lit by lanterns of *Crinodendron hookrianum* and white trumpets of datura; plants have interesting stories like the speckle leafed *Helleborus orientalis* **'Graigueconna'**, the fern given to the Browns by the celebrated gardener Graham Stuart Thomas, and *Brachyglottis maurii*, said to have been used by the Maoris as loo paper.

A soothing lawn with a pool at the centre offers a complete change of mood and a great habitat for decorative grasses and damp loving plants like the magenta flowered *Primula vialii*. An arboretum has intriguing species: the "dead rat tree", *Sorbus vilmorinii*, known for its stinking blooms, a snake bark, *Acer grosseri* var *hersii* and a pink Madeiran cow parsley, thought to be the only one in Ireland.

Other treats in store include a border of clematis and old roses like **'Phyllis Bide'** and *Rosa californica* **'Plena'** and, for true plant connoisseurs, there is a greenhouse full of propagating plants, and unusual numbers shaded by a veil of *Passiflora antioquiensis*.

Open May-Jul, by appointment; groups 4+ only. Not suitable for children, wheelchairs or dogs.
Directions: *Take exit for Bray from N11, second exit from roundabout turn right at lights Graigueconna is at the top on left.*

COUNTY WICKLOW

Killruddery House & Gardens

Hillsbrook **Bray** Co Wicklow
Tel: 0404 46024
Email: info@kilruddery.com Web: www.kilruddery.com

GARDEN

A unique 300 year old Baroque garden, with water features.

The venerable garden at Killruddery, beautifully situated on the flank of the Little Sugar Loaf, is a unique survivor of history. Edward de Brabazon commissioned a Monsieur Bonet, trained at Versailles, to create the formal gardens there in 1682.

The Brabazons may have been influenced by James Butler, 1st Duke of Ormonde, who returned from exile in France in 1662 after the Restoration, and introduced French baroque style to Ireland, notably in the Royal Hospital Kilmainham and at Kilkenny Castle. Other gardens from this period were swept away by "improvements" as French formality made way for romantic landscapes.

The main elements of the design are the 152m twin long ponds or miroirs d'eaux, similar to those at the Chateau de Courances, designed to reflect the house originally built in 1652 and Tudorized in 1820. Beyond them is a curious water feature known as the Stops, fed by an aqueduct from half a mile away, beyond them again an avenue of limes continues the perspective of the ponds.

Designed for symmetry and mastery of nature, gardens from this period were also about outdoor entertainment, witness the sylvan theatre screened by beech hedges and the Angles or Patte d'Oie (goose foot). A central point between triangular hedges offered viewers different perspectives on the surrounding countryside. A circular fountain pool, guarded by statues of the four seasons and encircled by a spectacular beech hedge, and a rectangular wood known as the Wilderness, also date from the period.

Later additions to the garden include the Statue Gallery and orangerie, designed by William Burns in 1852, with a dome by Turner and also an ornamental dairy by George Hodson, overlooking the Ribbon Garden.

Open daily May-Sep, 1-5. Supervised children welcome; no dogs; partial wheelchair access.
Directions: *Turn right at the roundabout on the Bray to Greystones Road and follow signs.*

Dunlavin
COUNTRY HOUSE / RESTAURANT

Rathsallagh House
Dunlavin Co Wicklow
Tel: 045 403 112 Fax: 045 403 343
Email: info@rathsallagh.com Web: www.rathsallagh.com

This large, rambling country house is just an hour from Dublin, but it could be in a different world. It is very professionally operated, but the O'Flynn family insist it is not an hotel and - although there is an 18-hole golf course with clubhouse in the grounds - the gentle rhythms of life around the country house and gardens ensure that the atmosphere is kept decidedly low-key. Day rooms are elegantly furnished in classic country house style, with lots of comfortable seating areas and open fires. Accommodation includes rooms in the original building, which vary, as is usual with old houses - some are very spacious with lovely country views while other smaller, simpler rooms in the stable yard have a special cottagey charm - and there are spacious rooms with luxurious bathrooms in a new block, which is already ageing gracefully to match the older buildings. Rathsallagh is renowned for its good food and guests enjoy the ritual of having an aperitif in the old kitchen bar while choosing from interesting menus that are based on local and seasonal produce, much of it from their own farm, tunnels and walled gardens. Head chef John Kosturk's cooking is sophisticated without being over complicated - and the graciously furnished dining room overlooking the gardens and golf course provides a fine setting for dinners which are never less than memorable - and, next morning, there's a magnificent Edwardian breakfast buffet to look forward too. Afterwards, a stroll around the grounds - including the lovely walled gardens - is recommended. Golf (18). Gardens, tennis, cycling, walking. Pool table. Swimming pool, steam & spa room. Pets allowed (by arrangement only). **Rooms 29** (1 suite, 1 for disabled). B&B c.€160pps, ss c.€65. No SC. * Short breaks offered, details on application. Open all year. Helipad. **Restaurant Seats 120** (private room, 48). Reservations essential. D daily, 7-9. Set 5-course D €60; house wine €18-20; SC discretionary. * Not suitable for children under 12. Lunch is available only for residents (12-3), **but food is served at Rathsallagh Golf Club, 9-9 daily**. Non-residents welcome for dinner, by reservation. Amex, Diners, MasterCard, Visa, Laser. **Directions:** 15 miles south of Naas off Carlow Road, take Kilcullen Bypass (M9), turn left 2 miles south of Priory Inn, follow signposts.

Powerscourt Gardens

Powerscourt House **Enniskerry** Co Wicklow
Tel: 01 204 6000
Email: carmel.byrne@powerscourt.net Web: www.powerscourt.ie

GARDEN

Formal gardens on a grand scale in a magnificent setting.

Justly famous for the glory of its setting and the grandeur of its scale, Powerscourt is Ireland's most visited garden. Parts of the plan date back to the 1740s when Richard Cassel, also architect of Leinster House, designed a series of terraces and a circular pool as a suitably imposing foil to the Palladian mansion he had created for Viscount Powerscourt.

A century later architect Daniel Robertson was commissioned to embellish the garden in the then fashionable Italianate style. The main elements of the design are an elegant stone staircase leading down from a broad terrace and adorned with a statuary walk, culminating in two magnificent pegasii guarding the lake. Featuring pebble mosaics in the shallow steps of the staircase and a Neptune fountain at its foot, the design is thought to be based on the gardens at the Villa Butera in Italy.

Further chapters in the garden's history included the addition of a woodland walk known as Tower Valley, planted with rhododendrons - including some magnificent large leaved varieties, conifers with a pepper pot tower as a focal point, and a 'Japanesey' garden. This European version of a Japanese garden is set in a hollow with two Japanese bridges, pools and acers, and has recently been restored and replanted. Beside it is a weeping grotto built from volcanic stone, where ferns and mosses flourish.

Beyond the lake, paths lead through groves of towering specimen trees and on to the Dolphin pond set in a sylvan glade. A very splendid gate adorned with gilded roses, thistles and shamrocks symbolising England Scotland and Ireland (but no leeks, perhaps for decorative reasons) provides the link back to the formal areas of the garden, via double herbaceous borders.

The entrance to the garden is now through the house, or what was the house, for the building was gutted by fire in 1974. The great reception hall has been restored and can be viewed but the rest of the building now houses a very successful shopping complex and restaurant (lunch on the terrace is recommended). The Greenhouse complex offers decorative homewares and a garden centre - altogether a very satisfying place for a day out. The Powerscourt Waterfall - Ireland's highest - is also nearby.

Open all year except Dec 25 & 26, 9.30-5 daily (to dusk in winter). Children and wheelchairs welcome; no dogs; shops restaurant and garden centre. Admission c. € 5-7 (winter rates gardens only).
Directions: *Near Enniskerry village - well-signed in area.*

Enniskerry
RESTAURANT

Powerscourt Terrace Café
Powerscourt House Enniskerry Co Wicklow
Tel: 01 204 6070 Fax: 01 204 6072
Email: simon@avoca.ie Web: www.avoca.ie

Situated in a stunning location overlooking the gardens and fountains of Powerscourt House, the Pratt family of Avoca Handweavers run this attractive self-service restaurant in a similar style to the original Avoca restaurant at Kilmacanogue. It is a delightfully relaxed space, with a large outdoor eating area as well as the 160-seater café, and the kitchen team ensures that everything is freshly made, using as many local ingredients as possible – including organic herbs and vegetables – so that they can consistently offer really appetising healthy food. Avoca cafés are renowned for interesting salads, home-bakes and good pastries, and also excellent vegetarian dishes many of which, such as oven-roasted vegetable and goat's cheese tart, have become specialities. Parking (some distance from the house). Children welcome. **Seats 160** (additional 140 outside terrace; private room 20-90). Toilets wheelchair accessible. Open daily 10-5 (Sun to 5.30). Licensed. Closed 25-26 Dec. **Also at: Kilmcanogue** (01 286 7466), **Avoca Village** (0402 35105) and **Dublin** (Wicklow Street, Dublin 2; 01 672 6019). Amex, Diners, MasterCard, Visa, Laser. **Directions:** 2 miles from Enniskerry Village.

Mir

8 New Russian Village **Kilquade** Co Wicklow
Tel: 01 281 0285
Email: dkehoe@eircom.net

GARDEN

A passion for plants and interesting design go happily hand in hand at this spring and summer garden

This a spring and summer garden where a passion for plants and interesting design go happily hand in hand. Dr Dermot Kehoe began the garden (his fourth) in 1999, to indulge his interest in collecting Alpines, herbaceous perennials and unusual shrubs.

His starting point was a double herbaceous border framing a vista down the garden. Visitors are drawn up steps and down a lawn passing between stately ranks of thalictrum, *Veratrum album*, *Chephalaria gigantean*. The serpentine tour leads around a lawn and shrub border, through a woodland garden with shade loving plants, back past a new border of grasses and round to an alpine bed and lily pond. One of the surprise elements is a hidden hill.

Raised beds situated around the garden to accommodate Alpines were a priority and among the eye catching treasures are orchids, cushions of *Dianthus erinaceus*, and the hardy, orchid *Bletilla striata*. In the front garden, mixed borders of salvias and digitalis are particular favourites, with eye catching Salvias *turkestana*, *forsskaolii* and *fulgens*, and brown flowered *Digitalis parviflora*. Other eye catching plants include *Incarvillea arguta*, and woodland *Dianella tasmanica*, laden with lapis lazuli berries in autumn.

Many of Dr Kehoe's plants are grown from seed, including the handsome pink flowered shrub *Vallea stipularis*, symphyandrums and campanulas. And there are many southern hemisphere plants, including widow's tear *Westrigia fructicosa*, *Grevillia rosmarinifolia* and, one of the most admired plants in the garden, the bluebell creeper *Sollya heterophylla*.

*Open several days in July, 2-5 (phone to check dates), also groups of 8+ welcome by appointment. Supervised children welcome; no dogs; partial wheelchair access. Plants for sale. Lecture tours with refreshments by appointment. Admission c. €6.50. **Directions:** Turn off the N11 at Kilquade.*

National Garden Exhibition Centre

Calumet Nurseries **Kilquade** Co Wicklow
Tel: 01 281 9890
Email: calumet@clubi.ie Web: www.clubi.ie/calumet

GARDEN

Twenty inspirational gardens for the price of one!

To describe the National Garden Exhibition Centre as inspirational would be an understatement. The brainchild of nurseryman Tim Wallace, his wife Suzanne and garden designer Gordon Ledbetter, the idea was to show the best in garden design for a variety of situations and budgets.

Now in its second decade, the Centre has matured and - like the best of gardens - it has evolved. Where once there were 14 gardens there are now 20, and some of the original ideas have been changed or replanted. They range from the informality of the ambitious Water and Woodland Garden, where the spectacular autumn colours of the swamp cypress *Taxodium distichium* and acers like *A.* **'Osakazuki'** are reflected in a lake, to the perfection of the small Knot Garden where the scent of old roses is trapped by the room-like hedges. Newest is the Gothic Garden, with a dramatic gothic window overlooking a pool and areas of different planting, and the Plantsman's Garden, featuring exciting plant combinations like the ponytail grass *Stipa Tenussima* with *Phylcia arborea* and *Artemesia ludoviciana*, with four different types of planting including a section of acid loving plants.

The Town Garden, with its pergola, raised beds and pond, is a lovely example of the kind of sanctuary which can be achieved in a small space, while the Japanese Garden remains a particular favourite, with informal beds set in gravel and soothing foliage textures and colours; hostas, grasses and berge-nias cosy up to the feet of diminutive *Acer palmatum aconitefolium*, *Abies koreana* and *Cornus mas* with its purple autumn leaves.

Many of the plants used in the display gardens can be bought in the excellent nursery and there is a tea room for light meals. What more could you want?

*Open all year, Mon-Sat 10-5.30, Sun 1-5.30. Group tours available. Supervised children welcome; wheelchair accessible; no dogs. Plant sales. Teas. Admission c.€4.50 **Directions:** Off the N11 just past the turn off for Delgany, take next left for Kilquade; the Centre is a mile down the road on the left.*

Kiltegan
COUNTRY HOUSE

Barraderry Country House

Barraderry Kiltegan Co Wicklow
Tel: 059 647 3209
Email: jo.hobson@oceanfree.net Web: www.barraderrycountryhouse.com

Olive and John Hobson's delightful Georgian house is in a quiet rural area close to the Wicklow Mountains and, once their family had grown up, the whole house was extensively refurbished and altered for the comfort of guests. Big bedrooms with country views are beautifully furnished with old family furniture and have well-finished shower rooms, and there's a spacious sitting room for guests' use too. Barraderry would make a good base for touring the gardens of Wicklow, Kildare, Carlow and Wexford and there are plenty of other things to do nearby, with six golf courses within a half hour drive, several hunts and equestrian centres within easy reach and also Punchestown, Curragh and Naas racecourses - and, of course, walking in the lovely Wicklow Mountains. Breakfast is the only meal served, but the Hobsons direct guests to a nearby restaurant. Garden; walking. Children welcome (cot available). No pets. **Rooms 4** (all en-suite, shower only & no smoking). B&B €45 pps; ss €5. (Restaurant 4 miles). Closed 15 Dec-15 Jan. MasterCard, Visa. **Directions:** N81 Dublin-Baltinglass; R 747 to Kiltegan (7km).

Macreddin
HOTEL / RESTAURANT

BrookLodge Hotel
Macreddin Village Co Wicklow
Tel: 0402 36444
Email: brooklodge@macreddin.ie Web: www.brooklodge.com

Built on the site of a deserted village in a Wicklow valley, the Doyle brothers' hotel and restaurant has earned a national recognition for its strong position on organic food and their little "street" is thriving, with an olde-worlde pub (Actons), a café, a micro-brewery and gift shops selling home-made produce and related quality products. Organic food markets, held on the first Sunday of the month (first and third in summer) have also proved a great success. Spacious and welcoming, the hotel has elegant country house furnishings, a luxurious small spa and – most importantly – Ireland's only all-organic restaurant, The Strawberry Tree (named after its pioneering 1990s predecessor in Killarney), reflecting the BrookLodge philosophy of sourcing only from producers using slow organic methods and harvesting in their correct season. There's a great buzz associated with the commitment to organic production at BrookLodge, and dining at the Strawberry Tree is a unique experience - and good informal meals can be equally enjoyable at The Orchard Café and Actons pub (both open noon-9pm daily). Children welcome. Pets allowed in some areas by arrangement. **Rooms 56** (19 suites/superior, 4 ground floor, 4 disabled, 35 no smoking). Lift. B&B from c. €110 pps; ss €40. **Restaurant: Seats 145.** Air conditioning. Toilets wheelchair accessible. D Mon-Sun, L Sun only. Light meals/bar food daily, 12-9. Open all year. Amex, Diners, MasterCard,Visa, Laser. **Directions:** Signed from Aughrim.

Warble Bank

Newtownmountkennedy Co Wicklow
Tel: 01 281 9298
Email: warblebank@yahoo.ie

GARDEN

Pleasant cottage style garden with an enviable collection of plants.

One of the most fortuitous things you could wish for in a garden is a mature setting combined with generations of gardeners. Warble Bank is blessed with both, and Anne Condell continues her late mother's tradition at her home, which has a history stretching back 300 years.

The sheltered garden has two sides to its character, part green with trees, shrubs and grasses amid lawns falling away from the front of the house, the other floriferous enough to satisfy serious planta-holics. This colourful drama is announced with a flourish by scarlet and crimson planting with lobelias and heucheras. In late summer visitors then run the gauntlet between ranks of stalwart gold and bronze *Crocosmia* **'Solfatare'**, helianthus and heleniums, before the lure of a deep border where blues predominate. Herbaceous clematis, early and late monkshood, and hardy geraniums form the supporting cast with star performers like *Campanula punctata* and *Salvia sclarea turkestancia*, *Veronica longifolia* clouds of *Geranium robustum* and *Aster* **'Twilight'**. Anne has an eye for choice varieties and collects campanula, asters and geraniums in particular, some of them grown from seed.

Beds are laid out as a series of grids with a pergola swathed in roses **'Kiftsgate'**, **'Francois Juranville'**, **'Paul's Himalayan Musk'**, backed up by venerable apples trees and *Magnolia soulangiana*. There are some lovely plant combinations here, dark ruby eupatorium, and sedums with perovskia and grasses or purple sage with regano and zauschneria. In spring the garden is full of bearded iris, early wallflowers and bulbs - daffodils, snowdrops, crocus. At the top of the garden there is a working kitchen garden, invaded in patches by the flowers Anne grows for cutting.

Open on various days through Jun-July (phone for dates), and other times by appointment. Supervised children welcome; no dogs; partial wheelchair access. Plants for sale. Admisson c. €5. **Directions:** *Go through village, gate is second on left up slight hill.*

Rathnew
HOTEL / RESTAURANT

Hunter's Hotel

Newrath Bridge Rathnew Co Wicklow
Tel: 0404 40106 Fax: 0404 40338
Email: reception@hunters.ie Web: indigo.ie/~hunters

A rambling old coaching inn set in lovely gardens alongside the River Vartry, this much-loved hotel has a long and fascinating history – it's one of Ireland's oldest coaching inns, with records indicating that it was built around 1720. In the same family now for five generations, the colourful Mrs Maureen Gelletlie takes pride in running the hotel on traditional lines with her sons Richard and Tom This means old-fashioned comfort and food based on local and home-grown produce – with the emphasis very much on 'old fashioned' – which is where its charm and character lie. There's a proper little bar, with chintzy loose-covered furniture and an open fire, a traditional dining room with fresh flowers – from the riverside garden where their famous afternoon tea is served alongside gorgeous old-world herbaceous borders in summer - and comfortable country bedrooms. There is nowhere else in Ireland like it. Children welcome. No pets. **Rooms 16** (1 junior suite, 1 shower only, 1 disabled). Wheelchair access. B&B from €95 pps, ss about €20. **Restaurant Seats 50**. Toilets wheelchair accessible. L daily, 1-3 (Sun 2 sittings: 12.45 & 2.30). D daily 7.30-9. Set D from €40. Set L from €23.50. No s.c. Afternoon tea c. €10. Open all year except 3 days at Christmas. Amex, Diners, MasterCard, Visa. **Directions:** Turn off N11 at Ashford or Rathnew.

Rathnew
HOTEL / RESTAURANT

Tinakilly Country House Hotel
Rathnew Co Wicklow
Tel: 0404 69274 Fax: 0404 67806
Email: reservations@tinakilly.ie Web: www.tinakilly.ie

This is a place of great local significance, having been built in the 1870s for Captain Robert Halpin, a local man who became Commander of The Great Eastern, which laid the first telegraph cable linking Europe and America. In more recent times, William and Bee Power first opened Tinakilly for guests in 1983, after a sensitive restoration programme - and it is now run by their son Raymond and his wife Josephine - who have retained much that earned its reputation, while also bringing a fresh enthusiasm and energy which has lightened the atmosphere. Tinakilly has become a favourite destination for business guests, but there is also a romantic side to its nature - most bedrooms have views across the gardens and a bird sanctuary to the sea, and there are also some impressive period rooms, some with four-posters. The hotel participates in the Wicklow Garden Festival and the gardens - which date back to the time when the house was built and retain a Victorian tone, with mature trees, shrubs and mixed flower beds - are open throughout the year. The lovely grounds, comfortable accommodation, friendly, well-trained staff, and a fine kitchen make this a very pleasant base for touring nearby gardens. Children welcome. No pets. **Rooms 51** (6 suites, 33 junior suites, 12 superior, 1 suitable for disabled). Lift. B&B c.€134 pps; ss €61. **Brunel Restaurant: Seats 80** (private room, 30). Reservations required. Air conditioning. Toilets wheelchair accessible. D Tue-Sat 7-9; D c.€55 (D Sun & Mon shorter 'Tinakilly House' à la carte menu). L Sun from 1pm. Light meals also available in bar. Open all year except 24-26 Dec. Gardens open daily except Christmas/ New Year. Amex, Diners, MasterCard, Visa, Laser. **Directions:** From N11 (main Dublin - Wexford road) to Rathnew village; Tinakilly is 500 metres from village on R750 to Wicklow town.

Roundwood   # Roundwood Inn
PUB / RESTAURANT   Roundwood Co Wicklow
Tel: 01 281 8107

Jurgen and Aine Schwalm have owned this 17th century inn in the highest village in the Wicklow Hills since 1980. There's a public bar at one end, with a snug and an open fire, and in the middle of the building the main bar food area, furnished in traditional style with wooden floors and big sturdy tables – a huge fireplace where a log fire always burns. The style that the Schwalms have developed over the years is their own unique blend of Irish and German influences: excellent bar food includes Hungarian goulash, fresh crab bisque, Galway oysters, smoked Wicklow trout, smoked salmon and hearty hot meals, notably the excellent house variation on Irish stew. The bar food at Roundwood has always had a special character, which together with the place itself and a consistently high standard of hospitality, has earned it an enviable reputation with hillwalkers, Dubliners out for the day and visitors alike – and it's only a short drive from south Dublin and County Wicklow gardens, including Mount Usher. The Restaurant is in the same style and only slightly more formal than the main bar, and is open by reservation. Long-standing favourites here include rack of Wicklow lamb, roast wild Wicklow venison, venison ragout, pheasant and other game; German influences are again evident in specialities such as smoked Westphalian ham and wiener schnitzel, but there are also classics which cross all the usual boundaries: roast stuffed goose often appears on winter menus, for example - and the roast suckling pig is not to be missed. An interesting mainly European wine list favours France and Germany, with many special bottles from Germany unlikely to be found elsewhere. Bar meals 12-9.30 daily. **Restaurant Seats 45** (private room 25), Open for groups by reservation and D Fri & Sat 7.30-9; à la carte; L Sun only 1-2 (Children welcome for lunch). Bar closed 25 Dec, Good Fri. Amex, MasterCard, Visa, Laser. **Directions:** N11; follow signs for Glendalough.

South East

Arthurstown
HOTEL / RESTAURANT

Dunbrody House Hotel
Arthurstown Co Wexford
Tel: 051 389 600 Fax: 051 389 601
Email: dunbrody@indigo.ie Web: www.dunbrodyhouse.com

Set in twenty acres of parkland and gardens on the Hook Peninsula, Catherine and Kevin Dundon's elegant Georgian manor is just across the estuary from Waterford city and, as it is close to the Ballyhack-Passage East car ferry, it is well situated for visiting gardens in the Waterford area as well as County Wexford. It was the ancestral home of the Chichester family and the long tradition of hospitality at this tranquil and luxurious retreat is very much alive and well; well-proportioned public rooms, which include an impressive entrance hall and gracious drawing room, are all beautifully furnished and decorated with stunning flower arrangements and the occasional unexpectedly modern piece that brings life to a fine collection of antiques. Spacious bedrooms offer all the comforts expected of such a house, and have fine views over the gardens to the estuary beyond. Kevin Dundon is an internationally acclaimed chef and good food is at the heart of this house: **The Harvest Room** restaurant is open to non-residents and looks out onto a pleasure garden and, beyond, to a promisingly productive organic vegetable and fruit garden - an interesting place to browse around before dinner and, perhaps, hazard a guess as to what will be on the evening's menu. Overnight guests may also look forward to an outstanding breakfast, offering a magnificent buffet - fresh juices, fruit compôtes, cheeses - as well as hot dishes from a tempting menu. There is plenty to do on site, with extensive grounds and gardens to explore - and stylishly converted outbuildings house a spa and beauty salon, and a cookery school; Kevin Dundon has recently written a lovely cookery book, **'Full On Irish'**, which features many of the dishes from the restaurant and cookery school at Dunbrody. Children welcome. No pets. **Rooms 22** (all suites & superior). B&B c. €135 pps; ss €25. **Restaurant: Seats 80** (outdoor seating, 10). Reservations required. Toilets wheelchair accessible. D Mon-Sat 6.30-9.15; L daily 1.30-2.30. D from €50 (early D from €35), Set L c. €35. Licensed. Not suitable for children after 8pm. Open all year except Christmas. Amex, Diners, MasterCard, Visa, Laser. **Directions:** N11 to Wexford, R733 from Wexford to Arthurstown.

Arthurstown
FARMHOUSE

Glendine Country House

Arthurstown New Ross Co Wexford
Tel 051 389 500
Email: Web: www.gendinehouse.com

Ann and Tom Crosbie's large nineteenth century farmhouse is approached up a driveway off the main road to Arthurstown, and has magnificent views across the estuary. It is a spacious house and makes a very comfortable and hospitable place to stay at a reasonable price; it would be a godsend for anyone travelling with children as there are sandy beaches nearby and there's a safe, enclosed playground for children beside the house - and they also enjoy the highland cows, Jacob sheep and horses which the Crosbies keep in paddocks around the house. But you don't have to have the family in tow to enjoy a stay here: a pleasant guest drawing room has plenty of comfortable seating for quiet relaxation and clear views down to the harbour, and across the estuary, and the immaculately maintained bedrooms are very large, as are the en-suite bathrooms. Five new guest rooms have recently been completed and they are really lovely - large, bright and airy, they are individually decorated but the tone is quite contemporary and they have smart bathrooms; for those who prefer a more traditional style, the original rooms have a cosy atmosphere, and all nine rooms have sea views. Service at Glendine House is a priority; the Crosbies take pride in giving their guests personal attention and lots of advice on local amenities - and sending everyone off well-fed for the day after a really good breakfast that offers home-baked breads, fresh and cooked fruits, organic porridge and a range of hot dishes include smoked salmon & scrambled eggs and French toast as well as the full Irish. Light meals are available all day and there's a choice of good restaurants nearby in the evening, including Dunbrody House and also Aldridge Lodge (051 389116) and Squigl (051 389188), both at nearby Duncannon (see www.ireland-guide.com for details). **Rooms 5** (4 shower only). B&B c. €50 pps, ss c. €15. Self-catering cottages also available. Open all year except Christmas. Diners, MasterCard, Visa, Laser. Directions: From Wexford turn right before Talbot Hotel onto R733. 22 miles to Arthurstown. Entrance on right before village.

The Chantry Restaurant & Scenic Gardens

Bunclody
RESTAURANT

Bunclody Co Wexford
Tel: 054 77482 Fax: 054 76130
Web: www.chantry-restaurant.com

The Chantry is especially attractively situated within the little town of Bunclody. Originally a Wesleyan chapel, it enjoys a position of unexpected serenity above its own lovely waterside gardens, where guests can relax and enjoy the fine trees and plants - hollies, rhododendrons, carmellias, ferns, hydrangeas and lilies among them, including many rare species. The River Clody joins the River Slaney nearby under the town bridge, and the ancient church well, with its abundant ferns, is a feature of the upper garden and provides a constant supply of crystal clear water. The restaurant is in a high room with a little gallery (just the right size for a grand piano) but, with its deep red walls, chandeliers and fascinating collection of old photographs and pictures of local interest, it doesn't feel too

churchy. Artwork on display around the building is for sale, and can include some very interesting work. Menus offered vary considerably depending on the time of day - all day food tends to be casual, with a carvery lunch from 12.30, but evening service is more formal - at dinner, the self-service buffet is removed and an à la carte menu with table service is offered instead. Typical main courses include a speciality of traditional honey-glazed baked Chantry ham, with fresh parsley sauce and there is always something for vegetarians; early bird specials are good value - and good home cooking is the common theme. Several little marquees (where smoking is allowed) are set up in the garden for outside dining - a pretty spot, looking down over the gardens to the river. The lovely situation and long opening hours make this a useful place to know about when visiting the area. **Seats: 50** (private room, 14). Children welcome. Toilets wheelchair accessible. Own parking. Pets allowed in some areas. Open 9am-9pm Mon-Sat, 10-6 Sun. (Sun L 12.30-4). Licensed. A la carte menu. Open all year (a phone call to check opening times is advised). **Directions:** In town centre.

Dunbrody Abbey Tea Rooms

Campile
CAFÉ

Dunbrody Visitor Centre Campile New Ross Co Wexford **Tel: 051 388933**
Email: theneptune@eircom.net Web: www.cookingireland.com

The 12th century Dunbrody Abbey, and adjacent Dunbrody Castle and visitor centre are very near Kilmokea Gardens, and make an interesting place to break a journey. Well-known chefs Pierce & Valerie McAuliffe (who offer all-year cookery courses, at the adjoining Dunbrody Abbey Cookery Centre) run the Tea Rooms in summer, and bake up a range of treats every day to make sure there's a fresh supply of simple good things to delight and refresh: usually a home-made soup of the day with Guinness & walnut brown soda bread, a selection of fresh filled rolls or sandwiches, home-made

biscuits, muffins, tarts and cakes and a choice of teas, coffees and hot chocolate. There's also a range of Dunbrody Abbey food products on sale (mustard dressing, ginger marmalade, hot pepper relish). **Seats 35.** Open 11-6 in high season (Jul/Aug), 12-5 shoulder season (May-Jun and Sep). Tea rooms closed late Sep-end Apr. Cookery centre open all year. Amex, MasterCard, Visa. **Directions:** On main New Ross-Hook Peninsula road; 3 miles from John F Kennedy Memorial Park, 2 miles from Passage East car ferry.

Campile
COUNTRY HOUSE / GARDENS

Kilmokea Country Manor & Gardens
Great Island Campile Co Wexford
Tel: 051 388 109 Fax: 051 388 776
Email: kilmokea@indigo.ie Web: www.kilmokea.com

COUNTY WEXFORD

Mark and Emma Hewlett's peaceful and relaxing late Georgian country house nestles above an estuary where the rivers Barrow and Nore meet, and is set in seven acres of Heritage Gardens, including formal walled gardens featuring topiary and strutting peacocks around the house, and the 'lower garden', which was started in 1947 and is now home to over 130 species of rare and tender trees and shrubs. The walled garden is laid out as a series of compartments leading into each other, with topiary and statuary marking the entrance to each new room: the Italian Loggia garden features a pool and stone pillars, the 'quarter garden' hosts a fine display of irises and roses, whilst the 'hot' herbaceous border is home to old-fashioned plants including the red Maltese cross lychnis. In 1968 the garden began expansion into a new area and, during the excavation for a large pond, a 7th century millstone and flume were discovered; the acid soil in this part of the garden provides perfect conditions for the cultivation of of rhododendrons, camellias, eucryphias, magnolias, and also echiums - the giant borage so closely associated with Kilmokea. The house is open to guests and is elegantly and comfortably furnished, with a drawing room overlooking the Italian Loggia, an honesty library bar, and dinner available by reservation in the main dining room. The individually-designed and immaculately maintained bedrooms command lovely views over the gardens and towards the estuary beyond; they have no television to disturb the tranquillity (though there is one in the drawing room). In an adjoining coach house there are newer rooms and self-catering suites; they have a separate entrance and some have been refurbished to match those in the main house. The property also has a tennis court, croquet lawn and spa for guests' use only (indoor swimming pool, gym, aromatherapy - Emma is a trained aromatherapist). And work continues on a large organic vegetable garden, planted in the traditional potager design - the revival of this charming fashion is very welcome. Children welcome. Pets allowed in some areas by arrangement. Fishing, tennis, walking; swimming pool, gym, spa, aromatherapy. Gardens open daily 1 Feb- 30 Nov, 10-6.30 (last entry 5pm).Light meals in conservatory Pink Teacup Café, 10-5 daily when house and gardens are open; wine licence; gift shop. **Rooms 6** (5 en-suite, 1 with private bathroom; 1 disabled; all no smoking). B&B c. €85 pps; ss €30. Self-catering also available. Closed Dec-Jan. MasterCard, Visa, Laser. **Directions:** Take R733 south from New Ross to Ballyhack, signposted for Kilmokea Gardens.

Enniscorthy
COUNTRY HOUSE

Ballinkeele House

Ballymurn Enniscorthy Co Wexford
Tel: 053 38105 Fax: 053 38468
Email: info@ballinkeele.com Web: www.ballinkeele.com

Set in 350 acres of parkland, game-filled woods, farmland and gardens, this historic house is a listed building; designed by Daniel Robertson, it has been the Maher family home since it was built in 1840 and remains at the centre of their working farm. It is a grand house, with a lovely old cut stone stable yard at the back and some wonderful features, including a lofty columned hall with a big open fire in the colder months, and beautifully proportioned reception rooms with fine ceilings and furnishings which have changed very little since the house was built. Nevertheless, it is essentially a family house with a refreshingly hospitable and down-to-earth atmosphere. Large bedrooms are furnished with antiques and have wonderful countryside views and this would make a very comfortable base for visiting local gardens, including The Ram House and The Bay Garden. Margaret, who is a keen cook and a member of Euro-Toques (the chefs' association, dedicated to defending the integrity of ingredients), enjoys preparing 4-course dinners for guests (nice little wine list to accompany too); she's also an enthusiastic amateur painter and runs small art workshops at Ballinkeele with Patricia Jorgensen, who is well-known for her botanical paintings. There's croquet on the lawn, a long sandy beach nearby

at Curracloe, and bicycles (and wellingtons!) are available for guests' use; horse riding, fishing and golf can be organised nearby. Not suitable for children under 5. No pets. **Rooms 5** (all en-suite, 4 shower only). B&B c. €90 pps; ss €20. Residents Set D €40 at 7.30 (book by noon; no D on Mon); licensed. Closed Dec-Jan. MasterCard, Visa. **Directions:** From Wexford N11, north to Oilgate Village, turn right at signpost.

Enniscorthy
COUNTRY HOUSE

Salville House

Enniscorthy Co Wexford **Tel: 054 35252**
Email: info@salvillehouse.com Web: www.salvillehouse.com

Set high on a hillside outside Enniscorthy, Gordon and Jane Parker's large mid-19th century house has sweeping views over the Slaney River Valley but the main point of interest is indoors in the dining room, where Gordon Parker's delicious dinners are served to guests around a communal table, elegantly set up with candles and fresh flowers in the evening - and where splendid breakfasts are served next morning. Seasonal dinners have an emphasis on local seafood and organic produce from the garden - but there isn't a formal menu with choices, so it's wise to mention any allergies or dislikes when booking. Gordon's cooking is modern and he seeks out superb ingredients, notably ultra fresh fish including shellfish from Kilmore Quay, and Slaney salmon. After dinner, guests can relax in front of the drawing room fire, or play a game of backgammon before heading up to one of the three large rooms in the main house, which have views over the Slaney and are comfortably furnished with some style, or one of two in a self-contained apartment at the back. (All have tea/coffee making facilities, but no TV). Laid back hospitality, great food and good value make this comfortable house a fine base for garden visits or simply exploring the area. **Rooms 5** (3 en-suite, 2 with private bathrooms, 1 shower only). B&B c. €50, ss €10. Residents' D €35 at 8pm (book a day ahead). No D on Sun. BYO wine. **No Credit Cards. Directions:** Off N11, 2 miles from Enniscorthy on the Wexford side (look out for the sign on the river side of the main road). Go up hill & turn left; house on left.

The Bay Garden

Camolin **Enniscorthy** Co Wexford
Tel: 053 938 3349
Email: thebaygarden@eircom.net Web: www.thebaygarden.com

GARDEN

Series of contrasting gardens each beautifully conceived and wonderfully planted.

Patience has paid off for Frances and Iain MacDonald. When they first bought their pretty Georgian farmhouse in 1989 the surrounding couple of acres was waist high with weeds and full of ash saplings. They cleared the site and grassed it to control the weeds before making new beds in 1992, spraying with weed killer three times, double digging, manuring and finally mulching around the new plants. Each time they opened a new area, they repeated the process

Now there isn't a sign of a weed in the six stunning compartmentalised designs. Each offers a complete change of mood from the devilish excitement of the Hot Border to mesmeric swaying of ornamental grasses in the Barn Garden. A place to admire individual plants, the Serpentine garden is laid out with wavy island beds where shrubs like the lovely *Cornus alternifolia* **'Argentia'** and *Parrottia persica* form the backbone, and smaller stars like *Dierama igneum* and *Perovskia* **'Blue Spire'** are the front row attractions. The deep bronze leaves of *Vitis vinifera purperea* that clothe the house together with the violet of *C* **'Perle d'Or'** are among the many happy plant associations.

The soothing silver,white and blue planting around the pond garden, with plants like wormwood, campanula, and the perfumed seclusion of the rose garden, where shrub roses are screened by a hedge of *Thuja plicata* and restrained by a cruciform of meticulously clipped box, are a complete contrast to both the sinister black plants of the Funereal Border: *Physocarpus opulifolius* **'Diabolo'**, *Pittisporum tenufolium* **'Nigricans'**, and the jazzy reds and yellows of the hot border - here punchy crocosmias, dahlias and day lilies are offset by cool green foliage and sober plum foliage plants.

But the perhaps the real attention grabber is the Barn Garden; planted in prairie style, it exerts a great fascination: silky fronds and tassels of grasses like *Calamagrostis* **'Carl Foerster'** and **'Overdam'**, *Stipa tenuissima* and *Miscanthus sinensis* **'Ferne Osten'** way in the breeze beside stately drifts of *Sanguisorba* **'Tanna's Seedling'** and sedums. Almost everyone tends to pause on a welcome seat in the shelter of a parrotia hedge to drink in the effect before moving on to the newest area which, with its informal beds and specimen trees and shrubs, promises to mature into a good example of a low maintenance garden. And there will always be some intriguing new plan afoot - both the MacDonalds are qualified horticulturists, and their lives revolve around gardening, designing gardens, leading garden tours all over the world and propagating plants from the garden for sale in the nursery.

Open May-Sep, Sun 2-5; Jun-Aug, Fri & Sun 2-5; groups by appointment at other times. Children and wheelchairs welcome; no dogs Plant sales. Tea c €2.50. Admission c. €5. **Directions:** *On N11 half a mile south of Camolin; on the left, travelling to Ferns.*

Gorey
COUNTRY HOUSE / RESTAURANT

Marlfield House
Courtown Road Gorey Co Wexford
Tel: 053 942 1124 Fax: 053 942 1572
Email: info@marlfieldhouse.ie Web: www.marlfieldhouse.com

Often quoted as 'the luxury country house hotel par excellence', this impressive house was once the residence of the Earls of Courtown, and was first opened as an hotel in 1978 by Mary and Ray Bowe who have lavished care and attention on this fine property ever since - imposing gates, a wooded drive, antiques and glittering chandeliers all promise guests a very special experience - and, although Mary and Ray are still very much involved, their daughters Margaret and Laura Bowe now continue the family tradition of hospitality established by their parents. The interior is luxurious in the extreme, with accommodation including six very grand state rooms, but the gardens are also a special point of interest: there is a lake and wildfowl reserve, a formal garden, kitchen garden, and beautiful woodland with extensive woodland walks - and a number of premier gardens are within easy access, including Mount Usher, Powerscourt, Altamont and Kilmokea. Dining is always an memorable experience at Marlfield - the graceful dining room and Turner style conservatory merge into one, allowing views out across the gardens, including the kitchen garden, which is Ray Bowe's particular point of pride and is a delight to the eye as well as providing a wide range of fresh produce for the restaurant. The conservatory, with its hanging baskets, plants and fresh flowers (not to mention the odd stone statue), is one of the most romantic spots in the whole of Ireland, further enhanced at night by candlelight – a wonderful setting in which to enjoy chef Micheál MacCurtain's accomplished cooking. His strongly seasonal menus are changed daily and outline the produce available in the kitchen garden and other ingredients used. Although contemporary in style and presentation, there is a strong classical background to the cooking, and it is all the better for that. **Rooms 20** (6 state rooms, 14 superior, 8 ground floor, all no smoking). B&B €137.50pps. Dogs and children are welcome by prior arrangement. Tennis, cycling, walking. Room service (limited hours). Closed mid Dec-1 Feb. Amex, Diners, MasterCard, Visa, Laser.

Ram House

Coolgreaney **Gorey** Co Wexford
Tel: 0402 32006

GARDEN

Densely planted country garden laid out in a series of contrasting garden rooms.

The Ram House, nestling behind a stone wall and a wicket gate, its Georgian fanlight draped in roses and clematis, looks like a Beatrix Potter illustration. The cottage style garden lives up to the image and is packed with interest and full of inspiring ideas.

One of those happy gardens that just grew over the years, its two acres are laid out as a series of contrasting areas where visitors are irresistibly drawn from one to the next. Lolo Stevens started with nothing more than a patchy lawn and a cypress tree... The lawn was gradually replaced with informal planting and gravel paths, and the cypress is now smothered in Clematis montana, one of the 50 varieties of clematis in the garden grown through trees and old roses.

There are gardens within gardens like Russian dolls. Inside the courtyard garden with its banks of old roses and clove scented dianthus, is a secret shady garden known as the Piggery, plus a pool garden, and a terrace garden with inviting seating. In a further Beatrix Potter touch, animal statues have been dotted about the garden with a Pigling Bland here and a Jemima Puddleduck there.

A pergola garden links the upper garden to two green gardens dominated by the soothing presence of a weeping willow with *Clematis* **'Perle d'Or'** growing through its tresses.

Beyond are the wilder parts of the garden where a stream cascades from pool to pool in the shade of a grove of silver birches, its banks lined with water loving plants and a host of candelabra primulas.

Local materials and plants are used in original ways; a variegated ivy forms the edging of a lawn, railway sleepers become steps, slate is set on edge in the gravel to make a starburst pattern. Plants are allowed to do their own thing: ajuga, saxifrage geraniums and lamium form carpets; southern hemisphere plants like osteospermums and helichrysum bask in sunny corners. The planting, which looks deceptively simple, is multi-layered and gives a wonderful display from spring through to the end of August. And, just to add to the perfection, Lolo Stevens is famous for her home made cakes.

Open Easter-end Aug, Sunday & bank hols; also Sat, Sun & Mon during the Wicklow Garden Festival, and to groups by appointment. Supervised children welcome; not suitable for wheelchairs; no dogs.
Directions: *Off the N11between Arklow and Gorey - turn off at Inch post office for Coolgreaney, the garden is on the edge of the village on the left.*

Rosslare
COUNTRY HOUSE

Churchtown House
Tagoat Rosslare Co Wexford
Tel: 053 32555
Email: info@churchtownhouse.com Web: www.churchtownhouse.com

Patricia and Austin Cody's Georgian house is extremely handy for the Rosslare ferryport, about four miles away, but it is a really lovely place and deserves a longer stay - it would make a beautifully relaxing base for a few days exploring the area. It's set in about eight and a half acres of wooded gardens and dates back to 1703 but it has been completely renovated by the Codys, and elegantly furnished to make a comfortable country house retreat for discerning guests. Public areas are spacious, with plenty of seating in rooms of different character allowing a choice of mood for guests. Bedrooms are equally pleasing - large, and furnished to the highest standards in country house style, with generous beds, phones, TV and well-finished bathrooms. The Codys are renowned for their hospitality and, if you're lucky enough to arrive at this well-run house at around teatime, you'll be served delicious home-made cake and
tea in the drawing room. Good food is an important feature here and a fine Irish breakfast is served in the bright dining room, where dinner is also served to residents (at separate tables), by arrangement. **Rooms 12** (1 junior suite, 5 shower only, all no smoking). B&B c. €65pps, ss €15; Residents' D 8pm (book by noon), c €40. Licensed. Closed Dec-Mar; weekends only in Nov. MasterCard, Visa, Laser. **Directions:** On R736, half a mile from N25, at Tagoat.

Bagenalstown
COUNTRY HOUSE

Kilgraney House

Borris Road Bagenalstown Co Carlow
Tel: 059 977 5283 Fax: 059 977 5595
Email: info@kilgraneyhouse.com Web: www.kilgraneyhouse.com

In a lovely site overlooking the Barrow Valley, Bryan Leech and Martin Marley's charming late Georgian house - which (encouragingly) takes its name from the Irish 'cill greíne', meaning 'sunny hill or wood' - is well-placed for garden visits in a wide area, and will also be a very pleasing destination in itself, as it is set in extensive wooded grounds with gardens that are open to the public by appointment and feature, among many delights, interconnecting herb gardens, a tea walk, a monastic garden - and a productive kitchen garden that provides much that Bryan will transform into delicious dinners. His cooking is contemporary and makes creative use of local and artisan produce, including their own home-smoked duck (with noodle salad & mirin/soy dressing, perhaps) and Lavistown cheese from Kilkenny - and your breakfast next morning will include other local foods. But it is for the sheer sense of style pervading both house and garden that Kilgraney is most famous - the enjoyment that Bryan and Martin have derived from their dedication to both is abundantly clear: elegant, yes, but with a great sense of fun too. Dinner is normally served at a communal table, but separate tables are available on request. Self-catering accommodation is also offered, in two courtyard suites and the gate lodge. Herbal treatment room (massage & aromatherapy). Not suitable for children under 12. **Rooms 8** (2 suites, 3 shower only, all no smoking). No dogs. B&B c. €70, ss about €10. D Wed-Sun, 8 pm (non-residents welcome by reservation); set 6-course D, c.€45. (Special dietary requirements on request.) Closed Mon & Tue & all Nov-Feb incl. Amex, MasterCard, Visa, Laser. **Directions:** Just off the R705, halfway between Bagenalstown and Borris.

Bagenalstown
COUNTRY HOUSE

Lorum Old Rectory

Kilgraney Bagenalstown Co Carlow
Tel: 059 977 5282 Fax: 059 977 5455
Email: reservations@lorum.com Web: www.lorum.com

This historic country house was built in 1863 of local cut granite, and discerning Dublin weekenders are among the many who appreciate its accessibility, relaxed atmosphere and proximity to so many places of interest, including a range of gardens - Altamont, of course, and also the great Kilkenny gardens such as Kilfane and Woodstock, the Japanese Gardens in County Kildare, and plenty more. Elegant and spacious, there's a lovely drawing room for guests and accommodation includes a bedroom with a four-poster - all are very comfortable, with big beds, phones and tea/coffee trays. But it is Bobbie Smith's hospitality that keeps bringing guests back: Bobbie, who is a member of the inter-national chefs' association, Euro-Toques, whose members are committed to defending local produce and suppliers, prepares good home cooking (rack of lamb, perhaps, with honey, mustard & rosemary glaze) based mainly on organic ingredients - dinner for residents is served at a long mahogany table (book by 3 pm). And those who like to travel with their dogs will be pleased to know that pets are welcome, by arrangement. Private parties/groups (10). Garden. Children welcome. Dogs permitted by arrangement. **Rooms 5** (all en-suite). B&B €60-75 pps, ss €20. Dinner for residents by arrangement (8pm). Closed 1 Dec-1 Feb. MasterCard, Visa, Laser. **Directions:** Midway between Borris & Bagenalstown on the R705.

Ballon Garden

Ballon Co Carlow
Tel: 059 915 9144
Email: gerardo@eircom.net

GARDEN

Established garden with a fine collection of dwarf conifers, perennials and shrubs.

Plants overflowing happily into the laneway signal the garden of an enthusiast. Stasia O'Neill and her husband began gardening 46 years ago, starting with a collection of choice shrubs and trees around the perimeter to provide much needed shelter. These now form the back row of a 20 foot deep chorus of thoroughly interesting plants, all vying for the attention of visitors. Gold and silvers predominate in mixed borders wrapped around a lawn while an impressive collection of dwarf conifers provide backbone and winter colour. Colchicums have colonised under birch trees and Dieramas seed freely round the rock garden.

It would be worth a visit just to make the better acquaintance of conifers alone, graceful *Cedrus atlantica* **'Glauca pendula'**, *Picea pungens* **'Globosa'** *Picea albertiana glauca* are just some of the representatives of a rewarding family that earn their keep throughout the year.

Like the best of gardens, this one evolved gradually, built up from cuttings, gifts, exchanges and irresistible purchases. Many of the plants came via Corona North at neighbouring Altamont and there are some particular choice varieties *Phlox* **'Nora Leigh'**, *Viola* **'Limelight'** *Rosa moyesii* **'Eddie's Jewel'** besides unusual plants that aren't even listed in the RHS encyclopedia of plants, but Mrs O'Neill - a knowledgeable plantswoman - is on first name terms with them all.

Open mid May-Jul, Sun & bank hols and during Wicklow Garden Festival, 2-6; groups 5+ by appointment only. Children and wheelchairs welcome; no dogs. **Directions:** *Off Bunclody-Carlow Road, just before Ballon on Bunclody side, at speed limit sign.*

Ballon
HOTEL

Ballykealey Manor Hotel
Ballon Co Carlow **Tel: 059 915 9288**
Email: ballykealeymanor@eircom.net Web: www.ballykealeymanor.com

Seat of the Lecky family for three centuries, the present house was designed by Thomas A Cobden (designer of Carlow cathedral) and built in the 1830s as a wedding present. Gothic arches and Tudor chimney stacks take you back to the architectural oddities of the time, but the house is set in well-maintained grounds and promising first impressions are well founded. Since taking over in 2003 the owners, Edward and Karen Egan, have completely refurbished the hotel - with considerable style - and improvements continue on an ongoing basis. Spacious reception rooms are furnished in a pleasingly elegant mixture of contemporary style and period features, combining comfort with a friendly atmosphere. Individually designed bedrooms, which are very pleasing to the eye, are luxuriously furnished and decorated in keeping with the character of the house and have all the expected amenities, including direct-dial phones and multi-channel TV. Wheelchair access; children welcome. **Rooms 12** (increasing to 42 by end 2006); 1 junior suite, 4 shower only, 2 non-smoking. B&B about €70pps, ss about €20; no SC. **Oak Room Restaurant:** D daily, L Sun only; informal meals available in the bar. Closed 24 Dec. MasterCard, Visa. **Directions:** On the N80, main Rosslare/Wexford road; coming from Carlow, about 18km on right, just before the village of Ballon.

Ballon
COUNTRY HOUSE

Sherwood Park House
Kilbride Ballon Co Carlow
Tel: 059 915 9117
Email: info@sherwoodparkhouse.ie Web: www.sherwoodparkhouse.ie

Built around 1700 by a Mr Arthur Baillie, this delightful Georgian farmhouse has sweeping views over the countryside and is well-placed for garden visits in the area - Altamont Gardens are on the doorstep (just 5 minutes away on foot). Patrick and Maureen Owens, who have welcomed guests here since 1991, accurately describe it as "an accessible country retreat for anyone who enjoys candlelit dinners, brass and canopy beds, and the relaxing experience of eating out while staying in". Spacious accommodation is furnished in period style and thoughtful in the details that count - and Maureen takes pride in offering guests real home cooking based on the best of local produce, including "best locally produced Carlow beef and lamb, from Ballon Meats" and fish from Kilmore Quay. There's a lovely garden and, as well as excellent garden visits, it's a good area for walking - and fishing the Slaney. Dinner is served at 8pm and is mainly for residents, although non-residents are welcome when there is room - and guests are welcome to bring their own wine and any other drinks.(Please give advance notice if you would like dinner.) **Rooms 5** (all en-suite), B&B c. €60-75pps, ss€20. D at 8pm by arrangement. Amex, MasterCard, Visa. **Directions:** Signed from the junction of the N80 and N81.

Borris
GUESTHOUSE

The Step House
Borris Co Carlow **Tel: 059 977 3209**
Email: cait@thestephouse.com Web: www.thestephouse.com

Stylishly decorated and furnished in period style, with antiques throughout, James and Cait Coady's attractive old house is well placed for exploring this beautiful area and visiting many of the gardens open to the public in parts of Kilkenny and Wexford as well as County Carlow. Well-proportioned reception rooms include a fine dining room (used for breakfast) and a matching drawing room that overlooks the back garden, which Cait enjoys and is gradually developing. One of the comfortable, elegant

bedrooms has a four-poster and all are furnished to a high standard with smart shower rooms, TV and tea/coffee facilities. The renovation and upgrading of this fine old house has been accomplished beautifully, including the conversion of the whole of the lower ground floor to make a magnificent kitchen of character, and a relaxed living room area with direct access to the garden - and a sunny decking area beside the dining room allows guests to enjoy breakfast outdoors on fine mornings. *At the time of going to press, The Coadys (who also one of Ireland's finest classic pubs, Tynans Bridge Bar, in Kilkenny city) are developing a hotel; meanwhile, The Step House will continue as before and guest accommodation is also available in a number of self-catering houses and apartments, which are available for short term letting, or B&B. NB: there are several flights of stairs, including steps up to the front door. **Rooms 5** (all with power shower only & no smoking). B&B c. €45, ss €10. Closed mid Dec-mid Mar. MasterCard, Visa, Laser. **Directions:** From main Carlow-Kilkenny road, take turning to Bagenalstown; 8 miles to Borris.

Carlow
GUESTHOUSE

Barrowville Townhouse
Kilkenny Road Carlow Co Carlow **Tel: 059 914 3324**
Email: barrowtownhouse@eircom.net Web: www.barrowtownhouse.com

This exceptionally comfortable and well-managed guesthouse just a few minutes walk from Carlow town centre will appeal to those who appreciate the convenience of being near facilities together with the space and relaxed atmosphere of a country house. It is a fine period house, set in lovely gardens and there is a pleasant residents' drawing room, with an open fire. The house is well maintained and bedrooms - which inevitably vary in size and character due to the age of the building - are comfortable and well-finished bathrooms. Breakfast is served in a handsome conservatory (complete with a large vine) overlooking the peaceful back garden. **Rooms 7** (2 shower only, all no smoking). B&B c. €47.50 pps. ss €12.50. Open all year. Amex, MasterCard, Visa. **Directions:** South side of Carlow town on the N9.

Carlow Town
PUB / RESTAURANT

Lennons Café Bar
121 Tullow Street Carlow Co Carlow
Tel: 059 913 1575

Sinéad Byrne runs this stylish modern café-bar with her husband, Liam, and their deliciously healthy, reasonably priced food is a hit with both locals and visitors to the town. In a manner reminiscent of that great Kerry speciality, the pub that gradually develops into a restaurant at the back without actually having a dedicated restaurant area, the design of the bar - which has a striking metal spiral staircase at the back - helps the atmosphere to shift into café gear as you move through it. Simple, uncluttered tables and speedy service of jugs of iced water bode well for menus that include a host of wholesome dishes ranging from full-flavoured soups and home-baked bread to hot specials like steak & kidney pie with champ, or cod & mussel bake. Consideration is shown to special dietary requirements - vegetarians are highlighted, gluten free bread is available for coeliacs - and everything is really wholesome and freshly made to order from top quality ingredients, with some local sources named on the menu. Home-made desserts might include more-ish hazelnut meringue roulade with raspberry sauce, perhaps, or hot apple crumble. Meals: Breakfast 10-11; L Mon-Fri 12-3, Sat 12-4; D Wed-Sat, 5-9. A la carte. Toilets wheelchair accessible. Closed 25 Dec, Good Fri. **Directions:** At junction of Tullow Street and Potato Market.

Leighlinbridge
CAFÉ

Mulberry's Restaurant
Arboretum Garden Centre Kilkenny Road Leighlinbridge Co Carlow
Tel 059 97 21558
Fax 059 97 21642 Web: www.arboretum.ie

This pleasant self-service restaurant is in the main hall of the garden centre at the Arboretum and, with a deck area for fine weather, it could make a good place to take a break between visits to the many gardens in the area. There's an attractive selection of wholesome, freshly-prepared food offered, ranging from home-baked scones and cakes (to have on the deck with a good cup of tea or coffee perhaps) to full hot or cold meals. Tables are simply set up, but every second table has fresh flowers; in addition to a blackboard menu, a self-service counter presents an appetising display of salads and

quick-serve dishes - everything is fresh and home-made with good ingredients, and there's a nice flair in the desserts (banoffi pie is a house speciality); there's wine by the glass, and a small choice of house wines and quarter bottles, also fruit drinks (including apple juice) and minerals. It's a good place to plan a journey break, as there's plenty of interest and a browse around is relaxing - and groups travelling together are welcome by arrangement. Ample parking (150). Wheelchair friendly. Children welcome. Wine licence. Open Mon-Sat 9-5, Sun 11-5. Closed 25 Dec & 1 Jan. **Directions:** From Carlow, take N9 towards Leighlinbridge.

Lisnavagh Gardens

Rathvilly Co Carlow
Tel: 059 916 1104
Email: r@lisnavagh.com

GARDEN

Large historic garden in a romantic setting.

Like Powerscourt Gardens, the house and gardens at Lisnavagh were designed by Daniel Robertson. Created to impress, the 10 acres of pleasure grounds, with views of the Wicklow Hills and Blackstairs mountains, consist of a formal framework of steps, terraces and walls in the same grey ashlar stone as the house, with walks shaded by fine specimen trees.

Jessica Rathdonnell has redesigned and replanted parts of the garden with a fine collection of herbaceous plants and shrubs. Near the house the main attraction is an L-shaped raised border, filled in summer with a host of delphiniums, roses and lilies and in spring with all manner of flowering bulbs. The other treat for plantspeople is the walled garden. Here a swimming pool converted from a pine pit (a historic gardening device for growing pineapples below ground level,) forms the central feature. Round the walls are deep beds with a profusion of damp loving plants: hostas in slug defying numbers, gunnera, rodgersia, tender shrubs and climbers like *Cytissus battandieri* and *Clematis seiboldii*. In the older part of the garden there is a magical yew walk where trees form an arch to frame the views of Mount Leinster, an azalea walk and huge flowering shrubs including camellias and *Drimys winteri*.

*Open to groups by appointment only, Jun-Aug. Supervised children permitted; not suitable for wheelchairs; no dogs. **Directions:** Signposted from the Rathvilly to Hacketstown road.*

St Mullins
B&B

Mulvarra House
St Mullins Co Carlow
Tel: 051 424936 Fax: 051 424969
Email: info@mulvarra.com Web: www.mulvarra.com

Harold and Noreen Ardill's friendly modern house is in a stunning location overlooking the River Barrow above the ancient and picturesque little harbour of St Mullins and, although it may seem unremarkable from the road, this relaxing place is full of surprises. Comfortably furnished bedrooms have balconies to take full advantage of views of the romantic Barrow Valley, for example, and, not only is there the luxury of (limited) room service but even a range of treatments (massage, mud wraps, refresher facials) to help guests unwind from the stresses of everyday life and make the most of this magical place. Noreen - an enthusiastic self-taught cook - prepares dinners for residents to enjoy in the dining room which also overlooks the river: quality produce, much of it local, is used in home-made soups, salmon mousse, roast stuffed pork steaks and Baileys bread & butter pudding, all of which are favourites, although menus are varied to suit guests' preferences. Genuinely hospitable and reasonably priced, this is a place where the hosts want their guests to relax and make the most of every moment - its relative remoteness is a large part of its charm, but it could make a good base for garden visits in the area, including Kilfane Glen & Waterfall, Woodstock Gardens (Inistioge) and Mount Juliet Estate. Pets permitted by arrangement. Children welcome. **Rooms 5** (all en-suite, shower-only & no-smoking; full bath in shared bathroom available to any guest). B&B c. €34, ss €6. Residents D nightly, €30 (7.30pm, by reservation). Closed mid Dec-mid Jan. MasterCard, Visa, Laser. **Directions:** 4.5 miles from Graiguenamagh; take R702 from Borris, turnright in Glynn; signposted from Glynn.

Altamont

Tullow Co Carlow
Tel: 059 915 9128
Email: altamontgardens@eagla.ie   Web: www.heritageireland.ie

GARDEN

Truly a heavenly garden with everything from herbaceous borders to a bluebell wood.

COUNTY CARLOW

There are places that have a special indefinable magic about them and Altamont is abundantly one of them. It could be attributed to the glorious setting, with views from the appealing 300 year old house across an ornamental lake to woods with Lugnaquilla mountain in the distance. It could be beguiling features like a Sunset Field temple and One Hundred Steps climbing through a bluebell wood. And it could be something to do with the benign spirit of Corona North who gave the garden in trust to the Nation.

There are many pleasures to be discovered: the cloistered hush of a Nuns' Walk through an aisle of beech trees carpeted with daffodils and cyclamen and the view framed by topiary peacocks and old roses of the lake reflecting clouds of rhododendron blooms.There is the irresistible invitation to follow the circular route round the lake, through the arboretum, swamp garden and on to the natural garden of an ice age glen leading to the River Slaney and back through the Sunset Field.

The history of the garden stretches back to the 1720s when the house was built by the St George family. Later the lake was dug out in the 1860s to give Famine relief work. In the 1920s Fielding Lecky Watson came to Altamont; he subscribed to plant hunting expeditions and the azaleas and rhododendrons around the lake were grown by him from seed. His daughter Corona North, an enthusiastic and knowledgeable plantswoman, continued to plant develop the garden adding features like the Sunset Temple. On her death the garden, just as she had planned, was taken in charge by the heritage section of the Office of Public Works and, in commemoration, a spectacular double herbaceous border was created with plants donated by her many friends.

Today the border - stretching in graduated colour combinations, to a circular pond and gazebo - is the glory of the walled garden. The colour combinations move through blues yellows and mauves, with campanula, thalictrum, delphinium, nepeta and helianthus, and then on to red pinks and plums with dahlias, penstemons and cosmos.

Fans of the garden will find much as it was: the pond in front of the house with beds of dwarf conifers patrolled by silky hens and the spectacular displays of cornus bracts and the handkerchief tree by the lake. Happily the garden continues to develop, some of the gardeners had worked with Mrs North and knew her hopes for the garden. The mixed border on one side of the lawn has new herbaceous planting as she would have wished, there is a new shady walk, where some of the 40 different varieties of snowdrop are to be found, and an area for carefully labelled shade loving plants like hellebore varieties. And, to round off the experience, many of the unusual plants grown in the garden have been propagated for sale. Make sure to bring walking shoes and leave room in the car for plant purchases.

Open daily mid Apr-end Oct; weekdays only Nov-Easter. Open from 9 am (closing times vary). Entrance free; children and wheelchairs welcome. Plant sales. **Directions:** *Well signed in area.*

Hardymount
Tullow Co Carlow
Tel: 059 915 1769

GARDEN

Old world walled garden packed with good herbaceous plants.

"Welcome to my garden," says the notice hanging on the gate, and indeed it is a welcoming place. The sight of Hardymount - a 1730s former road house with Regency bow ends added a century later - is enough to raise expectations. Set amid lawns, a sweeping drive and mature trees, the romantic house is veiled in old roses and the walled garden hides behind it like a child behind a mother's skirts.

Vistas down grass paths, espaliered apples trees, a wisteria pergola and a lily pond, its corners marked by topiary box, give the garden its formal structure. In between these features big rectangular beds barely contain the exuberant display of herbaceous perennials. In high summer *Hemerocallis* and *Lobelia tupa* and *Ligularia* provide gold and fire while roses with *Tradescantia* make unusual bed fellows.

Each turn in the grid of paths reveals something new, a little parterre of box with a sundial in the centre or a greenhouse sheltering ripe grapes. A pair of venerable *Hoheria* make a focal point at the end of the garden and the grassy paths lead to vistas of statues - and the discovery of a rustic gazebo, and a productive vegetable patch hidden away behind trellis. And there are also the kind of treasures you might expect to find in a long established garden: a peony bed with companion tree peonies, prolific old fashioned climbing roses, *Arisaema*, hollyhocks and foxgloves.

*Open May-Aug, Sun & bank hols, 2-6 and during Wicklow Garden Festival, also by appointment. Children and wheelchairs welcome. Tea by arrangement. Entrance about €4. **Directions:** Take Bunclody road from Tullow, right at Statoil, turn right at cross roads, entrance is 600m on right.*

Callan
COUNTY HOUSE

Ballaghtobin
Callan Co Kilkenny
Tel: 056 772 5227

Set in parkland in the middle of a five hundred acre working farm in lush countryside some 10 miles south-west of Kilkenny city, this immaculately maintained house has been in the Gabbett family for three hundred and fifty years. Graciously proportioned rooms are beautifully furnished and the spacious bedrooms - which Catherine Gabbett has decorated stylishly - all have antique furniture and every comfort, including lovely bathrooms with bath and overbath shower, and tea/coffee trays. The house is surrounded by large gardens, with a hard tennis court, a croquet lawn - and even a ruined Norman church - for guests' use. Dinner is not offered, but there is a good pub in Callan (Old Charter House, 056 775 5902), and a choice of restaurants within a short drive. Although not neighbouring any of the major gardens, this is a lovely place to be based for garden visits in counties Kilkenny and Tipperary, and travelling around this most beautiful part of the country is no hardship. Children welcome. Pets allowed by arrangment. **Rooms 3** (All en-suite & no smoking). B&B c. €45 pps, ss €10. Open all year except Christmas. MasterCard, Visa. **Directions:** Past Golf Club on left; after 2.3 miles bear left, then bear left at junction - entrance on leftt opposite Gate Lodge.

Inistioge
RESTAURANT

Bassetts at Woodstock
Woodstock Gardens & Arboretum
Inistioge Kilkenny
Tel: 056 775 8820

The historic and beautifully restored Woodstock Gardens & Arboretum offer the visitor a wide range of experiences, from one-offs such as the Monkey Puzzle Walk and the Noble Fir Walk to the delightful Flower Terraces, a Rustic Summer House and Fountain. And now, thanks to John Bassett, who grew up in Inistioge and recently returned to the area, and his partner Mijke Jansen, there is also a very special food experience here too, at Bassett's. This scenically located contemporary restaurant is in a modern building overlooking the Nore valley and, although conveniently situated beside the visitors' carpark, this is emphatically not just a 'garden visits café' but a fully fledge restaurant which, since opening in autumn 2005, has become a destination in its own right. The philosophy behind Bassett's is to use the very best produce available and, recognising the growing trend towards informal dining, John and Mijke, together with head chef Emilio Martin Castilla (previously at Kilkenny city's premier fine dining restaurant, Lacken House), the usual 'three course meal' format is by-passed. Departing from tradition, they offer a range of starter size dishes on menus that include some luxurious choices such as foie gras, and pheasant (in season) and are based on seasonal and mainly local produce - but what you get is a series of smaller dishes, more akin to the oriental style of eating, perhaps, except that the dishes you order arrive in progression rather than as a shared 'banquet, and there is a suggested wine (by the glass) to accompany each one. Good service and a concise, well chosen wine list enhance the beautiful location, warm atmosphere and good food - well worth a visit. **Open:** L Wed-Sun, 12-4 (Sun to 6); D Wed-Sat, from 7.30. Gardens open all year (summer 9-8; winter 10-4.30). MasterCard, Visa, Laser. **Directions:** Follow signs to Woodstock Gardens; passing ruins of the old house on the way up the hill, you will find Bassett's in a modern building beside the car park.

Kilkenny
GUESTHOUSE

Butler House

16 Patrick Street Kilkenny Co Kilkenny
Tel: 056 772 2828 Email: res@butler.ie Web: www.butler.ie

Located close to Kilkenny Castle, this elegant Georgian townhouse was restored by the Irish State Design Agency in the 1970s - and the resulting combination of what was at the time contemporary design and period architecture leads to some interesting discussions. However bedrooms are unusually spacious - some have bow windows overlooking the gardens and Kilkenny Castle - and the accommodation is very adequate, with all the amenities now expected of good guesthouse accommodation including large, if somewhat utilitarian, bathrooms. Three magnificent bow-windowed reception rooms are available for private functions such as receptions and dinners – and an excellent breakfast is served at the Kilkenny Design Centre (see below), which is just across the gardens. Children welcome. Parking. Garden. No pets. **Rooms 13** (1 suite, 4 superior,12 shower only). B&B c. €85, ss EUR70, sc discretionary. Off-season breaks offered. Closed 24-29 Dec. **Directions:** City centre, close to Kilkenny Castle.

Kilkenny
RESTAURANT

Kilkenny Design Centre

Castle Yard Kilkenny Co Kilkenny
Tel: 056 772 2118

Situated in what was once the stables and dairy of Kilkenny Castle - and overlooking the craft courtyard - this deservedly popular first floor self-service restaurant is situated above temptations of a different sort, on display in the famous craft shop. Wholesome and consistently delicious fare begins with breakfast for guests staying at Butler House (see entry), as well as non-resident visitors. The room is well-designed to allow attractive and accessible display of wonderful food, all freshly prepared every day: home baking is a strong point and, although there is plenty of hot food to choose from as well, salads, are a particular strength, always colourful and full of life - fresh beetroot, asparagus, spinach, red onion, coriander & crumbly Lavistown local cheese makes a salad worth travelling for, for example, and the selection changes all the time. Wines and beers are available, also gourmet coffees and herbal teas. Very reasonably priced too - well worth a visit. **Seats 220.** Toilets wheelchair accessible. Lift. Meals daily: Mon-Sat, 11-7, Sun & bank hols, 11-3.30. Self service. Off season (Jan-Mar), closed Sun & bank hols. Amex, Diners, MasterCard, Visa, Laser. **Directions:** Opposite Kilkenny Castle.

Maddoxtown
COUNTRY HOUSE

Blanchville House

Dunbell Maddoxtown Co Kilkenny
Tel: 056 772 7197 Fax: 056 772 7636
Email: mail@blanchville.ie Web: www.blanchville.ie

Tim and Monica Phelan's elegant Georgian house is just 5 miles out of Kilkenny city, surrounded by its own farmland and gardens. It's easy to spot - there's a folly in its grounds. It's a very friendly, welcoming place and the house has an airy atmosphere, with a fine dining room and drawing room on either side of the hall, and the big, comfortably furnished bedrooms in period style all overlook attractive countryside. Dinner is available to residents, if pre-arranged, and, like the next morning's excellent breakfast, is taken at the communal mahogany dining table. The Coach Yard has been renovated to make four self-catering coach houses, and the house can also be rented - an ideal arrangement for groups of 12-20 people, for family get-togethers or groups travelling together, as guests may have exclusive use of the house and coach yard. Garden visits, horseriding, fishing and other country pursuits are all nearby. Not suitable for children under 10. Pets permitted by arrangement. **Rooms 6** (5 en-suite, 1 with private bathroom, 2 shower only, all non-smoking). B&B €55-60 pps, ss €15. No SC. Residents D €37.50 by prior arrangement only. Closed 1 Nov-1 Mar. Amex, MasterCard, Visa, Laser. **Directions:** From Kilkenny take N10 (Carlow-Dublin road), 1st right 1/2 mile after 'ThePike' . Continue 2 miles to cross-roads (Connolly's pub). Take left, large stone entrance 1 mile on left.

Thomastown
COUNTRY HOUSE

Ballyduff House

Thomastown Co Kilkenny
Tel: 056 775 8488 Email: ballydhouse@eircom.net

Set in fine rolling countryside in its own farmland and grounds, Breda Thomas's lovely 18th century house overlooking the River Nore is blessed with an utterly restful location. Breda is a relaxed and welcoming host, and offers exceptionally spacious and comfortable accommodation in large period bedrooms with generous bathrooms and beautiful views over the river or gardens. Guests also have the use of large well-proportioned day rooms furnished with family antiques - and many return often, finding this rural retreat a warm and welcoming home from home. It is well situated for garden visits in the area, and there are beautiful walks on the estate. Fishing (salmon, trout); riding, hunting and other country pursuits can be arranged. Children welcome. *Self-catering accommodation also offered at Ballyduff Castle, adjoining Ballyduff House (2-4 bedrooms). **Rooms 3**. B&B about €40, ss about €10. Closed 1 Nov-1 Mar. **No Credit Cards. Directions:** 3 miles south of Thomastown.

Kilfane Glen & Waterfall

Thomastown Co Kilkenny
Tel: 056 772 4558
Email: susan@irishgardens.com

GARDEN

An 18th century woodland garden in the romantic manner, with a smaller modern garden

Kilfane is Ireland's answer to Marie Antoinette's Petit Trianon. This rediscovered treasure of gardening history was originally designed in the 1790s in the fashionably romantic style to embellish the gothic wonders of nature. Paths and rides had been laid out through the wooded demesne in the 18th century, with an attractive glen and stream with a series of pools and cascades forming the centrepiece.

This romantic garden was rescued from the undergrowth by Bennettsbridge potter, Nicholas Mosse, and his wife Susan. In the process, the couple rediscovered a grotto and the ruins of a cottage orné, all part of the idealised rural idyll - and an artificial waterfall opposite the cottage, fed by water diverted via pumps and canal. The cottage was restored with thatch and leaded window panes in keeping with a 1921 print, and with interiors designed by the late Sybil Connolly.

The other attractions of the garden include a sculpture trail through the woods and a series of contemporary gardens laid out around the Mosses home. There is a formal pool garden, a white moon garden, a blue orchard, a mysterious hall of mirrors and a wildlife pond.

Open July-Aug, 11-6 daily. Children welcome; partial wheelchair access; dogs on leads allowed; plant sales. **Directions:** *Well signed in the area.*

Thomastown
HOTEL / GARDEN

Mount Juliet Conrad
Thomastown Co Kilkenny
Tel: 056 777 3000
Email: mountjulietinfo@conradhotels.com Web: www.mountjuliet.com

Lying amidst 1500 acres of unspoilt woodland, pasture and formal gardens beside the River Nore, Mount Juliet House is one of Ireland's finest Georgian houses, and one of Europe's greatest country estates. Even today it retains an aura of eighteenth century grandeur, as the elegance of the old house has been painstakingly preserved - and the gardens, which are still in the care of Paddy Daly who looked after them when the property was in private ownership, remain reassuringly complete. Staying here should be a joy for any guests, but garden lovers find a day or two spent here especially enchanting; suites and bedrooms in the main house have period decor with all the comfort of modern facilities and there's additional accommodation in the Club Rooms at Hunters Yard, which is very close to the main house, and where most of the day-to-day activities of the estate take place. There are three main elements to the gardens, beginning with an informal stream and rockery area near the drive as you approach the house; then there's an old walled rose garden which has been replanted relatively recently with a mixture of modern and old-fashioned roses and, the highlight, a walled ornamental garden that has many charming features and is especially famous for its stunning double herbaceous borders which provide an ever-changing spectacle of colour from early summer to late autumn. The gardens at Mount Juliet are also maintained with the needs of the kitchen in mind, and include one of Ireland's largest herb gardens; good cooking based on the best of local produce is a point of pride at Mount Juliet, and there is a choice of fine dining in the **Lady Helen Dining Room** (a graceful high-ceilinged room in the main house, softly decorated in pastel shades and with sweeping views over the grounds; D daily, L Sun only) or an equally attractive contemporary option in the stylish **Kendals restau-**

rant (D daily) at Hunters Yard. Informal meals also available all day at The Club, Presidents Bar (12-9pm). (Although now best known for golf, the hotel is well located for exploring this beautiful area and there are woodlands to wander, new sports to try, and a spa/for pampering. Gardens open by appointment only; hotel open all year: **Rooms 58** (2 suites, 16 junior suites/superior rooms, 1 disabled; all no smoking). No lift. Room rate about €265. Self-catering accommodation is also offered, at the Rose Garden Lodges (close to Hunters Yard) and The Paddocks (at the tenth tee). **Directions:** M7 from Dublin, then M9 towrads Waterford, arriving at Thomastown on the N9 via Carlow and Gowran. (75 miles south of Dublin, 60 miles north of Rosslare).

COUNTY TIPPERARY

Ardcronney
COUNTRY HOUSE

Ashley Park House
Ardcronney Near Nenagh Co Tipperary
Tel: 067 38223
Email: margaret@ashleypark.com Web: www.ashleypark.com

From the moment you turn off the busy Nenagh-Borrisokane road, you enter a time warp. Margaret and P J Mounsey's home, Ashley Park, is one of those beautiful 18th century houses where all is elegance and comfort. It has the necessary mod cons (all the main bedrooms have en suite bathrooms) but this is a place which breathes an old-fashioned order, comfort and charm. The views of Lough Ourna, right in front of the house, with the distant Slieve Bloom Mountains looming up on the horizon, are stunningly lovely, and you can walk down to the lakeshore

or through the walled garden and grounds, past fairy forts and a gazebo... The gardens are under restoration, and guests have been known to come and spend their entire break helping out. A good night's rest in one of the old brass or mahogany beds will cure all worldly cares -if you want peace and comfort in splendid surroundings, this is the place. **Rooms 5** (all with private bathrooms). B&B c. €55, ss €10. Residents D c. €40 (book by noon). Open all year. **Directions:** On the N52, 4 miles north of Nenagh. Heading north, look for the lake on the left and go through the stone archway, past the gatehouse.

Cashel
HOTEL / RESTAURANT

Cashel Palace Hotel
Main Street Cashel Co Tipperary
Tel: 062 62707 Fax: 062 61521
Email: reception@cashel-palace.ie Web: www.cashel-palace.ie

One of Ireland's most famous hotels, and originally a bishop's residence, Cashel Palace is a large, graciously proportioned Queen Anne style house (dating from 1730), set well back from the road in the centre of Cashel town. The beautiful reception rooms and some of the spacious, elegantly furnished bedrooms overlook the immaculately maintained gardens and grounds (28 acres in total) surrounding the Rock of Cashel at the rear. The present owners, Patrick and Susan Murphy, took over the hotel in 1998 and, since then, have been gradually renovating and refurbishing both public areas and bedrooms; the whole hotel has been redecorated recently and each of the 23 guests rooms has retained its own individual character. Lunch and dinner are served every day in the vaulted basement restaurant, **The Bishops Buttery**, and there is also a formal ground floor restaurant, **The Dining Room**, which is serenely situated overlooking the gardens. The kitchen successfully juggles the various demands of a mixed clientèle ranging from passing trade to local business people, corporate guests, families out for a treat - and, of course, residents. Menus are well-balanced, offering the traditional choices like steak and chicken breast alongside more adventurous ones; cooking is sound and quite modern, with the generosity expected in country areas. Children welcome. No pets. Garden. **Rooms 23** (5 suites). Lift. B&B c. €115, ss c.€35. **Restaurant: Seats 60.** L & D served daily. Set D c. €45, also à la carte. Afternoon tea and light menus also available. **Directions:** From Dublin, N7 and N8; look for signs as you approach as the town has been bypassed. On the main street of Cashel - hotel is on the right heading towards Cork.

Killurney Garden

Ballypatrick **Clonmel** Co Tipperary
Tel: 052 33155

GARDEN

Prize winning informal garden in a gorgeous setting.

COUNTY TIPPERARY

A serene 1880 farmhouse with views south to the Comeraghs, a crystal stream flowing from Slieve Namon and the ruins of a 16th century church are some of the blessings of Killurney Garden. Complement them with imaginative design and the knowledge of a keen plantswoman and you can understand why this garden carries off prizes. Mildred Stokes began gardening seriously in the mid 1980s and her garden has been evolving ever since. The stream which runs along the side of the property was diverted to create a pool, an old orchard was rooted out, and bit by bit an informal area was created where paths wind through a wonderful collection of plants, with lovely vistas and plant combinations at every turn.

There are many unusual trees and shrubs, *Abies pinsapo* with a giant first cone, *Acer* **'Bloodgood'** and the Judas tree. Mildred got rid of her roses but somehow they have crept back in again and there are over 80 from *R* **'Bonica'** to *R* **'Souvenir to St Annes'**, there are collections of grasses, agapanthus, clematis and hellebores. Mildred likes to plant in colours with interesting combinations like *Agapanthus clauescens* against the glaucus foliage of *R rubrifolia*, mauve globes of allium amid waving violet *Verbena bonariensis* and deepest carmine *Astrantia major* **'Hadspen Blood'**, planted with reds and pinks.

Picture a rill lined with primrose globes of scented *Primula florindae* and diarama beside a scree bed, a shady peaceful area with ferns like the tatting fern and the painted fern, and damp loving plants beside the stream - and irresistible paths leading to a sundial or specimen tree. There are all kinds of inventive ideas, a clematis and rose arch leading to a seating area paved with old kitchen flags, a *Berberis thunbergii* treated as a topiary globe, and urns filled with ruby sedums.

In front of the house, a little farm gate at the end of a lawn surrounded by curving beds acts as a focal point. There's a blue bed with the heavenly shades of *Salvia patens* and inky *Agapanthus* **'Midnight Blue'**, and a gold bed with Anthemis tinctoria 'Sauce Hollandaise', golden lilies and Stipa calamagrostis. Truly a garden where everything - colour, sight, and form - pleases the senses.

Open by appointment, May-Sep. Supervised children, welcome; dogs, allowed. Partial wheelchair access; teas by arrangement. **Directions:** *Take N24 Waterford road from Clonmel, turn onto N76 for Kilkenny; take 2nd left at petrol pumps, 3rd right at sign for Killurney, then 1st left after school - the house is 1st on left.*

Fethard
COUNTRY HOUSE

Mobarnane House
Fethard Co Tipperary
Tel: 052 31962 Fax: 052 31962
Email: info@mobarnanehouse.com Web: www.mobarnanehouse.com

Richard and Sandra Craik-White's lovely 18th century home is approached up a stylish gravel drive with well-maintained grass verges and makes a wonderfully spacious house for guests, with a uniquely peaceful, away-from-it-all atmosphere - and is not far from gardens in the Cashel, Clonmel and Kilkenny areas. A large, beautifully furnished drawing room has plenty of comfortable seating for everyone when there's a full house - and the dining room, where Richard's good country cooking is served (usually at a communal table, although separate tables can be arranged on request), is equally impressive. Accommodation is to a similar standard: all rooms have lovely views and comfortable seating (two have separate sitting rooms), quality bedding and everything needed for a relaxing stay, including tea/coffee making facilities, phones and television. Bathrooms vary somewhat (bedrooms without sitting rooms have bigger bathrooms), but all are thoughtfully appointed and have quality towels and toiletries. An excellent breakfast gets the day off to a good start - and, as well as being well-placed to explore a large and interesting area blessed with beautiful scenery and gardens, an interesting history, local crafts and sports, there's plenty to do on-site including extensive walks in the grounds, tennis and croquet. Not suitable for children under 5 except babies. Pets by arrangement. **Rooms 4** (2 junior suites, all no smoking). B&B c. €90 pps, ss €30. Residents' 4-course D 8pm, c. €45; advance reservation essential. Licensed. SC discretionary. Closed end Nov-early Mar (except for groups). MasterCard, Visa. **Directions:** About halfway between Cashel and Clonmel: from Fethard, take the Cashel road for 3.5 miles; turn right, signed Ballinure and Thurles; 1.5 miles on the left.

Templemore Area
COUNTRY HOUSE

Saratoga Lodge
Barnane Templemore Co Tipperary
Tel: 0504 31886 Email: saratogalodge@eircom.net

In a particularly unspoilt and peaceful part of the country, just below the famous Devil's Bit in the Silvermine mountain range, Valerie Beamish's lovely classically proportioned house on a working stud farm is attractively situated on an open, sunny site looking out over her pleasant garden to the hills. Good equestrian paintings enhance the large, traditionally furnished reception rooms opening off a spacious hall and there is also a little TV room for children. Bedrooms are very comfortably furnished, although the bathroom arrangements are a little complicated: two share a well-appointed intercommunicating bathroom and the third shares with the hostess (who uses a downstairs bathroom if guests want it to themselves). However, guests seem to cope with this unusual arrangement quite happily - no doubt the breakfasts that Valerie takes great pride in are more important, also the fact that she's willing to cook 4-course dinners on request (using home-produced vegetables, herbs and honey), and make picnics - and be extremely hospitable all round. Garden visits, fishing, horse riding, hiking, racing (horses, greyhounds), cheesemakers and golf are all nearby. Children welcome. Pets allowed by arrangement. Garden, walking, cycling, tennis. **Rooms 3** (2 en-suite but shared, 1 shower only, 1 with private bathroom, all no smoking). B&B from c.€40pps, no ss. Residents' D c. €30, by arrangement. Wine licence. Open all year except Christmas/New Year. **Directions:** From Templemore, take the Nenagh road for 2 miles; take 2nd turn on right. 1.5 miles, left at junction; house is on the left.

Ballymacarbry
GUESTHOUSE / RESTAURANT

Hanora's Cottage

Nire Valley Ballymacarbry Co Waterford
Tel: 052 36134 Fax: 052 36540
Email: hanorascottage@eircom.net Web: www.hanorascottage.com

The appeal of the Wall family's wonderful country guesthouse is that it feels so gloriously remote, yet it is easily accessible and a number of special gardens are within a convenient distance, in the Clonmel, Lismore and Cappoquin areas. Foot-weary walkers and desk-weary city folk in need of some clear country air and real comfort find Hanora's equally appealing - and the genuine hospitality of the Wall family is matched by the luxurious accommodation and good food they provide. Comfortably furnished seating areas with sofas and big armchairs provide plenty of room to relax, and the spacious thoughtfully furnished bedrooms all have jacuzzi baths (one especially romantic room is perfect for honeymooners); there's also a spa tub in a conservatory overlooking the garden, with views of the mountains. And one of the best things about Hanora's is that people travel from far and wide to dine here, which adds an extra dimension to the atmosphere; guests mingle at the fireside over an an aperitif, choose from Eoin and Judith Wall's imaginative, well-balanced menus - then move through to the restaurant, which overlooks a secluded garden and riverside woodland. Enthusiastic supporters of small suppliers, Eoin and Judith use local produce whenever possible and credit them on the menu - fresh fish from Dunmore East, free range chickens from Stradbally and local cheeses, for example - and there's a separate vegetarian dinner menu on request. Overnight guests then begin the next day with Hanora's legendary breakfast buffet - it takes some time to get the measure of this feast, so make sure you get up in time to make the most of it. **Rooms 10** (1 suite, 3 junior suites, all no smoking). No pets. B&B from c. €75 pps. Not suitable for children under 12. Restaurant Seats 40 D Mon-Sat, 7-9, Set D c.€40, also à la carte. Licensed. Closed Sun, bank hols. House closed Christmas week. **Directions:** Take Clonmel/Dungarvan road (R67); turn off at Ballymacarbry.

Ballymacarbry
FARMHOUSE

Glasha

Ballymacarbry Nire Valley Co Waterford
Tel: 052 36108 Fax 052 36108
Email:glasha@eircom.net Web: www.glashafarmhouse.com

Away from it all, up in the hills in the serenely beautiful Nire Valley, Paddy and Olive O'Gorman's spacious farmhouse is set in its own lovely gardens and provides a very comfortable and hospitable base for garden visits in the area (Lismore and Clonmel are both nearby), or simply for a relaxed rural break. This is a place that will appeal to lovers of gardens and the great outdoors, and a stay here provides the perfect antidote to the stress of urban life: the Nire runs beside the farmhouse (fishing permits are available locally), and walking is a major attraction - Glasha links the Comeragh and there are walks suitable for all levels of fitness and experience; first time Knockmealdown sections of the famous Munster Way walking route - and visitors are invariably delighted at how unspoilt the area is, and pony trekking is another good way to enjoy it (also available nearby). Or you can just put your feet up and enjoy the conservatory and gardens... Glasha has been a national winner of the Bord Failte Irish Welcome Awards, and it is easy to see why: Olive thinks of everything that will help you feel at home and bedrooms - which are all en-suite, some with jacuzzi baths - have lots of little extras including spring water and magazines; There's plenty of comfortable lounging room for guests too - and the

nearest pub is just 3 minutes' walk from the house. **Rooms 9.** B&B c. €50pps. Residents' D c. €35. Open all year except Christmas. MasterCard, Visa. **Directions:** Just past Four-Mile-Water Church, off R671 on the Clonmel-Dungarvan road near Ballymacarbry.

Cappoquin House Gardens
Cappoquin Co. Waterford
Tel: 058 54004
Email: cappest@ercom.net

GARDEN

Four acre garden surrounding a Georgian country house

Cappoquin House was turned back to front, when the 1779 house was rebuilt after it was burnt in the Troubles in 1923. Both the house and the garden gained from the new orientation which makes the most of the magnificent prospect over the Blackwater River.

Raised beds and lawns sheltered by a beech hedge occupy the ground in front of the house while the less formal part of the garden rambles up the steep hillside with plantings of rhododendrons and azaleas - and an attractive conservatory gives shelter to tender plants, including velvet leafed tibouchina, oleander and pelargoniums. There is an intriguing 'mirror' garden laid out around a sundial, where penstemon, iris and lavender among other old fashioned favourites, are planted to echo each other. Bamboo lined paths create a sense of mystery and lead to different areas, like the very successful pond surrounded by damp loving plants. Tucked away in different corners are a bog garden, a rose garden with old favourites like **'William Lobb'** and *Rosa banksia*, and a spring garden.

The house, home to the Keane family for 200 years, has a fascinating history (it was once occupied by the Seventh Bicycle Brigade), and is open to the public.

Open Apr-Jul, 9-1 except Sun & bank hols. Supervised children welcome; no dogs; not suitable for wheelchairs. Admission c. €5. **Directions:** From the N72, turn right at the T junction in the town; the stone gateway into the garden is on the left.

Cappoquin
COUNTRY HOUSE / RESTAURANT

Richmond House
Cappoquin Co Waterford
Tel: 058 54278 Fax: 058 54988
Email: info@richmondhouse.net Web: www.richmondhouse.net

Genuine hospitality, comfort, caring service and excellent food are all to be found in the Deevy family's fine 18th century country house and restaurant just outside Cappoquin - no wonder this is a place so many people like to keep as a closely guarded secret. Arriving through parkland along a well-maintained driveway, you will find a profusion of climbing plants beside the door, a fine high-ceilinged hall with a warming wood-burning stove and, on chilly days, the scent of log fires burning in the well-proportioned, elegantly furnished drawing room and restaurant opening off it. Claire or Jean Deevy are usually there to welcome guests, and show you to one of the nine individually decorated bedrooms; they vary, as is the way with old houses - some guests love the smallest cottagey bedroom, while others may prefer the larger ones - but all are comfortably furnished and have full bathrooms. The **Restaurant** is the heart of Richmond House and non-residents usually make up a high proportion of the guests, which makes for a lively atmosphere. Paul Deevy is the chef and, an ardent supporter of local produce; his carefully sourced ingredients will always include home grown fruit, vegetables and herbs where possible - and daily-changed menus, which offer a balance between traditional country house cooking and more adventurous dishes inspired by international trends, include a separate vegetarian menu. And residents can also look forward to a memorable breakfast to set you up for the day - it is a wonderful area to explore, with garden visits including Cappoquin House and Lismore Castle nearby, and Richmond House makes an excellent base. Children welcome. No pets. Garden; walking. **Rooms 9** (1 junior suite, all with full bathrooms & no smoking). B&B c. €75 pps, ss €20. **Seats 40** (private room, 16). D 7-9 daily Set D c. €48, early D c. €30; licensed. Closed Christmas-early Jan. Amex, Diners, MasterCard, Visa, Laser. **Directions:** Half a mile outside Cappoquin on N72.

Millstreet
FARMHOUSE

The Castle Country House

Millstreet Dungarvan Co. Waterford
Tel: 058 68049 Fax: 058 68099
Email: castlefm@iol.ie Web: www.castlecountryhouse.com

Set in one and a half acres of recently landscaped gardens overlooking the River Finisk, the Nugent family's unusual and wonderfully hospitable farmhouse is in the 18th century wing of a 16th century castle. Although most of the house seems quite normal inside, it blends into the original building in places - so, for example, the dining room has walls five feet deep and an original castle archway. Spacious, comfortably appointed rooms have king size beds, television, tea/coffee facilities and neat shower rooms; (there is also a full bathroom available for any guest who prefers a bath). Meticulous housekeeping, a very pleasant guests' sitting room and fresh flowers everywhere all add up to a very appealing farmhouse indeed, and Joan uses their own produce - fruit, vegetables, meats and herbs - in her cooking. Excellent breakfasts, also dinner by arrangement. Children welcome. Pets permitted. Garden, walking, fishing. **Rooms 5** (all en-suite). B&B c. €45pps, ss €10. **Dining Room Seats 16**; Residents D €25. Closed 1 Nov-1 Mar. Diners, MasterCard, Visa. **Directions:** Off N72 on R671.

Sion Hill House & Gardens

Sion Hill **Ferrybank** Co Waterford
Tel: 051 851558
Email: info@sionhillhouse.com Web: www.sionhillhouse.com

GARDEN

Hillside garden with roses, daffodils and rhododendrons a special feature.

This is an enthusiast's garden with stories attached to everything from the plants George Kavanagh began collecting as a boy, to the house itself. Sion Hill (1746) is one of five houses built by the Pope family who made their fortune as wine merchants during the Napoleonic embargo. In present times, the Kavanagh family were devastated when their three acre garden in Waterford city was compulsorily purchased, and the house on the opposite hill became the focus of George's dreams. These were finally realised when George and Antoinette bought Sion Hill in 1995 and moved in, transplanting 2,000 plants from their previous garden. One of the first things they did was to plant 20,000 daffodils and over 400 species roses and - thanks to a map in the National Archives - rediscovered the original paths in the upper part of the garden, which lies in Kilkenny. They have been restoring and replanting ever since.

Tree ferns bought by George as a lad from Derreen for the grand sum of 2/6d are planted in tropical luxuriance around a hidden fountain pool, and new large leaved rhododendrons, cardiocrinums and tender shrubs are flourishing in the shelter of the woodland garden.

There is a walled area beside the house packed with George's treasures including a camellia that flowers pink white and red. There are commemorative trees planted by the family of a victim of 9/11, and by Desmond Guinness and Gerry Adams among others. Among them is the smallest rhododendron in the world, with quarter inch leaves.

Open 4 days June, 2-5 (Private Gardens of South East Festival) and by appointment. Supervised children welcome; partial wheelchair access; no dogs. Plant sales. Teas by arrangement. **Directions:** *Coming into Waterford city, the entrance is on the right opposite the Stat Oil garage just before Jurys Inn.*

Fairbrook House Gardens & Museum of Figurative Art
Kilmeaden Co Waterford
Tel: 051 38 4657
GARDEN

Intriguing compartmental garden in an old mill complex.

The water power of the River Dawn is the key to Fairbrook's history, first as a flour mill dating back to 1776 and, from 1846 to 1929, as a woollen mill. When Dutch artists Clary Mastenbroek and her late husband Wout Muller moved there only the house, old trees and mysterious ruins remained. Starting in 1994, they reclaimed the garden bit by bit from brambles and piles of stones, uncovering a spring well which became the basis for a water feature, laying a path and terrace by the trout filled river, and creating compartments with hedging and reclaimed stone, and making topiary features from box cuttings. Difficulties created by the stony old industrial site were turned to advantage - the old dye vats, for instance, were lined and turned into a swimming pool, self filtered by beds of reeds, iris and water plants.

Today it is a wonderfully structured garden which is constantly evolving. Off the central vista down a gravelled path intriguing areas await discovery, a hot garden planted with monarda, *Crocosmia* **'Lucifer'** and the curiously named rose **'Parkdirector Riggers'**. Further delights are an aromatic African garden with a Moroccan door, a berceau or fruit cage walk twined with crab apples and wisteria, a lily pool guarded by agapanthus and bonsais, a parterre planted with a trio of lavenders **'Munstead'**, **'Hidcote'** and *L angustifolia* and there is a sculpture garden, and even a maze designed by Clary.

Plants and materials are used in original ways: a trinity of *Prunus serrula* under planted with bergenia stands at the centre of a beech allée; mesh, used to reinforce concrete, is recycled as a framework for a blue climber walk for passion flower, solanum, clematis and *Billardiera* with its lapis lazuli berries. Box is sculpted into swirling spirals and undulating hedges, slates are made into sunbursts, and even the grass is mown into circular patterns under the trees. One of the most recent creations is a knot, its spaces filled with coloured marble and the corners punctuated by *Sorbus* **'Pink Pagoda'**. The garden is full of hidden corners and inviting seating areas and the latest project involves the restoration of the curious building where the raw wool was soaked in hot water.

The former warehouse has been converted into a studio and museum hung with Wout, Clary's and their daughter Tamara's paintings, and there is also their friend Eva's charming bric à brac shop.

Open by appointment only, May-Sep. Children over 12 welcome; not suitable for wheelchairs; no dogs; tea and lunch by arrangement. Shop. Admission c. €5. **Directions:** *Heading west on N25, take 4th turn after cheese factory in Kilmeaden.*

Mount Congreve
Kilmeaden Co Waterford
Tel: 051 384115
Email: congreve@eircom.net

GARDEN

Unforgettable massed planting of rhododendrons, shrubs and trees in a beautifully located demesne.

Mount Congreve represents gardening on a very grand scale indeed. And in late spring and early summer the 100 acre demesne is surely one of the wonders of the floral world to be ranked alongside sights like the flower carpets of Namaqualand.

At that time of the year one of the largest rhododendron collections in the world, the culmination of Ambrose Congreve's lifetime passion, reach their peak .

The estate overlooks a bend in the River Suir and the wooded hillside provides perfect growing conditions for over 300 different types of rhododendron, more than 600 types of camellia, 250 types of Japanese maple and 300 varieties of magnolia. There are also wonderful displays of prunus and euchryphia. Inspired by the Rothschilds' garden at Exbury Congreve's interest began at an early age and, where most of us plant by ones and twos, planting at Mount Congreve is done by the score. The result is to produce spectacular seas of blossom and banks of colour with wonderful contrasts between the foliage and forms of different genera.

The folds and slopes of the hills and valleys offer different prospects over the inspired planting and there are enchanting sights and scents at every turn. Views not to be missed include a view of a Japanese pagoda below a 100 foot cliff, clouds of the coral flowers of *Azalea* **'Favourite'** lining the path to a classical temple overlooking the river, and a natural amphitheatre peopled with dwarf *R yakushianum* overlooking a rock pool.

Flowering shrubs are only part of the story: bulbs - snowdrops, crocus, grape hyacinths, glory of the snow, daffodils and wild bluebells - provide carpets of colour before the tree canopy closes over. The impressive arboreal collection includes *Davidii involucrata* the handkerchief tree, *Metasequoia glyptostroboides*, the dawn redwood and *Nothofagus menziesii* the silver beech.

The walled gardens evoke previous eras with greenhouses dedicated to growing nectarines, grapes and flowers for the house, and with collections of exotic plants including orchids, bromeliads, clivias and fuchsias. Within the four walled acres there are borders dedicated to displays for the months of May, June, July and August, exemplary vegetable gardens, and collections of iris and hydrangeas. The whole estate is quite simply magnificent and is to be left to the nation.

Open Thu only, 9-4.30; also groups by appointment. Supervised childrenwelcome; no dogs; limited wheelchair access. **Directions:** *Off the main Cork/Waterford Road: five miles beyond Waterford turn right at the sign for Tramore; take the second turn to the left and the gates are on the right.*

Lismore Castle Gardens

Lismore Castle **Lismore** Co Waterford
Tel: 058 54424
Email: lismoreestates@eircom,net Web: www.lismorecastle.com

GARDEN

Historic garden dating back in parts to the 17th century

Chapter after chapter of history - peopled with high profile characters from King John, who had the first castle built there, to the first Protestant Archbishop (the notorious Myler McGrath) to Sir Walter Raleigh, who owned it at one point - has unfolded at Lismore Castle. Even without its colourful past the Castle has a dramatic enough setting to make it a star in its own right. James II is said to have almost fainted when he stayed the night there in 1689, looked out of the window and saw the sheer drop down to the River Blackwater.

The present early 19th century castle, designed by Paxton for the 6th Duke of Devonshire, incorporates parts of the medieval and17th century castles. The garden walls were once an important part of the castle's defences and within them the upper enclosure dates from the 1620s with a typical Jacobean raised terras for strolling. The orchards, with peach and nectarine trees, would have been a 'flowery mead' similar to today's wild flower meadows; here is a display of bluebells in the spring, and a yew walk dating to the early 17th century. The lower part of the garden was laid out as a Pleasure Ground for the 6th Duke, known as the Bachelor Duke, and is now planted with a host of flowering

shrubs: magnolias, rhododendrons, azaleas and flowering cherries. Part of the upper garden is laid out with formal beds, and has a central path and flights of steps running through a double shrub and herbaceous border backed by yew hedges, and by rose and lavender borders. Some of the original greenhouses, by Paxton of Crystal Palace fame, are still in use. The charming Riding House staircase links the two parts of the garden which has been enjoyed in its day by Lady Caroline Lamb, (on a visit to help her get over Byron) and Adèle Astair, the dancer and wife of the 9th Duke of Devonshire.

Open mid Apr-end Sep:Apr-May, 1.45- 4.45 daily. Jun-Sep from 11 am. **Directions:** *Entrance is from the town of Lismore.*

Waterford
FARMHOUSE

Foxmount Country House
Waterford Co Waterford
Tel: 051 874 308 Fax: 051 854 906
Email: info@foxmountcountryhouse.com Web: www.foxmountcountryhouse.com

The Kent family's 17th century home on the edge of Waterford is a haven of peace and tranquillity, and well situated for visiting gardens south of the city including Mount Congreve. The house is lovely, with classically proportioned reception rooms, and accommodation in five very different rooms which are all thoughtfully, and very comfortably, furnished - but, as peace and relaxation are the aim at Foxmount, don't expect phones or TVs in bedrooms, or a very early breakfast. However, Margaret Kent is a great cook and she loves baking, as guests quickly discover when offered afternoon tea in the drawing room - or in the morning, when freshly-baked breads are presented at breakfast. No evening meals are offered, but the restaurants of Waterford and Passage East are close by - and guests are welcome to bring their own wine and enjoy a glass at the log fire before going out for dinner. Children welcome. Pets by arrangement. Garden. **Rooms 5** (all with en-suite or private bathrooms, all no-smoking). B&B c. €55 pps, ss c. €15. Closed Nov-mid Mar. **No Credit Cards. Directions:** From Waterford city, take Dunmore Road - after 4 km, take Passage East road for 1 mile.

Waterford City
HOTEL / RESTAURANT

Waterford Castle Hotel
The Island Ballinakill Waterford Co Waterford
Tel: 051 878 203 Web: www.waterfordcastle.com

This delightful hotel dates back to the 15th century, and is uniquely situated on its own 310 acre wooded island (complete with 18-hole golf course), reached by a small private ferry. The hotel, which is surrounded by formal and informal gardens and woodland walks (and also productive tunnels which supply fresh produce to the kitchen), combines the elegance of earlier times with modern comfort, service and convenience - and the location is uniquely serene. All guest rooms have recently been refurbished and, although they inevitably vary in size and outlook, all are very comfortably furnished in a luxurious country house style. There are plans to extend the accommodation and add a health spa but, at the time of going to press, work on this development has not yet begun. Dining at the castle is a treat: the beautiful Munster Room restaurant is appointed to the highest standard and a fine kitchen brigade can be relied on to provide the food to match: menus are peppered with luxurious ingredients like lobster, foie gras, scallops, prawns, black sole, aged Irish beef and game, such as wild Irish venison; local produce is used as much as possible, including organic vegetables, and the cooking, in a modern classical style, is excellent. Golf, archery, clay pigeon shooting, fishing, tennis, walking, gardens. Children welcome. **Rooms 19** (8 suites,& junior suites, 4 ground floor, all no smoking). Lift. B&B c. €187.50pps, ss c. €77.50. **Restaurant Seats 60.** D daily; Set D c. €58 (priced by course) L Sun only, c. €30. Closed Jan. Amex, Diners, MasterCard, Visa, Laser. **Directions:** Outskirts of Waterford City, just off Dunmore East road.

South West

Glebe Gardens

The Glebe **Baltimore** Co Cork
Tel: 028 20232
Email: glebegardens@eircom.net   Web: www.glebegardens.com

GARDEN

Seaside garden with courtyard garden, wildflower meadow and organic kitchen produce

There is something very heartening about a productive garden, where all the plants are useful as well as decorative. Created by Jean and Peter Perry, this five acre seaside garden exists in happy synergy with their other enterprise, the **Courtyard Café**. Crops - including unusual varieties like Blauhilde French Beans and Golden Bush courgettes - are grown in their organic potager where the Perrys practise interesting techniques like companion planting to keep pests at bay, then find their way to the table as delicious soups, salads and puddings. Vegetables are grown in raised beds and mulched to keep moisture in and weeds out, and apple trees are trained as espaliers.

The herb garden, where medicinal and dye plants are grown in beds edged with silver santolina, also serves the café. Other areas of the garden earn their keep too, the cutting garden looks good and is full of excellent flowering plants for the vase like, dahlias, lupins and love in the mist.

Scents from the gravelled courtyard garden - roses, lilies and lemon verbena - billow into the house, and a raised lily pond and an olive tree provide the main focal interest. Further afield, the Harold Barry walk leads through woodland to an amphitheatre overlooking Church Strand Bay.

*Open mid-Apr-Sep, 1-6 (Apr Fri-Sun only; May & Sep Wed-Sun; Jun-Aug daily). Other times by appointment. Children welcome; no dogs; partial wheelchair access. Café. Admission c. €4. **Directions:** On the Skibbereen to Baltimore Road; the entrance is opposite the sign for Baltimore, on the way into the village.*

Baltimore
CAFÉ / RESTAURANT WITH ROOMS

Rolf's Restaurant & Wine Bar
Baltimore Co Cork
Tel: 028 20289 Fax: 028 20289
Email: rolfsholidays@eircom.net Web: www.rolfsholidays.com

The Haffner family have been at this pretty place up above Baltimore village for 20 years and, although part of the business is still a holiday hostel, it's a hostel with a difference; the complex has been extensively renovated and sensitively developed recently and, in addition to the restaurant and wine bar, which has earned a loyal following, now includes some en-suite rooms, and self-catering accommodation of character. For the casual visitor, the café is open during the day and serves an à la carte lunch, and a more extensive dinner menu is offered in the Restaurant 'Café Art' - which has views over Baltimore harbour, and is named after the contemporary art exhibitions held in the restaurant. Euro-Toques chef Johannes Haffner uses as much home-grown, organic and local produce as possible and all pastries, desserts and breads are home-made; wide-ranging menus include quite a few classics and retro dishes - starters like house paté with cranberry sauce & toast - and stunningly fresh fish simply cooked in the contemporary style; vegetarians are well looked after and there's also a better choice than in most other restaurants in the area for carnivores. Desserts include some continental treats - Flemish apple tart, "Linzer" almond tart - and coffees are delicious. The wine bar - with an open fire - is just the place for a drink before (or after) dinner; many wines not given on the wine list are available here by the glass. Garden terrace and sea view terrace available for fine weather. Accommodation: **Rooms 12** (4 en-suite, shower only), c. €60 per room (double). Self-catering accommodation also available. Children welcome. Pets permitted by arrangement. **Restaurant: Seats 50.** Toilets wheelchair accessible. L &D daily in summer. A la carte. Licensed. Closed Mon & Tue off season. Reservations advised. Open all year. MasterCard, Visa, Laser. **Directions:** On Baltimore Hill, 10 minute walk from village.

Baltimore
BAR/B&B

Bushe's Bar
The Square Baltimore Co Cork
Tel: 028 20125 Fax: 028 20596
Email: tom@bushesbar.com Web: www.bushesbar.com

Everyone, especially visiting and local sailors, feels at home in this famous old bar. It's choc-a-bloc with genuine maritime artefacts such as charts, tide tables, ships' clocks, compasses, lanterns, pennants et al - but it's the Bushe family's hospitality that makes it really special. Since Richard and Eileen took on the bar in 1973 it's been "home from home" for regular visitors to Baltimore, for whom a late morning call is de rigeur (in order to collect the ordered newspapers that are rolled up and stacked in the bar window each day). Now, it's in the safe hands of the next generation - Tom, Aidan and Marion Bushe - so all is humming nicely.

Simple, homely bar food starts early in the day with tea and coffee from 9.30, moving on to Marion's home-made soups and a range of sandwiches including home-cooked meats (ham, roast beef, corned beef), salmon, smoked mackerel or - the most popular by far - open crab sandwiches, served with home-baked brown bread. And all under €9. This is a terrific pub, at any time of year, and was a very worthy recipient of our Pub of the Year Award in 2000. Children not allowed after 10pm. Bar food served 9.30am-8.30pm daily (12.30-8.30 Sun). Bar closed 25 Dec & Good Fri. **Accommodation:** Over the bar, there are three big, comfortable bedrooms, all with a double and single bed, bath & shower, TV and a kitchenette with all that is needed to make your own continental breakfast. There are also showers provided for the use of sailors and fishermen. No pets.**Rooms 3.** B&B €27.50 pps, single rate €35. Amex, MasterCard, Visa, Laser. **Directions:** In the middle of Baltimore, on the square overlooking the harbour.

Baltimore
B&B

Slipway
The Cove Baltimore Co Cork
Tel: 028 20134 Fax: 028 20134
Email: theslipway@hotmail.com Web: www.theslipway.com

Quietly located away from the bustle around the square, but within easy walking distance of several excellent restaurants, Wilmie Owen's unusual house has uninterrupted views of the harbour and distant seascape from all the bedrooms, and also the first floor breakfast room, which has a balcony (a delightful room but only available to guests at breakfast time). There's a lovely garden and also a charming oyster bar in a converted outbuilding; very much intended for residents, it is only open when

Wilmie's husband, Dave, is not away on his travels. A self-catering cottage is also available for weekly rental (sleeps 2); details on application. Not suitable for children under 12; no pets. Garden. **Rooms 4** (all shower only & no-smoking). B&B c. €35 pps, ss c. €25. Closed Nov-Mar officially, but phone to check. **No Credit Cards**. **Directions:** Through Baltimore village, to the Cove, 500 metres.

Cois Cuain Gardens

Kilcrohane Nr. **Bantry** Co Cork
Tel: 027 67070
Email: marybobw@eircom.net Web: www.seasidegarden.net

GARDEN

Tender plants grown amid rocks and grass beside the shoreline.

Gardening in West Cork is definitely different. The Walshes may have had to use a pick axe rather than a spade to plant in their seaside garden but growing conditions, thanks to the greenhouse climate of the Gulf Stream, are incredible. Tender plants from Australasia and South Africa flourish in nooks between the rocks, and plants that normally need cosseting can safely be left out all winter.

Mary and Bob only began gardening seriously in 1991 when they retired to their holiday home overlooking Dunmanus Bay. They began in front of the house planting *Olieria macrondonta* as a wind break and then shrubs interspersed with plants. Quite without their ever intending it to happen, the garden has grown to three and a half acres, embracing a natural rockery area, a grassy stream garden planted with trees, a vegetable garden and a seaside path between fuchsias and camellias.

Little paths wind in between features, allowing the opportunity to admire the myriad tender and unusual plants. Restios, abutilon melianthus, hibiscus, yuccas, watsonias, leptospermum, aloes, agapanthus and kangaroo paw look all the more exotic near the wild seashore setting, and oleander, plumbago and tibouchina prosper in the greenhouse.

In the new stream and rock garden, exotic trees like *Acacia retinoides* and handsome species like *Picea breweriana* are keeping their heads down in the shelter of a hillock. Paths lead to viewing points, with seats made from driftwood or a telegraph pole where visitors simply have to pause and drink in the glorious combination of plants a scenery for, as Mary Walshe says, the place is all about peace and tranquillity.

Open 10-25 June, 11-6, Fri-Wed; otherwise by apointment. Children and dogs welcome; not suitable for wheelchairs. Entry c. €5. **Directions:** *3 miles out on road from Durrus to Ahakista; turn left after 9/10 mile and continue to sea shore; garden is on the right.*

Bantry Area   # Larchwood House Restaurant & Garden
RESTAURANT WITH ROOMS / GARDEN   Pearsons Bridge Bantry Co Cork
Tel: 027 66181

Aidan Vaughan's garden is his passion and his creation is a special point of interest here, complementing the restaurant, which is in a relatively modern house with both the traditionally-furnished lounge and dining room enjoying lovely views - the Ouvane River flows through the three acre woodland garden, which includes an island accessible via a footbridge and stepping stones. Sheila Vaughan, a Euro-Toques chef, presents seasonal dinner menus: smoked salmon with citrus salad, an unusual soup such as carrot & peach, quite traditional main courses such as loin of lamb with lemon and mint, and classical desserts like ice cream terrine or warm chocolate cake with caramel sauce - good cooking and, while the pace is leisurely, the view of the garden is a treat. This is a haven for garden lovers, who often make it a base when visiting the many gardens in the locality. **Accommodation:** B&B c. €40 pps, no ss. Gardens open daily all year. **Seats 25**. D Mon-Sat, 7-9.30. Set D c.€40. Closed Sun & Christmas week. (Limited opening in winter). Amex, Diners, MasterCard, Visa. **Directions:** Take the Kealkil Road off N71 at Ballylickey; after 2 miles signed just before the bridge.

Bantry Area
HOTEL / RESTAURANT

Seaview House Hotel
Ballylickey Bantry Co Cork
Tel: 027 50462 Fax: 027 51555
Email: info@seaviewhousehotel.com Web: www.seaviewhousehotel.com

Set in immaculately maintained gardens, with views over Bantry Bay, Kathleen O'Sullivan's country house hotel near Ballylickey Bridge is renowned for personal supervision and a warm welcome - and it would make a very comfortable base when visiting the many gardens in this area. Spacious, well-proportioned public rooms include a graciously decorated drawing room, a library, cocktail bar and television room, while generously-sized bedrooms - some especially luxurious ones in a new wing, and many with sea views - are all individually decorated, and most have good bathrooms. Family furniture and antiques enhance the hotel, and standards of maintenance and housekeeping are consistently high. The restaurant overlooks the garden, and is well-appointed with antiques, fresh flowers and plenty of privacy: the style is country house cooking, with the emphasis firmly on local produce, especially seafood, on menus that change daily and offer a wide choice on all courses; an informative wine list includes an extensive range of well chosen house wines, a generous choice of half bottles - and many treats. Service, as elsewhere in the hotel, is caring and professional. Children welcome. Pets permitted. **Rooms 25** (2 junior suites, 10 no smoking). 2 ground floor rooms suitable for less able guests; no lift. B&B c. €65 pps, ss c. €26. **Restaurant: Seats 50**. Toilets wheelchair accessible. D 7-9 daily, L Sun only 12.30-1.30; Set D c. €40, Set Sun L c.€23. Licensed. Hotel closed mid Nov-mid Mar. Amex, MasterCard, Visa, Laser. **Directions:** 10 minutes drive from Bantry, on N71 to Glengarriff.

Butlerstown
RESTAURANT WITH ROOMS

Otto's Creative Catering (O.C.C.)
Dunworley Butlerstown Bandon Co Cork
Tel: 023 40461
Email: ottokunze@eircom.net Web: www.ottoscreativecatering.com

Very close to the spot where they originally started the famous Dunworley Cottage restaurant many years ago, Hilde and Otto Kunze have created a dream of a place here. Otto and Hilde are deeply committed to the organic philosophy and members of both Euro-Toques and the Slow Food movement - and their vegetable gardens provide a beautiful and satisfying view from the vine-clad dining room, where meals of wonderful simplicity cooked by Otto are presented by Hilde. Take time to marvel at the sheer originality and ingenuity of their home over a drink (brought with you, if you like - no corkage is charged - or chosen from a short list of biodynamically produced wines) in the sitting room, while also pondering a unique dinner menu that offers several choices on each course. Their own organic farm supplies many of the ingredients for the kitchen, and a comprehensive list of producers and suppliers is presented with the menu. Typically your meal may start with a vegetarian salad platter, with organic leaves and several dips or, perhaps, a plate of Anthony Cresswell's smoked organic salmon. Freshly baked breads and butter, marvellous soups (based on whatever vegetable is especially prolific at the time, or perhaps Otto's wonderful beef consommé), wild salmon caught off the Seven Heads, organic T-bone steak well hung in local butcher Dan Moloney's cold room, and a vegetarian dish such as white organic asparagus with mustard greens and a freshly whisked sauce béarnaise are all typical... A magnificent selection of vegetables accompanies the main course and everything is presented with originality and palpable pleasure.To finish, if your visit is well-timed, there might be freshly picked top fruit, warm from the trees in the growing tunnels - cherries, plums, apricots, white peaches.....This wonderful food needs no embellishment, and it is outstanding value for the quality given. Accommodation is also offered: bedrooms are furnished in a simple Scandinavian style which, like the cleverly designed shower rooms, is intensely practical. And, of course, you will wake up in a most beau-

tiful place - and have more of that superb food to look forward to, at a breakfast that counts home-made sausages and home-produced rashers among its gems. **Rooms 4**. B&B c. €50, ss€20. Children welcome. Restaurant **Seats 30** (max table size 14). D Wed-Sun, by reservation (24 hours notice if possible); L Sun only. D c. €50; Sun L c. €35. Licensed; or BYO (no corkage). Wheechair access to restaurant & toilet. Closed Mon, Tue & mid Jan-Mar. MasterCard, Visa, Laser. **Directions:** Bandon to Timoleague to Dunworley.

Fota Arboretum & Gardens

Fota Island **Carrigtwohill** Co Cork
Tel: 021 4812728
Email: info@heritageireland.ie Web: www.heritageireland.ie

GARDEN

A historic arboretum and restored Italian walled gardens.

These pleasure grounds, set in a 780 acre estate on Fota Island, are proof of the T and M principle in gardening. Time and money can achieve wonderful results, and the Smith-Barry family had both. In 1820, John Smith-Barry had father and son Richard and Vitruvius Morrison enlarge an existing house on the island, and design the splendid interiors. In the mid 19th century, John's son James Hugh had the formal gardens laid out, started the arboretum, and had the orangery built .

Nothing if not competitive, the Smith-Barrys set out to make the arboretum one of the finest in these islands. Two subsequent generations continued to add to the collection of over 1,000 different species of trees and shrubs. Some of the oldest trees in the collection are among the earliest recorded introductions, as plant hunters brought back seeds and specimens from all over the world. There are wonderful collections of acers, magnolias and rhododendrons among the stately trees, and the curious fernery beside the gate was a traditional place for dalliance.

The two walled gardens beside the house have recently been restored. The rose garden has been planted in an open layout, with beds of modern hybrid tea roses in blocks of colour around a circular central feature; the borders around the walls are mainly reserved for herbaceous planting - there are zingy yellow and blue planting combinations with agapanthus, crocosmia, day lilies, yellow clematis and golden hops combined with the startling blue berries of dianella. Rambling roses are once again scrambling up the walls and there is an interesting section of new grasses, unfortunately not all labelled for the benefit of enthusiasts: among them *Phormium* **'Rainbow Maiden'**, *Miscanthus* **'Zebra'** and a collection of old roses - **'Madame Isaac Perrier'**, **'Reine des Violettes'** and **'Baron Girod de l'Ain'** - and there are some jolly dahlias too.

In the walled garden beside the house, a sunken Italian garden dating from the early 19th century has been unearthed, restored and planted with jazzy annuals, while the herbaceous borders around the walls are planted Jekyll fashion with drifts of soft colours. The south facing border has a more exotic scheme, with bananas flourishing among orange watsonias, agapanthus and hemerocallis.

*Popular Fota with it's wild life park has something for everyone, the house is open to the public, and there are tea rooms although the fare may not quite match up to the splendid surroundings. Arboretum open daily; garden Apr-Oct (times vary). Car park c. €2. **Directions:** Follow signs from the main Cork -Midleton road.*

Annes Grove Garden

Castletownroche Co Cork
Tel: 022 26145
Email: annesgrove@eircom.ie Web: www.annesgrovegardens.com

GARDEN

Romantic gardens and woodland, with walled Edwardian flower garden and luxuriant riverside fernery.

Annes Grove has many blessings, among them a long history in which generations of the Annesley family have enhanced the gardens plus a happy freak of nature which offers both lime and acid conditions in the sublime location by the River Awbeg.

The earliest element within 30 acres of 'pleasure grounds' is the walled garden, originally laid out in the 18th century with a curious viewing 'mount' typical of the period where a rustic summer house looks down on aptly named ribbon beds of clipped box. Later additions include a double herbaceous border planted with the soft shades of thalictrum, phlox and stachys, pergola walks and a lushly planted pond area within a framework of yew and beech hedges guarded by giant magnolias and eucryphias.

The 'Ornamental Glen', where the Awbeg flows through a limestone fault valley was first enhanced in the 1770s in the romantic manner. Rhododendrons were added to romance two generations ago when RA Grove Annesley, a subscriber to the then tremendously fashionable plant hunting expeditions planted the glen in the Robinsonian manner taking advantage of the pockets of neutral and acid soil. Some of the rhododendrons grown from seeds collected by Frank Kingdon Ward, on his expeditions to Burma, the Yunan and Tibet, are among earliest introductions to Ireland, (*R. wardii* is named for him.) Other spectacular flowering shrubs dating from this period include *Cornus cousa*, embothrium, eucryphia and hoheria.

There's a complete change of mood and vegetation in the luxuriant riverside garden amid a jungle of bamboos, gunnera, skunk cabbage and Himalayan primulas. Above this sub tropical area, limestone cliffs provide Mediterranean conditions and paths lead next to the multicoloured display around the 'Hydrangea Rock.'

Garden history continues to unfold, a new fernery is being created at the end of the woodland walk with over 300 different varieties of ferns, including the tree fern *Dicksonia antartica*. The 18th century Pen Pond beyond the riverside garden, once used for luring and trapping duck for the table, is being restored and there is now a nursery in the walled garden (Annes Grove Plants), specialising in herbaceous plants, including stock propagated from the garden.

Open mid Mar-end Sep; Mon-Sat 10-5, Sun 1-6. Children welcome, no dogs; partial wheelchair access. Plants for sale; entry about €6. Self catering accommodation available on the estate.
Directions: *In village of Castletownroache, turn right opposite Post Office; follow signs to gardens, Drive through entrance gates (about 1.5km from village) and on to car park.*

Castletownshend
B&B

Bow Hall
Main Street Castletownshend Co Cork
Tel: 028 36114
Email: dvickbowhall@eircom.net

Castletownshend is one of west Cork's prettiest villages and this very comfortable 17th century house on the hill is a wonderful place for discerning guests who enjoy a civilised atmosphere and old-fashioned comforts to stay. With a pleasant outlook over beautiful well-tended gardens to the sea, excellent home-cooking and a warm welcome by enthusiastic hosts, Dick and Barbara Vickery (who 'retired' here from Minnesota 25 years ago), a visit to this lovely home is a memorable experience. The house is full of interest - books, photographs, paintings - but its most outstanding features are perhaps the gardens and the food, which is not only imaginative but much of it is home-grown too. Residents' dinner, cooked by Barbara, is sometimes available by reservation; this treat will be a truly seasonal meal, based on their own produce fresh from the garden - potatoes, courgettes, swiss chard, salads, fresh herbs and fruit - picked just before serving, and cooked with other local specialities such as fresh crab or salmon. Breakfasts are also a highlight, with freshly squeezed orange juice,

Barb's 'just out of the oven scones', home-baked breads and muffins, home-made sausages, bramble jelly and other home-made preserves, pancakes, home-made sausage patties with rhubarb sauce, and eggs Florentine among the many delights. Non-smoking house. Children welcome. No pets. **Rooms 3** (1 en-suite, 2 with private bath or shower rooms, all no smoking), c. B&B €50, ss €5; min 2 night stay preferred. Advance bookings essential, especially in winter. Residents D 8 pm, by arrangement; €35 (no wine licence). Closed Christmas week. **No Credit Cards. Directions:** 5 miles from Skibbereen, on main street.

Lisselan Gardens

Lisselan Estate **Clonakilty** Co Cork
Tel: 023 33249
Email: info@lisselan.com Web: www.lisselan.com

GARDEN

Charming riverside garden in the Robinsonian manner.

To have a river running through a garden is a great blessing and Lisselan is a lovely case in point. The 30 acre garden is laid out on the banks of the River Adrigadeen, which provides gorgeous vistas along its sparkling expanse, to a wisteria covered bridge here and an island with a water lily pond there. Riverside walks to sooth the senses march beside the burbling water. The river is also responsible for the appealing topography, which suits the Robinsonian style of the garden, laid out for the Bence-Jones family around a house in French Chateau style by architect Lewis Vulliamy.

Reginald Bence-Jones caused the river to be widened to make a lake, and he and his wife were largely responsible for the garden on both sides of the river and also for the terrace below the house. Beneath it the steep sides of the valley provide a wonderful excuse for a rockery full of ferns, primula, cyclamen and dianthus.

Flagstone walks wind around the sides of the valley to different features, through the azalea garden and rose pergola, and through a stroll known as the Ladies' Mile lined with colourful shrubs, great banks of rhododendrons, Japanese maples, myrtles, Judas trees and robinia.

Open daily all year, 8 am to dusk. Supervised children welcome; teas by arrangement. **Directions:** *3km from Clonakilty, off the Cork road.*

Cork City
RESTAURANT WITH ROOMS

Café Paradiso

16 Lancaster Quay Western Road Cork Co Cork
Tel: 021 4277 939 Fax: 021 427 4973
Email: info@cafeparadiso.ie Web: www.cafeparadiso.ie

Devotees travel from all over Ireland - and beyond - to eat at Denis Cotter and Bridget Healy's ground-breaking vegetarian restaurant, where they produce such exciting mainstream cooking that even the most committed of carnivores admit to relishing every mouthful. House specialities that people cross the country for include delicious deep-fried courgette flowers with a fresh goats cheese & pinenut stuffing, olive & caper aoili and basil courgettes, which is a brilliant example of the cooking style at this colourful little restaurant. It's a lively place with a busy atmosphere and the staff, under the direction of Bridget Healy, are not only friendly and helpful but obviously enthusiastic about their work. Seasonal menus based on the best organic produce available are topped up by daily specials, which might include a modish dish like lime-grilled haloumi, with harissa sauce on a warm salad of couscous, cherry tomatoes, green beans & chickpeas & chermoula. The cooking is never less than stunning - and significantly, in this era of "cheffy" food and big egos, the

creator of this wonderful food describes himself simply as "owner cook"; many of Denis Cotter's creations are featured in his acclaimed books: Café Paradiso Cookbook and Café Paradiso Seasons. Café Paradiso may be small, but it packs a mighty punch.*__Paradiso Rooms__ offer accommodation over the restaurant; room rate c. €160. **Seats 45** (outdoor seating, 6). Toilets wheelchair accessible. L Tue-Sat, 12-3, D Tue-Sat 6.30-10.30. A la carte. Closed Sun, Mon, Christmas week. Amex, MasterCard, Visa, Laser. **Directions:** On Western Road, opposite Jurys Hotel.

Cork City
CAFÉ

Farmgate Café

English Market Cork Co Cork **Tel: 021 427 8134**
Fax: 021 427 8134 Email: knh@eircom.net

A sister restaurant to the Farmgate Country Store and Restaurant in Midleton, Kay Harte's Farmgate Café shares the same commitment to serving fresh, local food - and, as it is located in the gallery above the English Market, where ingredients are purchased daily, it doesn't come much fresher or more local than this. The atmosphere is lively and busy, with a comfortably down to earth atmosphere which suits the wholesome food they serve and, having highlighted the freshness of local ingredients for some time in dishes that were a mixture of modern and traditional, Kay Harte and her team have now decided to concentrate on the regional aspect of the food they buy in the market, and have introduced less well known foods such as corned mutton to their menus alongside famous old Cork ones with a special market connection like tripe & drisheen and corned beef & champ with green cabbage. Menus depend on what is available in the English Market each day, including "oysters to your table from the fish stall" and other fish - used, for example, in a chowder that market regulars keep coming back for. And there are delicious home-baked cakes and breads too, whether as a bite to accompany a coffee, or to finish off a meal, a wonderfully home-made seasonal sweet such as a classic raspberry sponge is always a treat. This is an interesting and lively place to enjoy good food - and it's great value for money. **Seats 110.** Meals Mon-Sat, from 8.30am - 5pm: B'fast 8.30-10.30, L 12-4. Licensed. Closed Sun, bank hols, Dec 25-3 Jan. Diners, MasterCard, Visa, Laser. **Directions:** English Market - off Oliver Plunkett Street and Grand Parade.

Cork
RESTAURANT WITH ROOMS

Flemings Restaurant
Silver Grange House Tivoli Cork
Tel: 021 482 1621 Fax: 021 482 1800
Email: flemingsrestaurant@iolfree.ie

Conveniently located on the eastern edge of the city and clearly signed off the main Cork-Dublin road, this large Georgian family house is home to one of Cork's finest restaurants, and also has four spacious en-suite bedrooms. On a hillside overlooking the river, the house is set in large grounds, including a kitchen garden which provides fruit, vegetables and herbs for the restaurant during the summer. It is a big property to maintain and the entrance can seem a little run down, but this is quickly forgotten when you enter the light, airy double dining room, which is decorated in an elegant low-key style that highlights its fine proportions, while well-appointed linen-clad tables provide a fine setting for Michael Fleming's classical and modern French cooking. The food here is invariably excellent, presentation elegant, and service both attentive and knowledgeable - at a time when ubiquitous multi-cultural menus are dragging so many restaurants down to a dull sameness, a visit to a classic restaurant like this is a treat to treasure. There's a good wine list too, and good value all round. **Seats 80** (private room 30; outside seating, 26). Children over 3 welcome before 8pm. L&D daily, 12-2.30, 6.30-10; reservations advised. Set L c. €28.50, Set D c. €38; also à la carte. Licensed. **Accommodation: Rooms 4**, comfortably furnished in a style appropriate to the age of the house (B&B c. €55 pps, ss €30). Open all year except Christmas. Amex, MasterCard, Visa, Laser. **Directions:** Off main Cork-Dublin route, 3 km from city centre.

Cork
HOTEL / RESTAURANTS

Hayfield Manor Hotel

Perrott Avenue College Road Cork Co Cork
Tel: 021 484 5900 Fax: 021 431 6839
Email: enquiries@hayfieldmanor.ie Web: www.hayfieldmanor.ie

Should you wish to stay in Cork city, this fine hotel set in two acres of gardens near University College Cork provides every comfort and a remarkable level of privacy and seclusion just a mile from the city centre. Although quite new - it only opened in 1996 - it has the feel of a large period house, and spacious bedrooms which vary in decor are beautifully furnished to a very high standard with antiques and have generous marbled bathrooms, many of them with separate bath and shower. Public areas are impressive and yet homely - and, since recent refurbishment, the lobby has taken on a classy contemporary tone which breathes new life into the traditional country house atmosphere of the original building. There is a Library and a Drawing Room for residents' use, and two restaurants offering equally good food in different styles: choose between **Perrotts**, a smart and relaxing contemporary restaurant

in a conservatory area at the front of the hotel, or **The Manor Room**, which offers a more formal option in a discreet position overlooking gardens at the back. Indoor swimming pool, spa. Children welcome. Pets permitted by arrangement. **Rooms 88** (4 suites, 9 junior suites, 40 no-smoking, 3 for disabled). Lift. Air conditioning. B&B c. €190 pps, ss c. €65. **Restaurants:** L&D offered daily in Perrotts and The Manor Room. Open all year. Amex, Diners, MasterCard, Visa, Laser. **Directions:** Opposite University College Cork - signed off College Road.

Lovetts Restaurant & Brasserie

Cork City
RESTAURANT

Churchyard Lane off Well Road Douglas Cork Co Cork
Tel: 021 429 4909 Email: lovetts@utvinternet.com

Home to both the restaurant and the Lovett family since 1977, this fine restaurant is in a late Georgian house situated in mature grounds, and is now run by Niamh Lovett and her business partner and head chef is Marie Harding. Just reading through Marie's list of suppliers is enough to whet the appetite: smoked salmon and eel from Cresswells of Ummera, Co Cork; mussels and oysters (in season) from Kellys of Clarenbridge; crab from Shellfish de la Mer, and most other fish from Denis Good, both in Castletownbere; Mrs Lombard of Minane Bridge supplies free range chickens, while ducks are from Barry's of Fort Farm, Fermoy and mushrooms from Fran & Jim Fraser. Better still, while the menus - which are based on daily availability, not over-extensive and admirably simple in style - are a mouth-watering read, the cooking matches the quality of ingredients, making for an outstanding dining experience. A blackboard menu offers around five fish dishes each day, and a separate vegetarian menu is very appealing; desserts are delicious too (loganberry bakewell tart, with cream, perhaps) and, of course, there's a fine Irish farmhouse cheese plate. There's a fully licensed bar (the extensive wine list is Niamh's father Dermod Lovett's particular passion) and The Brasserie operates at the same time as the restaurant, offering a more informal menu. **Seats 35.** (Private room 6-24). Toilet not wheelchair accessible. D Tue-Sat, 6.30-9.30. Closed Sun, Mon, 24-31 Dec, 2 weeks in Aug. **Directions:** Close to south Cork city-from Douglas Road take turning to Mahon and Blackrock and go through a roundabout. Take the fourth turn on the left.

The Maryborough House Hotel

Cork City
HOTEL

Maryborough Hill Douglas Cork Co Cork
Tel 021 436 5555 Web: www.maryborough.com

This hotel, which is quietly situated on the south of the city and very convenient to Cork airport and the Jack Lynch tunnel (ideal if you need to be in Cork city and want to visit gardens west of the city and in east Cork), has a fine country house at its heart and is set in its own gardens. The main entrance is via the original flight of steps up to the old front door and as a conventional reception area would intrude on the beautifully proportioned entrance hall, guests are welcome at a discreetly positioned desk just inside the front door. The original house has many fine features and is furnished in period style with antiques; spacious public areas now extend from it, right across to the new accommodation wing through the Garden Room, a spacious contemporary lounge overlooking gardens to the rear. Generously-sized guest rooms are in the new section; attractively designed – simple, bright, modern, with neat bathrooms, they feature Irish crafts and have a pleasantly leafy outlook and good amenities. The hotel restaurant, **Zings**, offers European cuisine with Mediterranean flavours; creative use of lighting separates areas within this design-led dining area without physical divisions - and the tables are considerably spot lit (ideal for lone diners who wish to read). Leisure centre (swimming pool); beauty salon; spa. Children welcome. No pets. Rooms 79 (5 suites/ junior suites, 20 no-smoking, 4 disabled). Lift. B&B c. €85, ss €25. **Restaurant Seats 120.** Air conditioned. L & D daily. Set L c. €25, D à la carte. Open all year except Christmas. Amex, Diners, MasterCard, Visa, Laser. **Directions:** Signed from the round-about where Rochestown Road meets Carrigaline Road.

Farran
COUNTRY HOUSE

Farran House

Farran Co Cork **Tel 021 733 1215**
Email info@farranhouse.com Web: www.farranhouse.com

Set in 12 acres of mature beech woodland and rhododendron gardens in the rolling hills of the Lee valley, this impressive house was built in the mid-18th century, although its present elegant Italianate style only dates back to 1863. It is beautifully situated with views over the medieval castle and abbey of Kilcrea and its location west of Cork city could make a good base for exploring Cork and Kerry. In the present ownership of Patricia Wiese and John Kehely, the house has been carefully restored and, although there are some contemporary touches as well as antiques, none of its original character has been lost. Despite its considerable size, there are just four bedrooms - all exceptionally spacious and decorated with style and comfort, as are their adjoining bathrooms (although without the complimentary toiletries and other small touches that are usually provided in this price range). There's a fine drawing room for guests' use (complete with grand piano) and a billiard room with full size table. The house is available all year for private rental by groups and this is, perhaps, its most attractive use. Children welcome. No pets. **Rooms 4** (all en-suite, 2 with separate bath & shower; all no smoking); B&B from c. €80 pps, ss €30 (advance bookings only); residents D c. €40 (24 hours notice; not available Sun or Mon, but Thady Inn nearby does good meals). Self-catering coach house available; house also available for self-catering groups of 8-9. Closed Nov-end Mar. MasterCard. Visa, Laser. **Directions:** Just off N22 between Macroom & Cork: heading west, 5 miles after Ballincollig, turn right to Farran village, up hill, 1st gate on left.

Doneraile
COUNTRY HOUSE

Creagh House

Main Street Doneraile Co Cork **Tel: 022 24433**
Email: creaghhouse@eircom.net Web: www.creaghhouse.ie

Michael O'Sullivan and Laura O'Mahony took on this Regency townhouse in need of renovation in 2000; since then, they have been giving it enormous amounts of TLC on an ongoing basis so that it may, one day, reach its full potential glory. A listed building, with notable historical and literary connections, stately reception rooms and huge bedrooms, its principal rooms are among the largest from this period outside Dublin, and have beautiful restored plasterwork. Yet it is a relaxed family home and place of work (Michael and Laura both have offices in restored outbuildings), and this hospitable couple clearly thrive on the challenge of the restoration process. Accommodation is wonderful, in vast rooms with huge antique furniture, crisp linen on comfortable beds, little extras (bowls of fruit, bottled water, tea/coffee/hot chocolate making facilities), and bathrooms to match - bath and separate shower, and big, soft towels. All modern partitions have been removed to restore the original scale, and 19th century furniture is used throughout, with 18th and 19th century prints and modern paintings. Anyone interested in architecture and/or history is in for a treat when staying here and Doneraile is well-placed for exploring a wide area - Cork, Cashel, Lismore and Killarney are all within an hour's drive. Garden lovers will be fascinated by the 2-acre walled garden behind Creagh House, which is under restoration ("black topsoil four feet deep!") and the house is beside Doneraile Court, which has 600 acres of estate parkland, free to the public. Creagh House is still a work in progress - but what a work! **Rooms 3** (all en-suite, with separate bath & shower, all no smoking). Residents' supper (2-course D, c. €25), available with 24 hrs notice. B&B c. €80pps, no ss. Closed Oct-Mar. Amex, MasterCard, Visa. Directions: Take N20 (Limerick road) from Mallow (8 miles).

Aultareagh Cottage Garden

Dunmanaway Co Cork **Tel: 023 55307**
Email: lesandchris@aultareaghcottagegarden.com
Web: www.aultareaghcottagegarden.com

GARDEN

A one acre garden packed with inspirational ideas and interesting plants.

There's nothing more encouraging than visiting enthusiasts' gardens, especially when starting a new garden. Christine and Les Wilson have had a wonderfully inventive approach to their one acre hilltop garden which is packed with choice plants and interesting ideas.

Features like their 100 foot double herbaceous borders grab the attention. Filled with perennials, mainly grown from seed: oriental poppies, Noble series lupins, thalictrum, campanulas, asters aconitum, agapanthus and choice crocosmias like **'Emily McKenzie'** have the Nowen and Shehy mountains as a backdrop.

Their pond garden and waterfall are a magnet for wildlife, the red waterlily **'Escarboucle'** rules the centre of the pond, in the margins are Iris ensata, flags and marsh marigolds.

A small walled garden area with a grotto provides shelter for tender plants; it has a 'hot' side and a 'cool' side, where the accent is on the accent on bluey green foliage with eucalyptus, guara and ozmanthus. A south wall border offers a display of *Liatris spicata*, *Ceanothus* **'Autumnal Blue'** and *Callistemon* **'Captain Cook'**, tiger flowers and *Indigofera heterantha*.

Part woodland, the garden also features a vegetable and fruit garden, a herb parterre, a willow arbour and a grass garden, all within the cleverly integrated whole.

Open May-Aug, 10-6 and by appointment. Children and wheelchairs welcome. No dogs. Plants for sale, around €5. Picnics welcome; teas available. **Directions:** *On the R587 Macroom road 4 miles north of Dunmanaway or, 200 yards off R585 Cork-Bantry Road. Follow garden signs.*

Durrus
RESTAURANT WITH ROOMS

Blairs Cove House
Durrus Co Cork **Tel: 027 61127**
Email: blairscove@eircom.net Web: www.blairscove.ie

Philippe and Sabine de Mey's beautiful property enjoys a stunning waterside location at the head of Dunmanus Bay. Although additions over the years have enlarged the restaurant considerably - including an elegant conservatory overlooking a courtyard garden - the original room is lofty, stone-walled and black-beamed. However, while characterful, any tendency to rusticity is immediately offset by the choice of a magnificent chandelier as a central feature, gilt-framed family portraits on the walls, generous use of candles - and the superb insouciance of using their famous grand piano to display an irresistible array of desserts. They have things down to a fine art at Blairs Cove - and what a formula: an enormous central buffet displays the legendary hors d'oeuvre selection, a speciality that is unrivalled in Ireland. Main course specialities of local seafood or the best of meat (rib eye of beef, perhaps) and poultry are char-grilled at a special wood-fired grill right in the restaurant and, in addition to those desserts on the piano, full justice is done to the ever-growing choice of local farmhouse cheese for which West Cork is renowned. An extensive wine list includes a good choice of house wines and half bottles. The food is terrific, service friendly and efficient, and the ambience atmospheric - magic. Accommodation (B&B or self-catering) is available in three small attractively furnished apartments, and also a cottage in the grounds. **Seats 85**. D Tue-Sat, 7.30-9.30. Reservations required. **Accommodation** c. €105 pps, ss €30. Closed Sun-Mon & Nov-Mar. MasterCard, Visa. **Directions:** 1.5 miles outside Durrus on the Malin Head road - blue gate on the right hand side.

Durrus
CAFÉ

Good Things Café
Ahakista Road Durrus Co Cork
Tel: 027 61426 Fax: 027 61425

Although not exactly a a gardeny place, great ingredients-led contemporary cooking is the magnet that draws those in the know to Carmel Somers' simple little café-restaurant just outside Durrus village - where there are recommended gardens to visit. Well-placed to make the most of fine west Cork produce, Carmel also sells some specialist foods from Ireland and abroad and a few books including the great little guide to Local Producers of Good Food in Cork, produced by Myrtle Allen and Cullen Allen for the Cork Free Choice Consumer Group, which details many of the artisan producers who supply Good Things Café. The daytime café menu offers a concise list including great salads (mixed leaves with fresh beetroot, fresh broad beans, cherry tomatoes, smoked salmon, quails eggs among the goodies), West Cork fish soup (available, like most dishes on the daytime menu, as a starter or main course), West Cork Ploughmans (a trio of local cheeses served with an onion cassis compôte), Durrus cheese, spinach & nutmeg pizza (a thin-based, crisp pizza with a delicious gourmet topping)...then there are irresistible desserts to choose from a display (raspberries and cream, St Emilion chocolate cups...) Dinner brings a more formal menu, with a choice of four on each course, and will feature some of the daytime treats along with more 'serious. main courses; ingredients are invariably superb and, at its best, a meal here can be memorable - this place is a one-off and it is well worth planning a stop here, especially during the day, when the bright atmosphere and white café furniture seems more appropriate. Cookery classes are also offered. **Seats 40** (plus 10 outside in fine weather). In summer open all day (10.30-5) Wed-Mon (daily in Aug & during Bantry Music Festival. L 12.30-3; also D Thu-Mon. A la carte. Licensed. Closed Tue & Nov-Easter (poss excepting some special dates). Reservations advised for D; a call to check times is wise, especially off season. MasterCard, Visa, Laser. **Directions:** Fron Durrus village, take the Ahakista/Kilcrohane road.

Carraig Abhainn Gardens

Durrus Co Cork
Tel: 027 61070
Email: carraigabhainn@eircom.net Web: www.carraigabhainngardens.com

GARDEN

Informal riverside garden with flowering shrubs and plenty of surprises.

People come from far and wide to visit Wiseman's emporium, a fine example of a nearly extinct breed of general store, stocking everything imaginable. Visitors - including bridal parties in search of a photogenic spot - also flock to the Wiseman's garden and it's easy to see why. Millions couldn't buy the wonderful setting beside the falls, pools and rapids of the Durrus River.

The Wisemans bought the two acre plot of 'genuine jungle' behind their shop in 1980 and began carving out a garden which "just happened". Inviting grass paths lead off through mixed shrub borders with azaleas, rhododendrons, acers, giant stands of gunnera and camellias, to gorgeous vistas of the river. They wind back via a gravel path where alders lean over the racing gold brown water to a wooden bridge over the old mill race with the mask of a mysterious river god topping a gnarled oak body. There are all manner of curiosities to be found in the garden, there's a temple with a mural overlooking a pool where an ocean liner made by the Wiseman's son-in-law Tommy Daly sails incongruously by Japanese bridges and an otter. There's a seat fit for a Sun God, and a fern garden in what was once a bog. Everything grows prolifically in this garden from Chilean holly - *Desfontania spinosa* - to a huge leaved eucalyptus quaintly named neglecta according to Eugene and the Wiseman's enthusiasm is infectious.

Open 1 Mar- 30 Oct, Mon-Sat 10-8; Sun by appointment. Children dogs and wheelchairs welcome. (Restaurant nearby). **Directions:** *In Durrus village.*

Kilravock Garden

Durrus Co Cork
Tel: 027 61111
Email: kilravock@eircom.net Web: www.kilravockgardens.com

GARDEN

Seaside garden laid out as a series of informal themed rooms, with stream, ferneries and sorbus walk.

Phemie Rose started the West Cork Gardening Trail in association with the Harold Barry Trust to show others just what could be done And the paradise Phemie has created with her husband Malcolm is proof indeed of just how special gardens there can be thanks to the benign climate.

Kilravock manages the hat trick, winning on all three counts of design, interest and an amazing collection of plants, many of them from the southern hemisphere. The Roses began work on their two and a half acres over 10 years ago. It wasn't an easy site and it was two years before they discovered they had the stream which is now a central feature, flowing into pools and along rills.

Laid out as a series of informal rooms the garden leads from an Oriental area which takes advantage of natural rock formations and features a host of acers and a curved bridge built by Malcolm, through a stream garden with hosts of primulas and hostas. Unusual species like the palm *Butia captitata*, and *Hakea saligna* prosper in mild shelter, a rill runs beside the fernery with exotic specimens like the graceful tree ferns *Cycathei cooperii/medularis* and *smithii*, the peacock like *Blechnum tabulare* and the Chinese lace fern.

The clever layout of the garden means that it is full of surprises and enchanting internal vistas. Malcom specialises in ferns, cordylines and sorbus (he has an azalea and sorbus walk carpeted with spring bulbs and with five Irish cultivars, including the rare *S* **'Molly Saunderson'**); Phemie grows Southern hemisphere plants from seed, including South African restios like Elegia capensis .

The big surprise is the Mediterranean garden with mosaic feature as the central focal point. It's miniature wonderland with plants that get curiouser and curiouser, there's the laughing plant *Cotyledon orbiculata*, spiky fans of *Puya chiliensis.* rosettes of *Aloe striata* and a palm with personality known as the 'Green Goddess'

Open 2 weeks in June (Tue-Sun, 12-7.30) & groups by appointment. Not suitable for children, dogs or wheelchairs. Plant sales, c. €5. Admission c. €3. **Directions:** *Just over a mile from Durrus on the Kilcrohane road (signed).*

Fermoy Area
COUNTRY HOUSE / GARDEN

Ballyvolane House
Castlelyons Fermoy Co Cork
Tel: 025 36349 Fax: 025 36781
Email: info@ballyvolanehouse.ie Web: www.ballyvolanehouse.ie

COUNTY CORK

The Greene family's gracious mansion is surrounded by its own farmland, magnificent wooded grounds, a recently restored trout lake and mature gardens, all carefully managed and well maintained. Garden lovers will find a stay here especially rewarding; an information leaflet detailing the garden and walks is available to guests, also one on other walks in the locality (there's also a comprehensive general information directory for guests which is exceptionally well-researched and up to date - a model of its kind). Ballyvolane is a member of the Blackwater Valley Garden Trail and the gardens - renowned for their terraced lawns and stunningly beautiful bluebell woods in spring, and also a walled garden - are open by appointment. The Italianate style of the present house - including a remarkable pillared hall with a baby grand piano and open fire - dates from the mid 19th century when modifications were made to the original house of 1728. This is a very lovely house, elegantly furnished and extremely comfortable, with central heating and big log fires; bedrooms vary according to their position in the house - all are roomy and, like the rest of the house, are furnished with family antiques and look out over the extensive gardens and grounds. Ballyvolane has private salmon fishing on 8km of the renowned River Blackwater, with a wide variety of spring and summer beats, and delicious food is another high point here, with modern Irish dinners served in style around a long mahogany table. There

is much of interest in the area and this makes a wonderful base for exploring the beautiful Blackwater Valley, with its many gardens and historic sites - including Lismore Castle, which is nearby. Jeremy and the late Merrie Greene's son, Justin, and his wife Jenny, now manage Ballyvolane - and Jeremy is still very much involved with the gardens and woodland, which are his great love; Justin has management experience in top hotels and they are committed to ensuring that the standards of hospitality, comfort and food for which this lovely house is renowned will be maintained, making this an excellent choice for a peaceful and very relaxing break. Children welcome. Pets permitted in some areas. Fishing; walking; cycling. **Rooms 6** (1 shower only). B&B c. €75 pps ss €30. Residents D c.€47.50 at 8pm, book by 10am; menu changes daily. Licensed. House open all year except Christmas. Gardens open by appointment. Amex, Diners, MasterCard, Visa, Laser, Switch. **Directions:** Turn right off main Dublin-Cork road N8 just south of Rathcormac (signed Midleton), following house signs on to R628 .

The Coach House

Glandore Co Cork
Tel: 028 33831

GARDEN

Walled garden with exotic southern hemisphere plants and wonderful views

It is as though subtropical house plants had escaped from their pots, marched outdoors to take advantage of the balmy West Cork climate and prospered mightily. Which is more or less exactly what has happened, for plantswoman Shirley Bendon has experimented by buying indoor plants and growing them in the sheltered walled garden of her 1836 home.

The central border in the beautifully situated garden overlooking Glandore Harbour is full of rare and exotic plants, some grown from seeds and cuttings. Walk down the central path and you feel as though you have strayed into South Africa or Madeira, for there are flourishing yuccas, aloes, puyas, vivid blue *Echium candicans*, *Trachycarpus fortunei*, *Osteospermums erythrina* (the Coral Tree) *Greyia sutherlandii* (the Natal bottlebrush). Their success is evidence of climatic change, and around the walls are kiwi trees dripping with fruit, fruiting olive trees and bananas.

Mrs Bendon started gardening seriously in 1990 and has created a garden with many changes of mood. There is a wooded areas full of the perfume of fragrant rhodendrons **'Fragrantissimum'** and **'Princess Alice'** in spring. There is a pond area with more southern hemisphere plants including: restios and tree ferns, an organic vegetable garden set out in nine foot plots and surrounded by a collection of salvias, a big herbaceous border and a cottage garden full of cheerful plants. Gravel and grass paths wind from one area to the next with the beguiling view of the harbour as a backdrop.

*Open by appointment only May-Aug. Supervised children; limited wheelchair access; no dogs; some plants for sale; teas for groups by arrangement. Admission c. €5. **Directions:** 2.5km from Leap, off the N71; 0.5 kilometre west of the pier at Glandore.*

Lakemount Gardens

Barnavara Hill **Glanmire** Co Cork
Tel: 021 4821052 / 086 8110241
Email: crossb@gofree.indigo.ie Web: www.lakemountgardens.com

GARDEN

Well-designed garden with extensive plant collection, cleverly planned to create constant changes of mood and style.

This hill top garden is rather like a very delicious box of chocolates, so full of different treats that it is hard to know which one to pick first. You could, for instance, be torn between the Millennium pond garden which links the terrace by the house to rest of the garden, and the gravel garden. Framed in Liscannor stone surrounded by raised beds filled with hydrangeas and dwarf rhododendrons, the formal pond harbours water lilies, *Iris ensata* and a cast iron sculpture of arum lilies. The exit to the lower garden is guarded by two dramatic columns of restios and the bank below is turned brilliant pink by nerines in autumn.

In contrast to the hard landscaping, the gravel garden shimmers with swaying grasses, *Verbena bonariensis*, *Diarama* **'Blackbird'** and bearded iris in late spring. Beyond this hot dry area, emerald green lawns lap around informal beds of mixed planting where contrasting forms and colours of shrubs act as the backdrop for the star performers out front.

Created over two generations by the late Mrs Margaret Cross and her son Brian, the garden is so cleverly planned with constant changes of mood and style that it seems much larger than two acres. There's an almost Californian brilliance to a side garden where the azure of the pool is offset by bright flowered azaleas, rhododendrons and primulas. The paved garden, its seclusion emphasised by wrought iron gates, contains a number of separate compartments with raised beds for alpines and structural plants like phormiums and inviting seats. Tucked away beside a formal area with topiaried box and bay, the conservatory is full of tender treasures, the tree poppy *Dendromecon rigida*, abutilon, pelargoniums and jasmine.

Open by appointment. Supervised children welcome; mostly wheelchair accessible. Entry c. €.50 (guided tour c. €6.50). **Directions:** *Just outside Cork city: from roundabout on Cork-Dublin road turn off for Glanmire, go through village, over bridge and turn left up hill; the house is at the top on the left.*

Illnacullin

Garinish Island **Glengarriff** Co Cork
Tel: 027 63040
Email: garinishisland@opw.ie Web: www.heritageireland.ie

GARDEN

Magnificent island garden combining formal and informal elements.

Most great gardens are the acolytes of grand houses, but Illnalcullin is the exception for the garden was created first and plans for a house were never realised. In 1910 Annan Bryce bought the then bare rocky island, previously a lookout during the Napoleonic War with a Martello tower, from the War Office.

The setting could hardly be more romantic. The island is nestled in the wooded arms of Glegarriff Harbour with glorious views across to the Caha Mountains and is reached by a short ferry journey past rocks draped with basking grey seals. It's a suitable overture to the most enchanting symphony of gardens, designed by architect and landscape designer Harold Peto and planted by Bryce in a garden made possible by dint of rock blasting, boatloads of top soil, a workforce of 100, plus shelter belts of conifers.

Each of the four main areas are as different in mood as Vivaldi's Four Seasons, yet work together as an intricate whole. There is the Italian garden with a classical loggia over-looking a formal pool guarded by venerable bonsai trees. Cypress and clipped yew provide a struc-tural element among a riot of blue clematis growing through the pinks and reds of leptospermum and callistemon.

A broad grass vista between fasci-nating shrubs and trees runs the full length of the island from the high point of the Martello tower to a Grecian Temple with views across Bantry Bay to the mountains. In between are the choice plants which were introduced from every corner of the globe - embothrium, the Chilean fire bush *Dacrydium franklinii* from Tasmania, cornus and redwoods from North America, rhododendrons *R. Macabeanum* from India and Yakushianum from Japan. Aptly know as the Happy Valley this area of Robinsonian planting dips down to a valley in the centre of the island where there is a lily pool and bog garden

There is a walled garden, with a splendid double herbaceous border full of traditional plants: asters, campanulas roses and verbascum, and a clock tower in the corner which look for all the world like an Italian campanile.

The central theme is set by the classical pavilion or casita (little house), its pillars wreathed in wisteria its shady stone interiors offering views over a tranquil green lawn. Much of the planting to be seen in the garden today was carried out by head gardener and plantsman Murdo MacKenzie for Annan's son Roland Bryce. In 1935 the Island was donated to the Nation and it is now in the care of the Heritage Division of the Office of Public Works.

Open daily Mar-Oct; times vary. Children welcome; no dogs; not suitable for wheelchairs. Admission c. €3. **Directions:** *Take the ferry from Glengariff.*

Kilbrittain
RESTAURANT

Casino House
Coolmain Bay Kilbrittain Co Cork
Tel: 023 49944 Fax: 023 49945 Email: chouse@eircom.net

Kerrin and Michael Relja's delightful restaurant is just a few miles west of Kinsale and it is well worth the effort of getting here, as it is one of the best in an area which takes great pride in the excellence of its food. It's a lovely old house and it has an unusually cool continental style in the decor, but Kerrin's hospitality is warm - and Michael's food is consistently excellent, in wide-ranging seasonal menus based on the finest local ingredients: Ummera smoked organic salmon, fresh seafood from nearby fishing ports (don't miss his wonderful speciality

lobster risotto) and Ballydehob duck all feature - a starter dish of four variations of duck is another speciality. Tempting vegetarian dishes are often listed ahead of the other main courses - spaghetti with basil oil, lamb's lettuce & feta cheese is typical - and nightly specials will include extra seafood dishes, all with individual vegetable garnishes and deliciously simple seasonal side vegetables. Variations on classic desserts are delicious (a delectable rhubarb & shortbread tartlet, with white chocolate & hazelnut crème and almond ice cream, for example) and local cheeses are always tempting in this area... An al fresco early summer dinner, or Sunday lunch, can be an especially memorable experience. **Casino Cottage:** sleeps two €85 per night (or €155 for 2 nights), everything provided except breakfast - which can be supplied if needed. Longer stays discounted; weekly & winter rates available. **Seats 35** (private room 22; outdoor dining 16). D Thu-Tue, 7-9, L Sun only, 1-2.30; all à la carte. Closed Wed, and 1 Jan-17 Mar. MasterCard, Visa, Laser. **Directions:** On R600 between Kinsale and Timoleague.

Kilbrittain
COUNTRY HOUSE

The Glen Country House
The Glen Kilbrittain Co Cork **Tel: 023 49862** Fax: 023 49862
Email: info@glencountryhouse.com Web: www.glencountryhouse.com

Although classified (correctly) as a farmhouse, Guy and Diana Scott's home is an elegant period house and they have recently renovated it to a high standard for guests. It is quietly located in a beautiful area, and the four large double bedrooms have lovely views across Courtmacsherry Bay. There's even a family suite (consisting of a double room and children's room, with interconnecting bathroom) and guests have the use of a comfortable sitting room, and a dining room where delicious breakfasts are served - a buffet with fresh and poached seasonal fruits, freshly squeezed orange juice, organic muesli and organic yoghurt, and a menu of hot dishes including free range eggs from their own hens. It's a relaxed place, where dogs are welcome to join the two house spaniels (guests' horses are welcome too!) and, although there are no dinners, evening meals and baby sitting are offered for children, allowing parents to go out to one of the excellent local restaurants - Casino House and Otto's at Dunworley are

both nearby. Strictly no smoking in bedrooms. Lots to do nearby - beautiful beaches, walking, golf - and a table tennis room has recently been added in a converted outhouse. Children welcome. Pets permitted outdoors. **Rooms, 5** (all en-suite & no smoking, 4 shower only). B&B c. €60 pps, ss €15. Closed Nov-Easter. MasterCard, Visa, Laser, Switch. **Directions:** Signposted off the R600, midway between Kinsale and Clonakilty.

Kinsale Area
COUNTRY HOUSE

Glebe Country House
Ballinadee Nr Kinsale Co Cork
Tel: 021 477 8294
Email: glebehse@indigo.ie Web: http://indigo.ie/~glebehse/

Set in two acres of beautiful, well-tended gardens (including a productive kitchen garden), this charming old rectory near Kinsale has a lovely wisteria at the front door and it is a place full of interest. The building dates back to 1690 (Church records provide interesting details: it was built for £250; repairs and alterations followed at various dates, and the present house was completed in 1857 at a cost of £1,160). More recently, under the hospitable ownership of Gill Good, this classically proportioned house has been providing a restful retreat for guests since 1989, and everybody loves it for its genuine country house feeling and relaxing atmosphere. Spacious reception rooms have the feeling of a large family home, and generous, stylishly decorated bedrooms have good bathrooms, phones and tea/coffee making facilities. The Rose Room, on the ground floor, has French doors to the garden. A 4-course candle-lit dinner for residents, much of it supplied by the garden, is served at a communal table (please book by noon). Although unlicensed, guests are encouraged to bring their own wine. Breakfasts are also delicious, and this can be a hard place to drag yourself away from in the morning although there is so much of interest to garden lovers in the area. An indoor heated swimming pool is under construction in the garden at the time of going to press. Two self-catering apartments are also available. **Rooms 4** (2 shower only, all no smoking) B&B c €50pps, ss€15. Residents D Mon-Sat c.€35. BYO wine.Open all year except Christmas. Diners, MasterCard, Visa, Laser. **Directions:** Take N71 west from Cork to Innishannon Bridge; follow signs for Ballinadee (6 miles). After village sign, first on right.

Kinsale Area
COUNTRY HOUSE

Walton Court

Oysterhaven Nr Kinsale Co Cork
Tel: 021 477 0878
Email: info@waltoncourt.com

Walton Court dates back to 1645 and when Paul and Janis Rafferty took it over on their return from Kenya in 1996, it was derelict. Five years of restoration work brought this listed building back to its former glory and the courtyard has been converted to provide stylish bedrooms and self-contained cottages, each with its own personality. There is also a small conference room), and a little bar with an open fireplace for guests' use. A plant-filled courtyard conservatory overlooking a courtyard garden at the back of the house is used for breakfast and, perhaps, dining, as an alternative to the restored Georgian dining room. As members of the Slow Food movement, Paul & Janis prepare everything using fresh organic and home-grown ingredients. This unusual place will please those who value character above the hotel conveniences and it helps to like animals as you will certainly be greeted by the dogs as well as their owners, and quite probably cats and other household animals too. Indoor exercise pool, sauna, treatment rooms. Pets permitted by arrangement. **Rooms 6** (all en-suite & no smoking). B&B c. €55, ss cc. €25. D by arrangement. Not suitable for children under 15, except in self-catering cottages. Open all year except Christmas. Garden open during West Cork Garden Trail (June). MasterCard, Visa, Laser. **Directions:** 6 miles from Kinsale (Cork side); R600 to Belgooly, signs to Oysterhaven.

Mallow
HOTEL / RESTAURANT / GARDEN

Longueville House & Gardens
Mallow Co. Cork
Tel: 022 47156 Fax: 022 47459
Email: info@longuevillehouse.ie Web: www.longuevillehouse.ie

When Michael and Jane O'Callaghan opened Longueville House to guests in 1967, it was one of the first Irish country houses to do so. Its history is wonderfully romantic, "the history of Ireland in miniature", and it is a story with a happy ending: having lost their lands in the Cromwellian Confiscation (1652-57), the O'Callaghans took up ownership again some 300 years later. The present house, a particularly elegant Georgian mansion of pleasingly human proportions, dates from 1720, (with wings added in 1800 and the lovely Turner conservatory - which has been completely renovated - in 1862), overlooks the ruins of their original home, Dromineen Castle. Very much a family enterprise, Longueville is now run by Michael and Jane's son William O'Callaghan, who is the chef, and his wife Aisling, who manages front of house. The location, overlooking the famous River Blackwater, is lovely.

The river, farm and garden supply fresh salmon in season, the famous Longueville lamb and kitchen garden produce. Longueville is a member of the Blackwater Valley Garden Trail, and the gardens are open to visitors by appointment; highlights include the two and a half acre walled garden, where 20 gardeners were once employed to keep the garden and glasshouses - today things are very different, but the walled garden still supplies the kitchen with most of its fruit, vegetables and herbs throughout the year. Like several other properties in the Blackwater Valley, Longueville has a small vineyard - and, in years when the weather is

COUNTY CORK

kind, the estate's crowning glory (and Michael O'Callaghan's, great enthusiasm) is their own house wine, a light refreshing white, "Coisreal Longueville". And this is also a wonderful place to stay - and dine. Graciously proportioned reception rooms include a bar and drawing room both elegantly furnished with beautiful fabrics and family antiques. Accommodation is equally sumptuous and, although - as is usual with old houses - they vary according to their position, bedrooms are generally spacious, superbly comfortable and stylishly decorated to the highest standards. And then there is **The Presidents Restaurant**, an elegant dining room which is named after the family collection of specially commissioned portraits of all of Ireland's presidents and leads into the beautifully renovated Turner conservatory, which makes a wonderfully romantic setting when candlelit at night; here guests savour the produce of the estate and surrounding area, in original culinary creations cooked by William

O'Callaghan and his team in this renowned kitchen - well worth a detour! Children welcome. No pets. **Rooms 20.** (1 suite, 2 junior suites, 4 superior rooms, all no-smoking). B&B c. €100pps, ss c.€45. **Restaurant Seats 110** (private room 20); open to non residents. D daily, 6.30-9; early D c. €35, Set D c.€55, Menu Gourmand c.€75; light meals 1-5 daily (set L c. €40 for groups of 20+). Licensed; SC discretionary. Gardens open by appointment. House usually closed early Jan-Mar, except for house parties. Amex, MasterCard, Visa, Laser. **Directions:** 3 miles west of Mallow via N72 to Killarney.

Cedar Lodge

Baneshane **Midleton** Co Cork
Tel: 021 461 3379
Email: nswilliams@eircom.net Web: www.irishgardentours.net

GARDEN

A 2 acre plantsman's garden with a collection full of interest: allow time!

Many people will remember Neil and Sonia Williams' excellent nursery at Carewswood, Midleton. The Williams have retired, but over 12,000 plants came with them when they moved to their new home in 1996. With a wealth of treasures to accommodate, the Williams planted shrubs and trees for shelter in the virgin site, then created a series of informal beds and island beds in their front garden.

This is a place to exclaim over VIP plants from collections of grasses to gorgeous day lilies. It would be worth a visit for some of the names of the plants alone, *Euphorbia* **'Silver Swan'**, *Miscanthus* **'Silver Feather'**, *Hosta* **'Sum and Substance'** (so big slugs can't reach the leaves), *Hemerocallis* **'Gentle Shepherd'**, *Achillea* **'Paprika'**, a breathtaking ensata iris called **'Caprician Butterfly'**. And then there is the insight afforded into new introductions and choice varieties like lilac and cream *Thalictrum* **'Elim'** or the curious Australian grass tree *Xanthorrhea*, a scarlet delphinium and a tiger flower which looks as though it has been painted in brilliant reds and yellows.

COUNTY CORK

A new bed will be of special interest to collectors of newly fashionable grasses with numbers of *Panicum* **'Warrior'** and **'Squaw'** or swaying pennisetums **'Carly Rose'** and *villosum* contrasting with canna leaves striped viridian, yellow and scarlet - yummy!

A pond and waterfall guarded by a weeping willow became the central feature of the back garden with a bridge made from the Williams' former hearth stone. Beside it waving tresses of pony tail grass *Stipa tenussima* and plumes of *S gigantean* contrast with the luxuriance of a bog garden with primulas and ligularias. Around the perimeter a deep double herbaceous and shrub border with particularly choice varieties. Trees play a starring role here with Paulownia the foxglove tree, the swamp cypress, and *Toona sinensis* grown for foliage which is pink in spring and yellow in autumn. There are over 80 varieties of hellebores in the garden, old fashioned varieties of plants from the collection of the late Nancy Minchum: including agapanthus, penstemons, watsonias, tradescantia and begonias.

A mixed shrub border with pieris, rhododendrons and bulbs loops around the front garden; there's a red border known as Africa and there is a newer small Zen garden of contemplation, with acers and bamboos planted in gravel. Now the nursery baton has been taken up by the next generation of the Williams family, and plants from the Perennial Plant Nursery beside Ballymaloe House can sometimes be bought at Cedar Lodge.

Open Apr-Sep, 10.30-4; other times by appointment. Children allowed under supervision; no dogs; partially wheelchair accessible; teas by arrangement. **Directions:** *From Midleton, take the access road to motorway to Cork; turn left at end of bridge, then first right; house is 6th on right.*

Midleton
RESTAURANT

Farmgate

The Coolbawn Midleton Co Cork **Tel: 021 463 2771**
Fax: 021 463 2771 Email: farmgaterestauarnt@eircom.net

This unique shop and restaurant has been drawing people to Midleton in growing numbers since 1985 and it's a great credit to sisters Maróg O'Brien and Kay Harte. Kay now runs the younger version at the English Market in Cork (Tel: 021 427 8134), while Maróg looks after Midleton - both are just the kind of places that garden lovers love to visit. The shop at the front is full of wonderful local seasonal produce - organic fruit and vegetables, cheeses, honey - and their own super home baking, while the evocatively decorated, comfortable restaurant at the back, with its old pine furniture and modern sculpture, is regularly transformed from bustling daytime café to sophisticated evening restaurant complete with string quartet (on Friday and Saturday). A tempting display of fresh home bakes is the first thing to catch your eye on entering and, as would be expected from the fresh produce on sale in the shop, wholesome vegetables and salads are always irresistible in the restaurant too. Maróg O'Brien is a founder and stall holder of the hugely successful Midleton Farmers Market, which is held on Saturday mornings, and is committed to handling only produce in season. **Open** Mon-Sat, L 12-4, D 6.30-9.45. A la carte. Closed Sun & bank hols, Christmas/New Year. MasterCard, Visa, Laser. **Directions:** Town centre.

Ballymaloe Cookery School Gardens

Shanagarry Nr. **Midleton** Co Cork
Tel: 021 464 6785
Email: enquiries@ballymaloe-cookeryschool .ie Web: www.cookingisfun.ie

GARDEN

A recent garden with parterre, potager, herbaceous borders maze and shell house.

The gardens at Ballymaloe are delicious - traditional with an original twist, just like Darina Allen's recipes. The first garden was made in the 1980s and, inspired by a the great French garden at Villandry, is laid out with a parterre of flower shaped beds filled with herbs and set in gravel surrounded by ancient beech hedges, the sole survivors of an earlier 19th century garden. A myrtle in honour of Myrtle Allen, founder of the Ballymaloe tradition, has pride of place in the centre of the garden. At the far end of the garden is a pond and a temple ingeniously made with the pillars of a demolished house. The garden has kept on growing one new area at a time, expanding to a potager planted with brilliant rows of vegetables planted in a pattern of squares and diamonds between herringbone brick paths. Edible flowers like marigolds and nasturtiums are used in salads or for garnishes in the restaurant, while leggy sunflowers and artichokes add to the colourful profusion.

The octagonal Shell House - which is based on the similar 18th century follies, its interior richly deco-rated with cockle, mussel, scallops and oyster shells by Charlotte Kerr Wilson - became a wonderful excuse for a another garden: thus deep, double herbaceous borders filled with shades of blue, gold and silver with delphiniums, hemerocallis, crocosmia and artemesia now lead to the shell house. Nearby a yew maze in Celtic swirls, designed by Peter Lamb and Lesley Beck, is maturing. A fruit garden, designed by Jim Reynolds with gravel walks where the trees are underplanted with spring bulbs, links the cookery school to the rest of the garden compartments. And of course there is always a new scheme: an Irish apple meadow, an arboretum and a rose garden are all part of the evolving scheme of things Darina Allen.

Open daily Apr-Sep, 10-6. Supervised children welcome; wheelchair access; no dogs; shop.
Directions: *Turn off the Cork-Waterford road at Castlemartyr for Ballycotton, and follow signs.*

Midleton Area
COUNTRY HOUSE / RESTAURANT

Ballymaloe House

Shanagarry Nr. Midleton Co Cork
Tel: 021 465 2531 Fax: 021 465 2021
Email: res@ballymaloe.ie Web: www.ballymaloe.ie

Ireland's most famous country house hotel, Ballymaloe was one of the first country houses to open its doors to guests when Myrtle and her husband, the late Ivan Allen, opened The Yeats Room restaurant in 1964. Accommodation followed in 1967 and since then a unique network of family enterprises has developed around Ballymaloe House - including not only the farmlands and gardens that supply so much of the kitchen produce, but also a craft and kitchenware shop, a company producing chutneys and sauce, the Crawford Gallery Café in Cork city, and Darina Allen's internationally acclaimed cookery school. Yet, despite the fame, Ballymaloe is still most remarkable for its unspoilt charm: Myrtle - now rightly receiving international recognition for a lifetime's work "recapturing forgotten flavours, and preserving those that may soon die"- is ably assisted by her children, and now their families too. The house, modestly described in its Blue Book (Irish Country House & Restaurants Association) entry as "a large family farmhouse", is indeed at the centre of the family's 400 acre farm, but the description fails to do justice to the gracious nature of the original house, or the sensitively designed later additions. The intensely restorative atmosphere of Ballymaloe is still as strong as ever; there are few greater pleasures than a fine Ballymaloe dinner followed by the relaxed comforts provided by a delightful, thoughtfully furnished (but not over decorated) country bedroom. For those with an historical bent it may be of interest to note that Ballymaloe has what must indisputably be Ireland's most ancient hotel room in the Gate House, a tiny one up (twin bedroom, with little iron beds) and one down (full bathroom and entrance foyer) in the original medieval wall of the old house: delightful and highly romantic! The gardens which surround the house are also delightfully relaxed; they include woodland walks with ponds and plenty of wildlife such as ducks, geese and peacocks, and a two acre walled vegetable and herb garden, where guests are welcome to stroll around. Children welcome. Pets allowed by arrangement. Outdoor swimming pool, tennis, walking, golf (9 hole). Shop. **Rooms 33** (all no smoking). Ground floor courtyard rooms are suitable for wheelchairs. B&B c.€125pps, ss€15. No lift. Some self-catering also available (details from Hazel Allen). **Restaurant: Seats 100.** L daily, D daily; Set D c. €62, Set L c.€38. Licensed. Buffet meals only on Sun. Reservations essential. House closed 23-26 Dec. Amex, Diners, MasterCard, Visa, Laser. **Directions:** Take signs to Ballycotton from N 25. Situated between Cloyne & Shanagarry.

Schull Area
Country House / Accommodation

Rock Cottage
Barnatonicane Schull Co Cork
Tel: 028 35538 Fax: 028 35538
Email: rockcottage@eircom.net Web: www.rockcottage.ie

Barbara Klotzer's beautiful slate-clad Georgian hunting lodge near Schull is an absolute delight. Garden-lovers, especially, will thrill to the immediate surroundings which are on a south-facing slope away from the sea (at nearby Dunmanus Bay) and offer a fascinating combination of well-tended lawns and riotous flower beds, the rocky outcrop which inspired its name - and even great estate trees in the 17 acres of parkland (complete with peacefully grazing sheep) that have survived from an earlier period of its history. The main house has style and comfort, with welcoming open fires and bright bedrooms which - although not especially large - have been thoughtfully furnished to allow little seating areas as well as the usual amenities. Behind the house a walled courtyard creates a wonderfully sheltered feeling and very appealing self-catering accommodation is offered in converted stables. And, as if all this were not enough, Barbara is an accomplished chef - so dinner at Rock Cottage is an experience to savour; a set menu based on the best of local produce might include starters like fresh crab salad or warm Ardsallagh goats cheese, main courses of Rock Cottage's own rack of lamb, monkfish kebab, or even lobster or seafood platters (prices for these options on request) and classic desserts like home-baked vanilla cheesecake or bread and butter pudding. Breakfast options include a Healthy Breakfast and a Fish Breakfast as well as traditional Irish and continental combinations - just make your choice before 8pm the night before. Not suitable for children under 10. No pets. **Rooms 3** (2 with en-suite showers, 1 with private bathroom, all no smoking). B&B from c.€60 pps, ss €20. Residents D, 7.30pm c. €40. No D on Sun. Open all year. MasterCard, Visa, Laser. **Directions:** From Schull, 6 miles, at Toormore, turn into R591 after 1.5 miles. Sign on left.

Lassanaroe Garden

Lissanroe **Skibbereen** Co Cork
Tel: 028 22563
Email: jstonard@iolfree.ie

GARDEN

Exotic garden with over a hundred species of bamboos and organic vegetables.

To garden with a single plant family is a magnif-icent obsession. While many gardeners reserve the best spot in the garden for the object of their particular passion, Robin and Janet Stonard have a whole two acre garden devoted to bamboos.

They began collecting 40 years ago, long before the various genera became fashionable. When the Stonards retired and moved to Cork in '98 the collection came with them. And in spring 2000 their two acre plot was planted with over a hundred species, varieties and cultivars, repre-senting 18 different genera. The bamboos were displayed to show off their individual habits around grass and gravel paths.

The whispering swaying collection includes both the rare and the new, with introductions like Roy Lancaster's Chinese find *Fargesia denudata*, with yellow green foliage and a weeping habit, or the striped version of the black bamboo *Phyllostachys nigra* **'Megurochiko'**, found only on the island of Awaji.

Other plants are now beginning to sneak into the scheme of things, particularly leptospermums, pittisporums, acacias and restios. There is also an organic vegetable garden, where ingenious methods include growing strawberries in hanging baskets to foil slugs.

To see the sheer variety in texture, colour and habit of bamboos ranging from Bhudda's belly (*Bambusa ventricosa*) to the small invasive yellow striped *Sasaella masamuneana aureostriata* from Japan is a revelation and the Stonards are extremely knowledgeable.

Open during West Cork Garden Trail (2 weeks June, 1-6 daily); otherwise by appointment. Partial wheelchair access. **Directions:** *From west end of Skibbereen N71 bypass, take exit signed NCT centre. Take left fork after 2.5 miles; take second left after 0.5 mile into narrow lane; the garden is 0.5 mile on the right.*

Youghal Area
FARMHOUSE

Ballymakeigh House
Killeagh Youghal Co Cork
Tel: 024 95184 Fax: 024 95370
Email: ballymakeigh@eircom.net Web: www.ballymakeighhouse.com

Ballymakeigh House is well located for garden visits in the east Cork and west Waterford areas, and it is one of the most outstanding establishments of its type in Ireland. Set at the heart of an east Cork dairy farm, this attractive old house is immaculately maintained and run by Margaret Browne, who is a Euro-Toques chef and author of a successful cookery book. The house is warm and homely with plenty of space for guests, who are welcome to enjoy the surrounding gardens and visit the farmyard.

The individually decorated bedrooms are full of character and all equally comfortable, and Margaret's hospitality is matched only by her energetic pursuit of excellence - ongoing improvements and developments are a constant characteristic of Ballymakeigh, which is set in lovely surroundings and offers a consistently high standard of comfort, food and hospitality. Margaret Browne has a national reputation for her cooking, and an impressive dinner menu is available every night - and self-catering accommodation is also offered nearby, in a restored Victorian house. **Rooms 5** (all en-suite & no smoking; 3 shower only) B&B c. €60 pps, ss €10. Residents' D daily, 7-8; set D c. €44. Licensed. House closed early Nov-early Mar. MasterCard, Visa. **Directions:** Off N25 between Youghal and Killeagh (signed at Old Thatch pub).

Caragh Lake
HOTEL/RESTAURANT

Ard-na-Sidhe

Caragh Lake Killorglin Co Kerry
Tel: 066 976 9105

Set in woodland and among award-winning gardens, this peaceful Victorian retreat is in a beautiful mountain location overlooking Caragh Lake. Decorated throughout in a soothing country house style, very comfortable antique-filled day rooms provide plenty of lounging space for quiet indoor relaxation and a terrace for fine weather – all with wonderful views. Bedrooms – shared between the main house and some with private patios in the garden house – are spacious and elegantly furnished in traditional style, with excellent en-suite bathrooms. Like the rest of the hotel, the dining room – known as the Fairyhill Restaurant - has intimacy and character and, after an aperitif on the terrace or at the fireside, this is a delightful place to spend an hour or two. There's a pleasing emphasis on local ingredients and updated interpretations of traditional Irish themes in specialities that might include the house boxty (traditional Irish potato cake with an onion and mustard sauce), for example, and a main course of Kerry mountain lamb – although there will be seafood choices, there is a stronger emphasis on meats than is usual in the area. Coffee and petits fours can be served beside the drawing room fire, where welcoming chintzy armchairs await. Non residents are welcome by reservation. This is a sister hotel to Dunloe Castle (see entry) and the Hotel Europe, whose leisure facilities are also available to guests. **Rooms 18** (3 suites, 1 family room, 5 ground floor, 6 no smoking) B&B c. €85 pps, ss c. €50. D available Mon-Sat. Hotel closed Oct-Apr. Amex, Diners, MasterCard, Visa, Laser. **Directions:** Off N70 Ring of Kerry road, signed 5km west of Killorglin.

Caragh Lake

Carrig Country House & Restaurant

COUNTRY HOUSE / RESTAURANT / GARDEN

Caragh Lake Killorglin Co Kerry
Tel: 066 976 9100 Fax: 066 976 9166
Email: info@carrighouse.com Web: www.carrighouse.com

At the heart of Frank and Mary Slattery's sensitively extended Victorian house lies a hunting lodge once owned by Lord Brocket - and he chose well, as it is very attractive and handsomely set in fine gardens with the lake and mountains providing a dramatic backdrop. The house is welcoming and well-maintained, with friendly staff (Frank himself carries the luggage to your room) and a very relaxed atmosphere, notably in a series of sitting rooms where you can chat beside the fire or have a drink before dinner. This is a place where you can lose yourself for hours with a book, or playing chess, cards or board games in the games room, or boating out on the lake. Individually decorated bedrooms furnished with antiques (some with their own patio) are large, high-ceilinged and airy, with generous, well-designed bathrooms with bath and shower - a Presidential Suite has a sitting room with panoramic views across the lake to the Magillicuddy Reeks, two separate dressing rooms and jacuzzi bath. **The Lakeside Restaurant** is in a fine big room with well-spaced tables, beautifully situated overlooking the lake. A strong kitchen team led by head chef Helen Vickers and pastry chef Patricia Teahan have been steadily building the reputation of Carrig House as a dining destination since 2003, and menus offer a growing range of specialities based on local meats (especially Kerry lamb) and seafood - and, of course, produce from their own kitchen garden. The extensive gardens are of great interest and a laminated map is available, naming the various areas - Waterfall Garden, Pond Garden, Rock Walk etc - and the main plantings in each; a more detailed list is available on request, and personalised tours can be arranged with head gardener Mark Skidmore. Not suitable for children under 8 except small babies. Dogs allowed in some areas. Swimming (lake), fishing (ghillie & boat available), walking, garden, croquet. **Rooms 16** (1 suite, 1 junior suite, 3 no smoking); B&B c. €80 , ss €50. **Lakeside Restaurant: Seats 50** (private room, 15). D daily, 6.30-9. Extensive à la carte. Licensed. Non-residents welcome (reservations essential). Establishment closed Dec-Feb. Diners, MasterCard, Visa, Laser. **Directions:** Left after 2.5 miles on Killorglin/Glenbeigh Road N70 (Ring of Kerry).

Dingle
B&B

Captains House

The Mall Dingle Co Kerry
Tel: 066 915 1531 Fax: 066 915 1079
Email: captigh@eircom.net Web: homepage.eircom.net/ncaptigh/

Dingle could not in all honesty be described as a garden lovers place, but many people visiting gardens in the south-west will want to visit Dingle and, if so, there's only one place for you - it has to be the Captain's House. When Jim, a retired sea captain, and Mary Milhench bought this guesthouse in the late '80s they were renewing a seafaring tradition going back to the original captain, Tom Williams, who first took lodgers here in 1886. Today this charming house is as relaxed and hospitable a place as could be wished for: approached via a little bridge over the Mall River then through a lovely garden, it has been renovated and furnished with the antiques and curios collected by Jim on his voyages. The age and nature of the building - which extends into the next door premises - has created a higgledy-piggledy arrangement of rooms that adds to the charm; rooms vary considerably, as would be expected, but all have comfort (orthopaedic beds, phones, satellite TV, hospitality trays, plenty of hot water) as well as character. A welcoming turf fire in the reception area encourages guests to linger over tea, or with a book, and breakfast - which is a very special feature of a stay here - is served in the conservatory. But the real surprise is Jim's garden centre, just across the road from the back door. It's a revelation! Not suitable for children. No pets.* Self-catering also available, in a large bungalow with privacy, sea views, garden, slipway & boat dock; 1 mile from Dingle town. **Rooms 8** (7 shower only, all no smoking). B&B c. €50pps, ss €10. Closed 1 Nov-16 Mar. MasterCard, Visa, Laser. **Directions:** Turn right at town entrance roundabout; Captains House is 100 metres up on left.

Kenmare
HOTEL / RESTAURANT

Park Hotel Kenmare

Kenmare Co Kerry
Tel: 064 41200 Fax: 064 41402
Email: info@parkkenmare.com Web: www.parkkenmare.com

Francis Brennan's renowned hotel enjoys a magnificent waterside location in the midst of Ireland's most scenic landscape, with views over gardens to the ever-changing mountains across the bay - yet it is only a short stroll to the Heritage Town of Kenmare and its quality shops, characterful pubs and fine restaurants. Many travellers from all over the world have found a home from home here since the hotel was built in 1897 by the Great Southern and Western Railway Company as an overnight stop for passengers travelling to Parknasilla, 17 miles away. Today it is a luxurious, hospitable and relaxing place, where a warm welcome and the ever-burning fire in the hall set the tone for a stay in which guests can relax in great comfort, cared for by outstandingly friendly and professional staff. Guest accommodation is in spacious suites and bedrooms individually furnished to the highest standards, with personally selected antiques and many special details. The Park is also home to a deluxe destination spa, Sámas, which translates from the Gaelic as 'indulgence of the senses' - a true world class spa, unlike anything else offered in Ireland, Sámas adjoins the hotel on a wooded knoll and is designed to rejuvenate the body, mind and spirit; lifestyle programmes incorporating spa treatments with other activities in the area - walking on the Kerry Way, golf, fishing, horse trekking - offer a unique way to enjoy the deeply peaceful atmosphere of this luxurious hotel. Then, innovative as always, the folk at the Park have come up with yet another little treat for guests: the Reel Room; and no, it is not a display of fishing memorabilia, but a private 12-seater cinema...And, as for the food offered here, the hotel is renowned for its table, and discerning guests who have tired of the ubiquitous contemporary style will relish the opportunity of a fine dinner in this refreshingly classical restaurant - and the views from window tables are simply lovely. And, to prepare you for a long day out and about, they also serve one of the best breakfasts in Ireland here. Golf club adjacent (18 hole). Horse riding, sea and game angling, mountain walks, stunning coastal drives and garden visits are all nearby. Garden, tennis, croquet, cycling, walking, snooker. **Rooms 46** (9 suites, 27 junior suites, 46 no smoking, 1 for disabled). Lift. 24 hour room service. Children welcome. No pets (but kennels available on grounds). B&B c. €215 pps, (single occupancy c. €242); holistic retreats from c. €855. **Restaurant: Seats 80** (private room, 40). D, 7-9 daily; Set D menus about €49-67; also à la carte. Lounge menu, 11am-6pm. SC discretionary. Restaurant not suitable for children under 12 after 8 pm. Hotel closed late Nov-23 Dec & early Jan-mid Feb. Amex, Diners, MasterCard, Visa. **Directions:** Top of the town.

Kenmare
HOTEL / RESTAURANT

Sheen Falls Lodge
Kenmare Co Kerry
Tel: 064 41600 Fax: 064 41386
Email: info@sheenfallslodge.ie Web: www.sheenfallslodge.ie

Set in a 300-acre estate just across the river from Kenmare town, this luxurious, classically contemporary hotel is in a beautiful waterside location - and welcoming fires always burn in the elegant foyer and in several of the spacious, elegantly furnished reception rooms, including a lounge bar area overlooking the tumbling waterfall. Sheen Falls offers traditional luxury with a modern lightness of touch; accommodation in spacious bedrooms - and suites, which include a presidential suite - is seriously luxurious: all rooms have superb amenities, including video/DVD and CD players, beautiful marbled bathrooms and views of the cascading river or Kenmare Bay. Outstanding facilities include an equestrian centre (treks around the 300 acre estate) and The Queen's Walk (named after Queen Victoria), which takes you through lush woodland. A Health & Fitness Spa includes a pretty 15 metre pool (and an extensive range of treatments including seaweed wraps and aromatherapy massages) and, alongside it, there's an evening bar and bistro, **'Oscars'**, which has its own separate entrance as well as direct access from the hotel and offers an informal dining alternative to the tiered fine-dining restaurant, **La Cascade**.* Two luxuriously appointed self-contained two-bedroomed thatched cottages, Little Hay Cottage and Garden Cottage, are also available to rent, singly or together. Snooker, equestrian, walking, fishing, gardens, tennis, cycling. Children welcome. No pets. **Rooms 66** (11 suites, 8 junior suites,10 no-smoking bedrooms, 1 disabled). Lift. 24 hour room service. B&B c.€215 pps, ss c.€90 **Restaurants: La Cascade Seats 120** (private room, 24; outdoor seating, 50). Pianist, evenings.Toilets wheelchair accessible. D daily 7-9.30. Set D c. €65..*Light lunches and afternoon tea are available in the sun lounge, 12-6 daily, and the informal **Oscar's Bar & Bistro** open every evening, 6-10pm. SC discretionary. Hotel closed all Jan. Amex, Diners, MasterCard, Visa, Laser. **Directions:** Take N71 Kenmare (Glengariff road); turn left at Riversdale Hotel.

Kenmare
COUNTRY HOUSE

Shelburne Lodge

Cork Road Kenmare Co Kerry
Tel: 064 41013 Fax: 064 42135
Email: shelbourne@kenmare.com Web: www.kenmare.net/shelbourne

Tom and Maura Foley's fine stone house on the edge of the town is well set back from the road, in its own grounds and lovely gardens. It is the oldest house in Kenmare and has great style and attention to detail; spacious day rooms include an elegant, comfortable furnished drawing room with plenty of seating, an inviting log fire and interesting books for guests to read - it is really lovely, and the feeling is of being a guest in a private country house. Spacious, well-proportioned guest rooms are individually decorated and extremely comfortable; everything (especially beds and bedding) is of the

highest quality and, except for the more informal conversion at the back of the house, which is especially suitable for families and has neat shower rooms, the excellent bathrooms all have full bath. But perhaps the best is saved until last, in the large, well-appointed dining room where excellent breakfasts are served; no other meals are served but Kenmare offers what is probably the best choice of quality dining in Ireland for a town of its size: for dinner, residents are directed to the family's restaurant, **Packie's** (Tel 064 41508) and, for daytime meals, a visit to Maura's sister Grainne O'Connell's informal restaurant and **The Purple Heather** bar on Henry Street (Tel 064 41016) is always a pleasure - open since 1964, it was among the first to establish a reputation for good food in Kenmare. **Rooms 9** (2 shower only). B&B c. €75, ss €15. Closed Dec-mid-Mar. MasterCard, Visa. **Directions:** On the edge of Kenmare, on the Cork road, R569.

Kenmare Area
COUNTRY HOUSE

Muxnaw Lodge

Castletownbehre Haven Road Kenmare Co Kerry
Tel: 064 41252
Email: muxnawlodge@eircom.net

Within walking distance from the town in good weather, Mrs Hannah Boland's cosy and welcoming house was built in 1801 and enjoys spectacular views across Kenmare Bay. This is very much a home where you can relax in the TV lounge or outside in the sloping gardens (you can even play tennis on the all-weather court). A couple of superior new rooms came on stream recently and, although the original ones now seem old-fashioned by comparison, all the bedrooms are tranquil and comfortable, individually furnished with

free-standing period pieces and pleasant fabrics - and have cleverly hidden tea/coffee-making facilities. Notice is required by noon if you would like dinner – a typical meal cooked in and on the Aga might be carrot soup, oven-baked salmon and apple pie, but guests are always asked what they like beforehand. Not suitable for children. Garden. **Rooms 5** (all en-suite & no-smoking). B&B c.€40. Residents D c.€20. Open all year except Christmas. MasterCard, Visa. **Directions:** 2 minutes drive from Kenmare Town - first right past the double-arched bridge towards Bantry.

Killarney
HOTEL

Cahernane House Hotel
Muckross Road Killarney Co Kerry
Tel: 064 31895 Fax: 064 34340
Email: info@cahernane.com Web: www.cahernane.com

This family-owned and managed hotel is in a lovely quiet location adjacent to Killarney's National Park, convenient to the town yet - thanks to a long tree-lined avenue and private parkland which stretches down to the water - with a charmingly other-worldly atmosphere. The original house was built by the Herbert family, Earls of Pembroke, in the 17th century, and accommodation is divided between fine old rooms (including some suites and junior suites) in the main house, and more contemporary rooms in a recent extension. The hotel has many attractive features, not least its classically elegant dining room, and a characterful cellar bar - complete with a real old-fashioned wine cellar. Children welcome. No pets. Garden, walking, fishing, tennis. Golf nearby. **Rooms 38** (28 with separate bath & shower, 15 no smoking). B&B c. €135 pps, ss c. €32. **Restaurant:** D daily, c €50. Light meals 12-6.* Off-season breaks offered. Amex, Diners, MasterCard, Visa, Laser. **Directions:** Ouskirts of Killarney, off the N71 near Muckross Park.

Derreen Garden
Lauragh **Killarney** Co Kerry
Tel: 064 83588

GARDEN

Large domain with subtropical conditions where exotic trees and shrubs flourish.

The passion of an Edwardian grandee for shrubs and trees collected from around the globe and lush sub tropical growth promoted by the Gulf Stream combine to make this an unforgettable place. Not for ideas which can be copied in the average garden, to be sure, but for a store of indelible memories.

Among them are the sight of huge rhododendrons in bloom like so many vividly coloured clouds that have come to rest improbably on the wild shores around Kilmacillogue Harbour. Or an island linked by an extraordinary plank bridge to the shore, and veritable thickets of tree ferns in sheltered, green twilight where you might expect dinosaurs to come crashing through the primeval-looking growth.

The sights are a reminder that a wider range of plants can be grown in Ireland than anywhere else at the same latitude. A fact which no doubt spurred on the 5th Marquis of Landsdowne when he planted 400 acres of woodland to shelter a collection of shrubs and specimen trees, many of them brought back from his sojourns as Viceroy of India and Governor General of Canada.

The estate, now owned by the Hon David Bigham, is still in the same family, and head gardener Jacky Ward's father was head gardener before him This is a place for stout walking shoes, the better to explore the labelled paths starting with the Big Rock and leading to the evocatively named 'Kings Oozy' (a boggy area where Edward VII planted a tree), or the viewing point known as Knockatee Seat - or to get up close and personal with shrubs which include camellias, magnolias, crinodendrons and hoherias.

Open Apr-Oct, 10-6 daily (Aug: Fri-Sun only). Supervised children welcome; dogs on leads allowed; tea by arrangement. **Directions:** *Off the Kenmare - Castletownbere road.*

Killarney
HOTEL

Great Southern Hotel Killarney

East Avenue Road Killarney Co Kerry
Tel: 064 31262 Fax: 064 31642
Email: res@killarney-gsh.com Web: www.greatsouthernhotels.com

Belying its central position in Killarney town, this classic Victorian railway hotel hotel is set in 20 acres of landscaped gardens, providing peace and relaxation on the premises. It was established in 1854 and its pillared entrance and ivy-clad facade still convey a sense of occasion - and, since a major refurbishment programme, which was completed with due respect for its age and history, the sparkle has also been restored to the interior of this fine building. A welcoming open fire just inside the door draws guests through to a spacious grandly-pillared foyer (where afternoon tea is served), and the adjacent areas - including a homely residents' drawing room and a fine bar, which has also been redeveloped- are also elegant, high-ceilinged rooms with some sense of grandeur, and a soothing atmosphere which makes a refreshing contrast to the bustle of Killarney town. Fine bedroom corridors originally built wide enough 'to allow two ladies in hooped dresses to pass comfortably' set the tone for suites and executive rooms that have regained their old sense of grandeur in generously-proportioned rooms, elegantly furnished to individual designs - with, of course, all the necessary modern facilities (email, mini-bar etc). But the pièce de résistance in restoration terms is the great gilt-domed Garden Room Restaurant which, with its marbled pillars and intricately gold-leafed ceiling, is a prime example of Victorian opulence - and makes the perfect contrast for the hotel's smaller contemporary restaurant, Peppers which is a popular dining destination for locals. Aside from the extensive gardens, recreational facilities include the Innisfallen Spa, with 18 metre pool, jacuzzi, steam room, plunge pool and gym, and tennis. Children welcome. Pets allowed by arrangement. **Rooms 172** (2 suites, 34 junior suites, 70 superior rooms, 120 no smoking, 4 disabled). Lift. B&B c. €140 pps, ss c. €30; no SC. **Peppers: Seats 60.** D Tue-Sat, 6.30-9.30; advance reservations advised. Open all year. Amex, Diners, MasterCard, Visa, Laser. **Directions:** In the heart of Killarney town beside railway station.

Killarney Area
COUNTRY HOUSE

Coolclogher House
Killarney Co Kerry
Tel: **064 35996** Fax: 064 30933
Email: info@coolclogherhouse.com Web: www.coolclogherhouse.com

Mary and Maurice Harnett's beautiful early Victorian house is just on the edge of Killarney town and yet, tucked away on its 68 acre walled estate, it is an oasis of peace and tranquillity. The house has been extensively restored in recent years and has many interesting features, including an original conservatory built around a 170 year-old specimen camellia - when camellias were first introduced to Europe, they were mistakenly thought to be tender plants; it is now quite remarkable to see this large tree growing under glass. It is an impressive yet relaxed house, with well-proportioned, spacious reception rooms stylishly furnished and comfortable for guests, with newspapers, books, fresh flowers - and open fires in inclement weather - while the four large bedrooms have scenic views over gardens, parkland and mountains. Gazing out from this peaceful place, it is easy to forget that the hustle and bustle of Killarney town is just a few minutes' drive away; it could just as well be in another world. Mary and Maurice enjoy sharing their local knowledge with guests to help them get the most of their stay at what they quite reasonably call 'perhaps the most exclusive accommodation available in Killarney'. **Rooms 4** (all en-suite & no smoking). B&B from c.€95pps, ss €50. Also available for private rental (groups of 10-12). **Directions:** Leaving Killarney town, take Muckross Road and turn left between the Brehon and Gleneagles Hotels, onto Mill Road. Gates are on the right after half a mile.

Killarney Area
HOTEL / GARDEN

Hotel Dunloe Castle & Gardens
Beaufort Killarney Co Kerry Tel: **064 44111**
Email: sales@liebherr.com Web: www.killarneyhotels.ie

Although the original castle - the shell of the MacThomas' medieval keep - is part of the development, this beautifully located hotel is mainly modern; it is a sister hotel to the Hotel Europe (Fossa) and the pretty Ard-na-Sidhe (Caragh Lake), either of which would also make an appealing base for visiting this area, and has much in common with the larger Europe: the style is similar, the scale is generous throughout, and standards of maintenance and housekeeping are exemplary. Like the Europe, the atmosphere is distinctly continental; some of the exceptionally spacious guest rooms have dining areas, and all have magnificent views, air conditioning and many extras. The surrounding park is home to an extensive arboretum and a unique botanical collection, which includes many sub-tropical and rare specimens including Australian gum trees, New Zealand cabbage trees, and the Chinese swamp cypress - and a fine collection of camellias, magnolias, rhododendrons and roses, all catalogued by broadcaster and plantsman Roy Lancaster (a booklet is available from the hotel). The gardens surround the old castle, and the mountain setting - looking straight towards the Gap of Dunloe - is highly dramatic. Golf is, of course, a major attraction here too, and there is an equestrian centre on site, also fishing on the River Laune, which is free of charge to residents. Other on site amenities include a fine leisure centre with swimming pool. Children welcome. No pets. **Rooms 110** (1 suite, 40 no smoking). Lift. B&B from c. €95pps. Short breaks offered. **Gardens** open daily, May-Oct. Hotel closed Oct-mid Apr. Amex, Diners, MasterCard, Visa. **Directions:** Off the main Ring of Kerry road.

Sneem
HOTEL

Great Southern Hotel, Parknasilla

Sneem Co Kerry **Tel: 064 45122**

Email: res@parknasillagsh.com Web: www.gshhotels.com

Set in 300 acres of sub-tropical parkland, overlooking Kenmare Bay, this classic Victorian hotel is blessed with one of the most beautiful locations in Ireland. The spacious foyer with its antiques and fresh flowers sets a tone of quiet luxury, enhanced by the hotel's impressive collection of original art (currently being catalogued). Whether activity or relaxation is required there are excellent amenities at hand – including an outdoor swimming pool and Canadian hot tub - and an abundance of comfortable places for a quiet read or afternoon tea. Public rooms include the classical Pygmalion Restaurant and although bedrooms vary in size and outlook, most have been upgraded recently. Afternoon tea at Parknasilla is a relaxing affair, served in the spacious interconnecting lounges along the front of the hotel. An impressive range of outdoor activities available on-site includes cruises on the hotel's own boat, Parknasilla Princess - this is a place to slow down and take time for yourself. Children welcome. Golf (12 hole), tennis, fishing, equestrian, walking. No pets. **Rooms 83** (2 for disabled). Lift. B&B c. €105, ss c. €30. Open all year. **Directions:** 25 km west of Kenmare, on Ring of Kerry.

Sneem
GUESTHOUSE

Tahilla Cove Country House

Tahilla Cove Sneem Co Kerry
Tel: 064 45204 Fax: 064 45104
Email: tahillacove@eircom.net Web: www.tahillacove.com

Although it has been much added to over the years and has a blocky annexe in the garden, this family-run guesthouse has an old house in there somewhere. There's a proper bar, with its own entrance (which is used by locals as well as residents) and this, together with quite an official looking reception desk just inside the front door, makes it feel more like an hotel than a guesthouse Yet this is a refreshingly low-key place, and it has two very special features: the location, which is genuinely waterside, is really lovely and away-from-it-all; and the owners, James and Deirdre Waterhouse. Tahilla Cove has been in the family since 1948, and run since 1987 by James and Deirdre – who have the wisdom to understand why their many regulars love it just the way it is and, apart from regular maintenance (and some recent major refurbishment) little is allowed to change. Comfort and quiet relaxation are the priorities. All the public rooms have sea views, including the dining room and also a large sitting room, with plenty of armchairs and sofas, which opens onto a terrace (where there are patio tables and chairs overlooking the garden and the cove with its little stone jetty). Accommodation is divided between the main house and the annexe, which is very close by; rooms vary considerably but all except two have sea views, many have private balconies, and all are en-suite, with bathrooms of varying sizes and appointments (only one single is shower-only). All rooms have phone, TV, hair-dryer and individually controlled heating. Food is prepared personally by James and Deirdre and, although the dining room (20) is mainly intended for residents, others

are welcome to share their Irish home cooking when there is room – simple 5-course menus change daily. It's also a lovely place to drop into for a cup of tea overlooking the little harbour. **Rooms 9** (1 shower only, all no smoking) B&B c. €70 pps, ss€25. D at 74.45, c. €30. Non-residents welcome by reservation.No D Tue & Wed. Closed mid Oct-Easter. Amex, MasterCard, Visa, Laser. **Directions:** 11 miles west of of kenmare and 5 miles east of Sneem (N70).

Glanleam House & Subtropical Garden

Valentia Island Co Kerry
Tel: 066 947 6176
Email: info@glanleam.com Web: www.glanleam.com

GARDEN

Exotic woodland gardens with bamboo forests and ferns

Experiencing this garden is like straying into a benign jungle where the most exotic of plants rule in wild profusion. And if ever there was a place to give a sense of other worldliness it is Glanleam. The 40 acre site on an east facing bay on Valentia Island was created in the 19th century by the 19th Knight of Kerry, with plants sent back by plant collectors from all over the world, particularly Australasia.

Much of the collection and its descendants survive, spreading and growing to enormous proportions in the warming breath of the Gulf Stream, proving the point that things grow faster in Ireland than at anywhere else at this latitude. Paths wiggle through luxuriant growth past cordylines, bamboo forests, *Beschorneria yuccoides*, groves of tree ferns, embothrium and myrtles (including the variant *Luma apiculata* **'Glanleam Gold'** with cream bordered leaves which originated in the garden.)

Ferns, much collected by Victorians, are a particular feature and include species like the chain fern and the Killarney fern.

The garden is long and narrow in shape with paths winding back and forth between different features and prospects. There is an upper walk through thickets of camellias, a sea walk edged with bluebells and primulas, and a gunnera walk near the house. Streams and water features throughout the garden add to the interest. Restoration work is ongoing by current owners Meta and Jessica Kressig and, while storm damage which uprooted scores of trees posed challenges, it has also opened up new areas and opportunities.

*Open by appointment Easter to Sep, 10 -5. Supervised children welcome; dogs allowed on leads. Not suitable for wheelchairs. * Glanleam House is a member of Hidden Ireland and offers accommodation (6 rooms, B&B from c. €70pps), and dinner is available if booked the previous day. **Directions:** From Ring of Kerry, take car ferry (Caherciveen) or road bridge (near Portmagee) to Valentia Island. On the island, take the road for Knightstown: turn left in village; Glanleam is signposted on the right.*

Lower Shannon

Adare Manor Hotel

Adare
HOTEL

Adare Co Limerick **Tel: 061 396566**
Email: reservations@adaremanor.com Web: www.adaremanor.com

The former home of the Earls of Dunraven, this magnificent neo-Gothic mansion is set in 900 acres on the banks of the River Maigue. Grand public areas include the Gallery, named after the Palace of Versailles (unique 15th century choir stalls and fine stained glass windows), a splendid chandeliered drawing room and the glazed cloister of the Oak Room Restaurant which have views over the box-hedged French Formal Gardens to the meandering River Maigue. Luxurious bedrooms have individual hand carved fireplaces, fine locally-made mahogany furniture, cut-glass table lamps and impressive marble bathrooms with powerful showers over huge bathtubs. Recent additions include a state of the art Spa, which offers a

wide variety of massage and beauty treatments, and a "golf village" of two and four bedroom townhouses that offers a comfortable accommodation option for longer stays, groups and families. Extensive amenities are provided but with beautiful formal gardens to stroll in and parkland for walking, what more could anyone want? Children welcome. No pets. **Rooms 63** (1 state room, 5 suites). Lift. Room rate from c. €215. Open all year. **Restaurant Seats 76.** D daily; Set D c. €60, also à la carte. * Informal bistro style dining is offered all day at the Clubhouse Bar & Restaurant. Amex, MasterCard, Visa, Laser. Open all year. **Directions:** Adare village centre.

Carrabawn Guesthouse

Adare
GUESTHOUSE

Killarney Road Adare Co Limerick
Tel: 061 396067
Email: carrabawn@indigo.ie Web: www.carrabawnhouseadare.com

In an area known for high standards, with prices to match, this immaculate owner-run establishment set in large mature gardens provides a moderately-priced alternative to the luxury accommodation nearby - and should be a pleasing choice for garden lovers. Bedrooms are very well maintained with all the amenities required and Bernard and Bridget Lohan have been welcoming guests here since 1984 - many of them return on an annual basis because of the high level of comfort and friendly service provided. A

good Irish breakfast is served in a conservatory dining room overlooking lovely gardens and - although the restaurants of Adare are very close by - light evening meals can be provided by arrangement. Children welcome. No pets. **Rooms 8** (all shower only & no smoking). Room service (limited hours). B&B c. €45 pps, ss €20. Open all year except Christmas. MasterCard, Visa, Laser. **Directions:** On N21, 8 miles south of Limerick

Ballingarry
COUNTRY HOUSE / RESTAURANT / GARDEN

The Mustard Seed at Echo Lodge

Ballingarry Co Limerick
Tel: 069 68508 Fax: 069 68511
Email: mustard@indigo.ie Web: www.mustardseed.ie

Dan Mullane's famous restaurant The Mustard Seed started life in Adare in 1985 and quickly gained fame for both the quality of food and hospitality, and as one of the country's prettiest and most characterful restaurants. Ten years later Dan moved a short distance away to Echo Lodge, a spacious Victorian country residence dating from 1884, set on seven acres; both house and garden were in serious decline at the time, so Dan set about the daunting task of restoration, with the aim of creating a stylish small country house hotel complete with a working garden providing pleasure grounds, flowers for the house and culinary produce for the kitchen. Remnants of the original gardens include old box hedging, beberis, and mature trees including copper beech, ash, sycamore and a magnificent laburnum; younger trees of interest include *gingka biloba*, *acer palmatum dissectum* and *cornus* (the wedding cake tree). The present gardens are laid out on eight acres: four are under tree plantation of oak and ash, which are maturing nicely, the remainder consist of lawn, pond, shrubberies, orchard, vegetable garden, tunnel, herb garden, herbaceous borders, roses and a new courtyard area with with a limestone fountain. Good food is the main raison d'etre at The Mustard Seed, thus the orchard and kitchen garden produce all the familiar crops and many less usual ones too: alongside the apples, pears and plums, you will find figs and a range of soft fruits including loganberries, for example, and the tunnel provides ideal conditions for kiwi fruit and a grapevine as well as cucumber, courgettes and tomatoes. Outside vegetables thrive on the sloping site-early potatoes (Sharpe's Express, Duke of York), artichokes, pumpkins and squash all take their place alongside more everyday vegetables, and the herb garden is carpeted with a wide range of cultivars including several types of mint, comfrey and stately angelica...mingled with the herbs and vegetables are rows of fragrant sweet peas for the dining room, and many different varieties of rose - climbers like **'Schoolgirl'** and **'Dublin Bay'**, shrub roses including **'Graham Thomas'** and **'Gertrude Jekyll'** - also both pink and blue hydrangeas thrive here. A pond area is home to bamboos, gunneras, hostas, agapanthus, lilies and pentstemons - each season brings new colour and interest to this wonderful garden and Dan Mullane and his team are justifiably proud of the work they have put into its restoration and development. Indoors, elegance, comfort and generosity are the key features - seen through decor and furnishings which bear the mark of a seasoned traveller whose eye has found much to delight in while wandering the world; in addition to the luxurious traditional accommodation in the main house, an old schoolhouse in the garden has been converted to offer three more contemporary suites, with their own residents' lounge and a small leisure centre with sauna and massage room; this stylish development is in great demand from regulars who make Echo Lodge their base for golf and fishing holidays. Then there is the restaurant...food and hospitality are at the heart of Echo Lodge and

it is in ensuring a memorable dining experience that Dan Mullane's great qualities as a host emerge. To this, add head chef Tony Schwartz's stylish modern Irish cooking - and all that wonderful organic produce that is grown for him within sight of his kitchen window - and it becomes clear that no visit to Echo Lodge is complete without dinner. **Rooms 18** (3 suites, 5 shower only, 10 no smoking, 1 for disabled). c. B&B €90 pps, ss €20. **Restaurant Seats 60.** Reservations required; non residents welcome; restaurant not suitable for children. D 7-9.30. D c.€35-50. Licensed. Closed Christmas week, 2 weeks Feb. Amex, MasterCard, Visa, Laser. **Directions:** From top of Adare village take first turn to left, follow signs to Ballingarry - 8 miles; in village.

Glin Castle & Pleasure Grounds

Glin Co Limerick
Tel: 068 34173
Email: knight@iol.ie Web: www.glincastle.com

GARDEN

Restored gardens dating back over two centuries, with walled garden.

The fortunes of the Norman FitzGerald family and their various castles stretching back to 1197 rises and falls like the tides in the Shannon estuary beyond the sugar white castellated house. The history of the garden is relatively recent, dating to the time the present house was built in 1780. The 25th Knight of Glin, John Fraunceis FitzGerald, known as the Knight of the Women, embellished the estate in the 1820s with the walled garden, woods, Gothic lodges, a folly and a hermitage in the pleasure grounds. It was restored with additions by the grandmother and mother of the present Knight of Glin, Desmond FitzGerald.

The formal lawn, with curlicues of yew around a sundial terrace, is bordered with flowering shrubs - cherries, magnolias, cornus, *Drimys winterii* and hydrangeas - before giving way to the wilder areas. There is a hill dancing with daffodils in spring, carpets of bluebells under moss covered oaks, tree ferns and bamboos in the dappled shade around the hermitage, and a ring of mock standing stones in the pleasure ground.

The productive walled garden is laid out with traditional cruciform paths and a yew walk marching down the centre. In the kitchen garden and orchard sections all manner of fruit and vegetables are grown for the castle table, where guests are offered every imaginable treat, from asparagus to sea kale. Recent additions include a Gothic hen house and a rustic temple sheltering a statue of Andromeda - and the Edwardian seat overlooking a pond is a good place to drink in the perfection of it all.

Not only are the gardens a joy, but the house is also open for visits at certain times - and it is a wonderful place to stay (Mar-Nov); when the Knight is at home he will take visitors on a tour of the house, which has superb interiors and decorative plasterwork, and show them all his wonderful pictures and old furniture. And, not to be missed while in Glin is **Thomas O'Shaughnessy's Pub** (Tel 068 34115), just outside the castle walls; one of the finest pubs in Ireland, it is now in its sixth generation of family ownership and precious little has changed in the last hundred years - except that the gardens hidden away at the back have been given a lot of TLC in recent years.

*Garden open mid Mar-Nov by appointment. Supervised children welcome; partial wheelchair access; no dogs. Accommodation (15 luxurious rooms, B&B c. €140 pps; Residents' D c. €48, reservations required); garden visits and meals by arrangement; shop. **Directions:** Glin is between Foynes and Tarbert, on the N69.*

Ballyvaughan
HOTEL / RESTAURANT

Gregans Castle Hotel
Bllyvaughan Co Clare
Tel: 065 707 7005 Fax: 065 707 7111
Email: info@gregans.ie Web: www.gregans.ie

Although not close to any of our recommended gardens, this is a wonderful place to stay when visiting The Burren, with its annual display of rare flora which is at its height in early summer. Gregans Castle has a long and interesting history, going back to a tower house, or small castle, which was built by the O'Loughlen clan (the region's principal tribe) between the 10th and 17th centuries and is still intact. The present house dates from the late 18th century and has been added to many times; it was opened as a country house hotel in 1976 by Peter and Moira Haden who (true to the traditions of the house) continued to develop and improve it, together with their son Simon, who is now proprietor. The exterior is grey and stark, in keeping with the lunar landscape of the surrounding Burren - the contrast between first impressions and the warmth, comfort and hospitality to be found within is one of the great joys of arriving at Gregans Castle. Peace and quiet are the dominant themes: spacious rooms are furnished to a very high standard, with excellent bathrooms and lovely countryside views - and deliberately left without the worldly interference of television. Yet this luxurious hotel is not too formal or at all intimidating; non-residents are welcome to drop in for lunch or afternoon tea in the **Corkscrew Bar** - named after a nearby hill road which, incidentally, provides the most scenic approach to Ballyvaughan - and, in fine weather, guests can sit out beside the Celtic Cross rose garden and watch patches of sun and shade chasing across the hills. In **The Dining Room**, with lovely views over the Burren (where there can be very special light effects as the sun sets over Galway Bay on summer evenings), a commitment to using local and organic produce, when available, is stated on the menu - all fish is caught locally around Galway Bay, and Burren lamb and beef come from local butchers. Wide-ranging menus reflect this philosophy in fresh, colourful dishes that blend traditional values and contemporary style - in dinners that are never less than a treat. **Rooms 21** (3 suites, 3 junior suites). B&B c. €105 pps, ss c. €73. **Restaurant: Seats 50**. D daily; non residents welcome. A la carte. Licensed. Light lunch menu offered in The Corkscrew Bar. Afternoon Tea daily 3-5. Hotel closed early Nov-late Mar. Amex, MasterCard, Visa, Laser. **Directions:** On N67, 3.25 miles south of Ballyvaughan.

Carron
RESTAURANT

Burren Perfumery Tea Rooms
Carron Co Clare
Tel: 065 708 9102 Fax: 065 708 9200
Email: burrenperfumery@eircom.net Web: www.burrenperfumery.com

When touring Clare you will be pleased to find this charming spot - the perfumery is beautifully laid out, with a herb garden (where many native plants are grown - and later used in the organic herbal teas), pleasing old buildings and lovely biody-
namic scents. The little tea rooms open onto a courtyard, opposite the perfumery shop - and beside the distillation room, where essential oils are extracted in a traditional still. Although small and simple, the tea rooms are pretty, with floral waxed tablecloths, fresh flowers and cups and saucers all creating a happy mismatch of pastels - and what they do is of high quality, made freshly on the premises, and uses local organic produce. At lunch time there might be summer minestrone & herbs soup with brown bread, or salad plates - a home-made organic goat's cheese & spinach quiche served with mixed salad - or, from a range of traditional home baking, you could just have a home-made scone with butter and Maureen's jam. All kinds of teas and tisanes are offered, also natural juices - and coffee is served in individual cafetières. Tea Rooms: **Seats 20**, open 9-5pm, May-Sep. [Perfumery open daily all year except Christmas; high season (Jun-Sep) open 9-7, off season 9-5. MasterCard, Visa, Laser. **Directions:** In the Burren, east of Gort - off R480 & N67.

Vandeleur Walled Garden

Kilrush Co Clare
Tel: 065 905 1760
Email: vandeleurwalledgarden@eircom.net Web: www.kilrush.ie

GARDEN

Restored walled garden with rare and tender plants

The secret world of the walled gardens at Vandeleur, Kilrush had lain forgotten for years. The house belonging to the surrounding 420 acres of wooded demesne was first planted in 1712, the house was burnt in 1887 and finally demolished in 1973. But now, thanks to funding from the Great Gardens of Ireland Restoration Scheme, and to Kilrush Amenity Trust and Kilrush Urban District Council, the gardens have risen again phoenix-like, bringing jobs and tourism in their wake.

Laid out in part with geometric beds set in gravel paths amid lawns and partly with winding paths running between informal beds, the garden and planting scheme was designed in conjunction with Belinda Jupp. There is a an intriguing collection of plants from South Africa, including reed-like restios, tipped to become popular plants of the future and other rare and tender plants. Opened in 2000, the garden has unusual water features, a horizontal maze and a tree collection. With woodland trails riverside views, a visitor centre, restaurant and gift shop, it's a good place for a family outing - and, as it is close to the Killimer car ferry, it could make a day trip if you are based in County Limerick or North Kerry.

Open all year: Apr-Sep, 10-6 daily. Oct-Mar 10-7. Entrance about €5. Children welcome; suitable for wheelchairs. **Directions:** *Signed from Kilrush.*

stock image

Lisdoonvarna
HOTEL / RESTAURANT

Sheedy's Country House Hotel
Lisdoonvarna Co Clare
Tel: 065 707 4026 Fax: 065 707 4555
Email: info@sheedys.com Web: www.sheedys.com

John and Martina Sheedy run one of the west of Ireland's best loved small hotels here and, although not close to gardens open to the public, it would make a fine base for anyone interested in in the natural display of flora on the nearby Burren. Sheedys offers some of the most luxurious accommodation and the best food in the area, yet it still has the warm ambience and friendly hands-on management, which make a hotel special. The sunny foyer has a comfortable seating area - and an open fire for chillier days - and all the bedrooms are spacious and individually designed to a high standard. Fine food and warm hospitality remain constant qualities however - and the gardens in front of the hotel have been developed to include an original feature that has already enhanced the exterior in a way that is as practical as it is pleasing to the eye: a rose garden, and also a potager, which supplies leeks, swiss chard, beetroot and cabbage to John Sheedys renowned kitchen. Sheedy's Restaurant is a must-visit destination for discerning diners who appreciate John's cooking of beautifully presented meals that showcase local produce, especially seafood. No pets. Not suitable for children, except babies. **Rooms 11** (3 juniior suites, 1 disabled, all no smoking); B&B c. €70pps, ss €20. **Restaurant: Seats 27.** D daily. A la carte. Licensed. MasterCard, Visa, Laser. **Directions:** 200 metre from town square, on road to Sulphur Wells.

Newmarket-on-Fergus
HOTEL / RESTAURANTS

Dromoland Castle Hotel
Newmarket-on-Fergus Co Clare
Tel 061 368 144 Fax 061 363 355
Email: sales@dromoland.ie Web: www.dromoland.ie

The ancestral home of the O'Briens, barons of Inchiquin and direct descendants of Brian Boru, High King of Ireland, this is one of the few Irish estates tracing its history back to Gaelic royal families, and it is now one of Ireland's grandest hotels, and one of the best-loved. Despite the grandeur of the surroundings, it is a relaxing hotel, where the surrounding lakes, parkland and gardens, and the magnificent furnishings to be expected of a real Irish castle all enhance the pleasure for guests - and it would make a very comfortable base for visiting gardens such as Glin Castle and Vandeleur, or simply as a treat. Aside from luxurious accommodation and wonderful public rooms, Dromoland Castle has earned an exceptional reputation for its food in both the magnificent **Earl of Thomond Restaurant** (gleaming crystal, gilding and rich fabrics abound here, and the food and service match the surroundings) and in the less formal **Fig Tree Restaurant** at the Dromoland Golf and Country Club, which is very close to the hotel – and makes a lovely place to plan a lunch break if you are travelling. Executive Head Chef David McCann has overall responsibility for both areas – and also for the delicious Gallery Menu which offers a choice of lighter dishes at the castle, throughout the day – and the cooking is invariably excellent. And, with so much to do on site and in the area, a stay here will be very tempting. Children welcome. Leisure centre (indoor pool, spa, beauty salon, hairdressing); golf (18); fishing, tennis, cycling, walking. Snooker, pool table; gift shop, boutique all on site. Wheelchair accessible Air conditioning. **Rooms 100** (27 suites/junior suites, 2 disabled, all no smoking) Room rate c. €446. **Meals:** Earl of Thomond, D daily, L Sun only; Gallery Menu, 11-7 daily; Fig Tree Restaurant open 9am-9.30pm daily. Reservations advised. Open all year. Amex, Diners, MasterCard, Visa, Laser. **Directions:** Off N18 between Limerick and Ennis; exit at Dromoland interchange and follow signage.

West

Aran Islands
B&B

Man of Aran
Kilmurvey Inis Mór Aran Islands Co Galway
Tel: 099 61301 Fax: 099 61324
Email: manofaran@eircom.net

While the Aran Islands may not be an obvious destination for garden visits, many garden lovers will want to come here while in the area and, despite the rugged location, you will be in for a pleasant surprise at this traditional cottage. For, despite its fame - this is where the film Man of Aran was made - Joe and Maura Wolfe make visiting their home a genuine and personal experience. Their three little bedrooms are basic but full of quaint, cottagey charm and they're very comfortable, although only one is en-suite. The cottage is right beside the sea and Kilmurvey beach, surrounded by wild flowers, and Joe has somehow managed to make a productive garden in this exposed location, so their meals usually include his organically grown vegetables (even artichokes and asparagus), salads, nasturtium flowers and young nettle leaves as well as Maura's home-made soups, stews and freshly-baked bread and cakes. Dinner is served in the little dining room but there are benches in the garden, with stunning views across the sea towards the mountains, where you can enjoy an aperitif, or even eat outside on fine summer evenings.

Breakfast will probably be a well cooked full-Irish - made special by Joe's beautifully sweet home-grown cherry tomatoes if you are lucky - although they'll do something different if you like – and packed lunches are available too. Children welcome. No pets. **Rooms 3.** B&B €40, ss c. €20. D at 7.30 (one sitting) is mainly for residents, but non-resident guests are also welcome by reservation (no regular weekly closures, but check availability of meals when booking). Set D c. €30; licensed. Closed Nov-Feb. **No credit cards.**

Ardcarraig

Oranswell **Bushy Park** Co Galway
Tel: 091 524336
Email: oranswell@eircom.net

GARDEN

Rare and unusual plants mingling happily with native species among rocks and heather

There is nothing quite like Ardcarraig, perhaps because people don't try to garden in such apparently inhospitable spots among the rocks and heather. Yet the sights to be seen in this 5 acres of hillside where Lorna McMahon has developed her own style of gardening with nature, are every bit as breathtaking as the most contrived of gardens. Acers, hostas and a Japanese snow viewing lantern are reflected in a rock fringed mountain pool as though they just happened to be there. Dazzling splashes of violet *Iris ensata* and magenta *Primula poissonii*, line a stream against a backdrop of moorland.

But of course these lovely effects didn't just happen: years of back-breaking work have gone into the garden. Lorna opened up clearings, planted hazel and holly as shelter, and made rustic steps up and down the hillside coaxing things to grow between rocks.

Things started traditionally enough 35 years ago when Lorna planted a dwarf conifer garden beside the house, helped by a load of lime top soil. But before long the garden grew beyond a bluebell and hazel wood to take in a new areas each year The Mary O'Connor Garden (named for a gardening friend) is planted with rambling roses like Kifsgate, and summer flowering hoherias and eucryphias. Azalea lined steps lead on to the Primula Garden where some of the 40 varieties represented surround a pool with stands of phormium. Royal ferns add to the lushness and the dawn redwood and snakebark maples provide autumn colour.

The streamside bog garden, full of water loving plants gives way to the Japanese Garden where, beside a cascade, an obliging rock represents Mount Fuji. When Mrs McMahon sadly lost her husband Harry in '96, trees and shrubs given by friends began to appear on her doorstep, so she began another garden in his memory. More trees and shrubs arrived and were planted in the natural rock garden beside the stream in what promises to be the loveliest of all the areas.

The more formal side of the garden grew too with a sunken circular enclosure sheltering tender plants in commemoration of Lorna's gardening aunts. An old mill wheel and a Cretan jar act as focal points. A former tennis court took on a new lease of life as a knot garden filled by herbs with a Shakespearean and Biblical theme. There are many rare and unusual plants mingling happily with native species, all planted so densely that the garden almost cares for itself. Lorna now has a new house overlooking her lovely creation.

*Open May-July by appointment; Open Day (c. 17 May). Supervised children welcome; not suitable for wheelchairs. Plants for sale on open day. Admission c. €5. **Directions:** On the Oughterard-Clifden road, 5km out of Galway - 2nd left after Glenlo Abbey.*

Bushy Park
COUNTRY HOUSE

Killeen House
Bushy Park Galway Co Galway
Tel: 091 524 179 Fax: 091 528 065
Email: killeenhouse@ireland.com Web: www.killeenhousegalway.com

Catherine Doyle's delightful, spacious 1840s house enjoys the best of both worlds: it's on the Clifden road just on the edge of Galway city yet, with 25 acres of private grounds and gardens reaching right down to the shores of Lough Corrib, offers all the advantages of the country, too. Catherine's thoughtful hospitality and meticulous standards make a stay here very special, beginning with tea on arrival, served on a beautifully arranged tray with fine linen and polished silver - a house speciality extending to the usually mundane tray provided in your bedroom. Guest rooms are luxuriously and individually furnished, each in a different period, e.g. Regency, Edwardian and (most fun this one) Art Nouveau; the bedding is exquisite, bathrooms are lovely and there are many small touches to make you feel at home. And, although the menu is not exceptionally extensive, breakfast is a delight. Not suitable for children under 12. No pets. **Rooms 6** (1 shower only). Lift. B&B c. €90pps, ss €50. Open all year except Christmas. Amex, Diners, MasterCard, Visa. **Directions:** On N59 between Galway city and Moycullen village.

Cashel
HOTEL / RESTAURANT / GARDENS

Cashel House Hotel & Gardens

Cashel Co Galway
Tel: 095 31001 Fax: 095 31077
Email: info@cashel-house-hotel.com Web: www.cashel-house-hotel.com

Standing at the head of Cashel Bay, Dermot and Kay McEvilly's gracious property has been run an an hotel since 1968 and comfort abounds here, even luxury, yet it's tempered by common sense, a love of gardening and the genuine sense of hospitality that ensures each guest will benefit as much as possible from their stay. The award-winning gardens, which run down to their own little private beach, contribute greatly to the atmosphere, and the accommodation includes especially comfortable ground floor garden suites, which are also suitable for less able guests (wheelchair accessible, but no special grab rails etc in bathrooms). Relaxed hospitality combined with professionalism have earned an international reputation for this outstanding hotel and its qualities are perhaps best seen in details - log fires that burn throughout the year, day rooms furnished with antiques and filled with fresh flowers from the garden, rooms that are individually decorated with many thoughtful touches. Service is impeccable, and the superb breakfasts for which they are renowned will set you up for the most demanding schedule of garden visits. The hotel is covered in a soft cloak of climbing plants - jasmine, ivy, clematis and roses, with some planting of pelargonium and antirrhinum

into the rocky base, and a long flower bed in front of the house contains a colourful display of viola, canna lilies, antirrhinum, phlox and chocolate cosmos. The gardens, which are informal and quietly secluded, are open to the public for most of the year and they are a delight, with their paths and small walks covered in 'mind your own business' (*soleirolia soleirollii*) and edged with moss covered rocks - an enchanting setting for exquisite flowering shrubs, many of them imported from Tibet, including azaleas, camellias, eucryphia, old-fashioned and modern roses, and rare and beautiful magnolias. A fine Beech Walk leads up to the herb and vegetable gardens, and the walled garden, now known as The Secret Garden, was an orchard until 1919 when the apple trees were felled and replaced with rare trees and shrubs from all over the world; the Irish Tree Society has recently compiled a list of all the rare trees in the gardens. The gardens are over 200 years old and the McEvillys see them as a work in progress - a beautiful New Garden was started several years ago and, in recognition of Kay's sister Mary's garden in Belgium, there are mainly herbaceous plants there. **Gardens open** Feb-end Oct. Admission €5 (to charity). **Rooms 32** (13 suites, 9 superior rooms, 1 shower only, 4 suitable for less-able guests). B&B €120pps, no ss. * Self-catering accommodation is also offered, in a 3-bedroom house and 2-bedroom traditional cottage nearby; details on application. **Restaurant Seats 70.** D daily, 7-8.30; Set D c.€48; also à la carte. (Bar L 12-2.30, Afternoon Tea 2-5). 12.5% s.c. Hotel closed early Jan-early Feb. Amex, MasterCard, Visa, Laser, Switch. **Directions:** South off N59 (Galway-Clifden road), 1 mile west of Recess turn left.

Cashel
HOTEL / RESTAURANT

Zetland Country House

Cashel Bay Cashel Co Galway
Tel: 095 31111 Fax: 095 31117
Email: zetland@iol.ie Web: www.zetland.com

Originally built as a sporting lodge in the early 19th century, Zetland House is on an elevated site with views over Cashel Bay; its unusual name dates back to a time when the Shetland Islands were under Norwegian rule, and known as the Zetlands - the Earl of Zetland (Lord Viceroy, 1888-1890) was a frequent visitor here, hence the name. Now in the second generation of ownership by the Prendergast family, it still makes a good base for fishing holidays, and is well located for visiting the many fine gardens in the area, most of which (including the Zetland Hotel) are members of the Connemara Garden Trail. This is a charming and hospitable house, with a light and airy atmosphere and an elegance bordering on luxury, in both its spacious antique-furnished public areas and bedrooms. The latter are individually decorated in a relaxed country house style, and include two lovely newer rooms, which were opened in 2004. The gardens surrounding the hotel are very lovely, their well-tended flowers, trees and shrubs greatly enhancing the peaceful atmosphere of the house - and the productive kitchen garden supplies fresh seasonal vegetables and herbs for use in the restaurant, which is beautifully located overlooking Cashel Bay and is known for serving the best of local produce, notably lobster - and also game, in season. Children welcome. Pets permitted by arrangement in some areas. **Rooms 19** (10 superior rooms, 5 no smoking). B&B c. €110pps, ss €25; **Restaurant** D daily, Set D c. €56; snack lunches available 12-2 daily. SC12.5%. Wheelchair accessible. Amex, Diners, MasterCard, Visa, Laser. **Directions:** N59 from Galway. Turn left after Recess.

Clifden
B&B

Sea Mist House
Clifden Co Galway
Tel: 095 21441 Email: sgriffin@eircom.net
Web: www.accommodation-connemara-ireland.com

Sheila Griffin's attractive house was built in 1825, using local quarried stone. Major renovations undertaken over the last few years have retained its character while adding modern comforts, allowing her to offer stylish and comfortable accommodation which will appeal especially to garden lovers. A recently added conservatory has made a lovely, a spacious room overlooking the garden, where guests can relax - and fruit from the garden is used in spiced fruit compôtes and preserves which appear at breakfast along with home-made breads, American-style pancakes with fresh fruit salsa and scrambled eggs with smoked salmon and a special of the day which brings an element of surprise to the menu each morning. The pretty cottage garden adjacent to the house has been developing over the years and is now reaching maturity - guests are welcome to wander through it and soak in the tranquil atmosphere, and this would make an agreeable base for visiting the many other gardens nearby (the Connemara Garden Trail). Private parking (3). No pets. **Rooms 4** (all shower only & no-smoking). c. B&B €50pps, ss €15. Closed Christmas, also mid-week off season. MasterCard, Visa. **Directions:** Left at square, a little down on the right.

Kylemore Abbey
& Victorian Walled Garden

Letterfrack Co Galway
Tel: 095 41146
Email: info@kylemoreabbey.ie Web: www.kylemoreabbey.com

GARDEN

Restored formal garden and kitchen garden in romantic setting

With a loughside setting under the wooded lee of the Twelve Bens in Connemara, Kylemore looks for all the world like a moody Victorian painting and the 19th century castle has a story to match. Built as a romantic indulgence by Liverpool merchant Mitchell Henry for his wife Margaret, the spell was broken when she died less than a decade later. The castle and ambitious demesne was then owned by the Duke of Manchester before the Irish Benedictine nuns returned from Ypres and opened a school there after World War I.

The 6 acre walled gardens, which originally took three years to complete, have now been restored with help from the Great Gardens Restoration Programme, the European Regional Development Fund and work by FAS. Photographs from the historic Lawrence Collection were used as reference. Planting - with carpet bedding, cordyline palms and a ring of floral arches - shows how much fashions in gardening have changed.

The garden is divided in two with a stream and woodland garden and a double herbaceous border to shield the gentry in the formal garden from views of the vegetable garden. There were originally 18 glasshouses and a bothy house for the garden boys, who had to ensure the boilers remained lit, and the East Vinery has been restored. With woodland walks, the dramatic backdrop of Diamond Hill, a miniature Gothic cathedral, a shop and museum, there is plenty for the family to see and do - not surprisingly, it can be very busy in summer.

Gardens open Easter-Oct, 10.30-4.30; tours by arrangement. Supervised children and wheelchairs welcome. Admission charge applies. (Abbey, craft shop & restaurant open all year except Christmas week & Good Friday.) **Directions:** *On the N 59, between Leenane and Clifden.*

Letterfrack
COUNTRY HOUSE

Rosleague Manor Hotel
Letterfrack Co Galway
Tel: 353 95 41101 Fax: 353 95 41168
Email: rosleaguemanor@eircom.net Web: www.rosleague.com

A lovely pink-washed Regency house of gracious proportions and sensitive modernisation, Rosleague looks out over a tidal inlet through gardens of early 19th century origin which have many rare shrubs and plants, and are especially known for their wonderful hydrangeas. The woodland walks reach down to the waters edge, and these beautiful surroundings convey a deep sense of peace - it is hard to imagine anywhere better to recharge the soul. The hotel changed hands within the Foyle family quite recently, and it now has an energetic young owner manager, Mark Foyle, who has undertaken considerable refurbishment - not only in the house but also the gardens (already extensive) which have been further developed to make new paths and establish a wild flower meadow.This is a very pleasant, peaceful place to stay and the restaurant - a lovely classical dining room, with mahogany furniture and a fine collection of plates on the walls - is open to non-residents by reservation; the style is quite traditional, as befits a country house and, afterwards, you can relax in one of two drawing rooms, or in the bar. Member of the Connemara Garden Trail; gardens open mid-Apr-mid Oct, 12-6. admission c. €2.50. Tennis, fishing, walking. Children welcome. Pets permitted by arrangement. **Rooms 20** (4 junior suites). B&B c. €110pps, ss €30. **Restaurant Seats 50.** D 7.30-9 daily, by reservation; Set D c. €45; Light L,12-3. Wheelchair accessible. Closed Dec-Mar. Amex, MasterCard, Visa, Laser. **Directions:** On N59 main road, 7 miles north-west of Clifden.

Oughterard
COUNTRY HOUSE

Currarevagh House
Glann Road Oughterard Co Galway
Tel: 091 552 312 Fax: 091 552 731
Email: currarevagh@ireland.com Web: www.currarevagh.com

Tranquillity, trout and tea in the drawing room - these are the things that draw guests back to the Hodgson family's gracious, but not especially luxurious early Victorian manor overlooking Lough Corrib. Currarevagh, which was built in 1846 as a wedding present for Harry Hodgson's great, great, great grandfather, is set in 150 acres of woodlands and gardens with sporting rights over 5,000 acres. Guests have been welcomed here for over half a century; the present owners, Harry and June Hodgson, are founder members of the Irish Country Houses and Restaurants Association (known as Ireland's Blue Book), and now joined by their son Henry. Yet, while the emphasis is on old-fashioned service and hospitality, the Hodgsons are adamant that the atmosphere should be more like a private house party than an hotel, and their restful rituals underline the differences: the day begins with a breakfast worthy of its Edwardian origins, laid out on the sideboard in the dining room; lunch may be one of the renowned picnic hampers required by sporting folk. Then there's afternoon tea, followed by a leisurely dinner. Fishing is the ruling passion, of course - notably brown trout, pike, perch and salmon - but there are plenty of other pursuits, including garden visits, to assist in building up an appetite for June's good home cooking, all based on fresh local produce. Not suitable for children under 10. Walking, tennis. **Rooms 15** (all en-suite). B&B c.€95, ss c.€35. D c.€42.50, at 8pm (non residents welcome by reservation). Wine licence. Closed mid Oct-early Apr. MasterCard, Visa, Laser. **Directions:** Take N59 to Oughterard. Turn right in village square and follow Glann Road for 4 miles.

Oughterard
HOTEL

Ross Lake House Hotel
Rosscahill Oughterard Co Galway
Tel: 091 550109 Fax: 091 550 184
Email: rosslake@iol.ie Web: www. rosslakehotel.com

Quietly situated in six acres of beautiful gardens - and well located for vsiting other gardens in the area - this charming country house was built in 1850 and is now a protected building. The current owners, Henry and Elaine Reid, bought the property in 1981 and have gradually refurbished it, so the hotel now offers luxurious accommodation in spacious rooms and suites individually furnished

with antiques - including some with four-poster beds. While graciously-proportioned and impressively furnished, hands-on management and the warm interest of the proprietors and their staff ensure a welcoming and surprisingly homely atmosphere. Weddings are a speciality, especially off season. Children welcome. Pets allowed in some areas by arrangement. Garden visits nearby. Tennis. Walking, cycling, fishing. **Rooms 13** (1 suite, 1 junior suite, 3 superior, 1 shower only, 10 no smoking) B&B c.€85pps, ss c. €30. Closed early Nov-mid Mar. Amex, MasterCard, Visa, Laser. **Directions:** Signed off Galway-Oughterard road.

Oughterard Area

Brigit's Garden & Café

Pollagh Roscahill Co Galway **Tel: 091 550905**
Email: info@galwaygarden.com Web: www.galwaygarden.com

Jenny Beale's beautiful themed garden near Oughterard reflects the Celtic festivals and, in addition to woodland trails, ring fort and stone chamber has a café that is worth a visit in its own right. A pine-ceilinged modern room that also acts as reception/shop has a small kitchen open to view at one end, and is set up with tables covered in old-fashioned oil cloth; everything is very simple, with plain white crockery and stainless cutlery and paper serviettes and, in fine weather, there is seating outside too. A short (vegetarian) blackboard menu offers a daily soup chunky, wholesome vegetable with thyme, perhaps, a meal in itself with brown bread & butter, and a special such as home-grown chard and blue cheese pasta. Lovely toasted sandwiches are generously filled with salad and a choice of fillings (egg mayonnaise, goats cheese & herb, hummus & olive, cheese & scallion), and great home bakes include delicious scones with jam & cream, and a luscious, walnut & apricot carrot cake, which is nutty and moist. Good coffee, tea or tisanes, and soft drinks like cranberry or lemon juice - just the kind of place you need to know about when exploring the area. Good toilets too, including baby changing facilities.

Garden open mid Apr-Sep. 9.30-5.30 daily. Other times by arrangement. Wheelchair accessible. Café open 11-5 daily; seats 35 (+20 outdoors). Visa, MasterCard, Laser. **Directions:** Just off the N59 between Moycullen and Oughterard.

Recess
HOTEL / RESTAURANT / GARDEN

Ballynahinch Castle Hotel
Recess Co Galway
Tel: 095 31006 Fax: 095 31085
Email: bhinch@iol.ie Web: www.ballynahinch-castle.com

This crenellated Victorian mansion is renowned as a fishing hotel and enjoys a most romantic position in 450 acres of ancient woodland on the banks of the Ballynahinch River. It is also home to one of Connemara's oldest gardens - set out among mature trees and shrubs, on many levels, the extensive landscaped gardens here have long been a point of pride and are open to the public every day throughout the season (there is a small charge, donated to local charities). Although impressive by any standards, the atmosphere is relaxed and the castle would make a very comfortable base for

a few days - and it is also a lovely place to take a break during the day, as excellent food is served in the hotel's characterful bar, a mighty high-ceilinged room with a huge fireplace, and many mementoes of the pleasures of rod and hunt. The tone is set in the foyer, with its huge stone fireplace and ever-burning log fire (which is a cosy place to enjoy afternoon tea), and the many necessary renovations and extensions through the years have been undertaken with great attention to period detail, a policy also carried through successfully in furnishing both public areas and bedrooms, many of which have lovely views over the river. Fine dinners are served every evening in **The Owenmore Restaurant**, a bright and elegant room with the classic atmosphere of a splendidly old-fashioned dining room - it is carefully organised to allow as many tables as possible to enjoy its uniquely beautiful river setting and, in the unlikely event that service should ever falter, it could well go unnoticed by guests lost in fascinated observation of happy fisherfolk claiming the last of the fading daylight on the rocks below. A stay here is always a restorative treat and, after a restful night's sleep, a Ballynahinch breakfast will give you a good start ahead of a day's fishing, wilderness walks on the estate, visiting nearby gardens or simply touring the area. Fishing: 3 miles of private fly fishing for Atlantic salmon, sea trout and brown trout. Members of Connemara Garden Trail. Cycling, walking; Children welcome. No pets. Golf nearby. **Rooms 40** (3 suites, 12 with separate bath & shower). No lift. 24 hr room service. B&B c. €120 pps, ss c. €30; SC10%. **Owenmore Restaurant:** D daily, 6.30-9 (Set D c. €49). Bar meals 12.30-3 & 6.30-9 daily. Closed Christmas & Feb. Amex, Visa, Diners, MasterCard, Laser. **Directions:** N59 from Galway - Clifden; left after Recess (Roundstone road), 2 km.

Renvyle
HOTEL / RESTAURANT

Renvyle House Hotel
Renvyle Co Galway
Tel: 095 43511 Fax: 095 43515
Email: info@renvyle.com Web: www.renvyle.com

In one of the country's most appealingly remote and beautiful areas, this famous Lutyens-esque house has a romantic and fascinating history, having been home to people as diverse as a Gaelic chieftan and Oliver St John Gogarty - and becoming one of Ireland's earliest country house hotels, in 1883. It is approached via a stunning scenic drive along a mountain road with views down into a blue-green sea of unparalleled clarity. However, once reached, the hotel seems to be snuggling down for shelter and has only limited views, but the surroundings are charming and have been given a lot of TLC in recent years. The sheltered feeling is reinforced by the cosy atmosphere of the original building, with its dark beams, rug strewn floors and open fires - and a snug conservatory where guests can survey the garden and landscape beyond from a comfortable vantage point. The grounds and gardens around the hotel are a special point of interest at Renvyle, and come as a delightful contrast to the magnificently rugged surrounding scenery. Photographs and mementoes recording visits from the many famous people who have stayed here - Augustus John, Lady Gregory, Yeats and Churchill among them - keep guests happily occupied for hours, but there is plenty to distract you from this enjoyable activity, with masses of things to do on site and nearby. Just loafing around is perhaps what guests are best at here, however, and there's little need to do much else. Head chef Tim O'Sullivan looks after the inner man admirably in lovely dinners featuring local seafood and Connemara produce, including Renvyle rack of lamb, local lobster and game in season - and the hotel's bar food is also excellent. All this, plus the scent of a turf fire and a comfortable armchair, can be magic. Continuing improvements have brought bedrooms up to a high standard, and special breaks (midweek, weekend and bank holiday) are very good value. Children welcome. Outdoor swimming pool, archery, all-weather tennis court, clay pigeon shooting, croquet, lawn bowls, snooker. **Rooms 69** (6 suites, 40 no smoking, 1 for disabled). B&B c.€115pps, no ss, no SC. **Restaurant** open 7-9 daily (Set D c.€45). **Bar meals** 11-7 daily (excl 25 Dec, Good Fri). Closed Jan. Amex, Diners, MasterCard, Visa, Laser. **Directions:** 12 miles north of Clifden.

Roundstone Area
COUNTRY HOUSE

The Angler's Return

Toombeola Roundstone Co Galway
Tel: 095 31091
Fax: 095 31091

This charming and unusual house near Roundstone was built as a sporting lodge in the eighteenth century and, as the name implies, fishing remains a major attraction to this day. But you don't have to be a fisherperson to warm to the special charms of The Anglers Return: peace and tranquillity, the opportunity to slow down in a quiet, caring atmosphere in this most beautiful area - this is its particular appeal. The house is set in three acres of natural gardens (open every day in spring and summer; best in late spring) and makes a good base for the Connemara Garden Trail. Bedrooms are bright and comfortably furnished in a fresh country house style, although only one is en-suite (the other four share two bathrooms between them); this is not a major problem and the overall level of comfort is high. However, bathroom arrangements are gradually being improved - one now features a restored Victorian ball & claw cast-iron bath. As well as garden visits and fishing, there is golf nearby, and riding and boat trips can be arranged for guests - and there are maps and information for walkers too. Tea and snacks are available at any time during the day or evening, (out in the secluded back garden in fine

weather, or beside the fire in the soothing drawing room, perhaps); dinner is available for groups staying several days, otherwise bookings can be made in nearby restaurants. Breakfast will include treats from the garden - and you are even invited to collect your own egg. Infants and children over 7 welcome. **Rooms 5** (1 en-suite, 4 with shared bathrooms; all no smoking). B&B c. €48, ss by arrangement. Closed late Nov-early Mar. **No Credit Cards. Directions:** From Galway, N59 Clifden road; turn left onto R341 Roundstone road for 4 miles; house is on the left.

Castlecoote
COUNTRY HOUSE / GARDEN

Castlecoote House & Gardens
Castlecoote Co Roscommon
Tel: **0906 663794** / 0906 663795 Fax: 0906 663795
Email: info@castlecootehouse.com Web: www.castlecootehouse.com

This fine Georgian residence overlooking the beautiful River Suck was built in the enclosure of a medieval castle between 1690 and 1720, and is of historic interest - not least as the birthplace of the Gunning sisters, who became the Duchess of Hamilton (and later, of Argyll) and Countess of Coventry; celebrated for their beauty; their portaits by Sir Joshua Reynolds hang in the main hall. Having restored the house to its former glory, the present owners, Sarah Lane and Kevin Finnerty, now offer magnificent country house accommodation and they are members of the Ireland West Garden Trail - guided tours of the gardens, which include an orchard of rare apple trees, the towers of the ruined castle, a medieval bridge and even an ice house, are offered by appointment. Tennis, crocquet, fishing. Gardens open by appointment Apr-Sep. Not suitable for children or wheelchairs. Rooms 4 (all ensuite & no smoking); gate lodge also available. B&B c. €115pps, ss €35. Residents' D c. €45 (reservations required on the previous day). MasterCard, Visa, Laser. **Directions:** From Dublin: N4, N6 and N61 to Roscommon; take the R366 (south-west) to Castlecoote village; cross bridge, bear right - gates are directly ahead.

Castlerea
COUNTRY HOUSE

Clonalis House
Castlerea Co Roscommon **Tel: 094 962 0014**
Email: clonalis@iol.ie Web: www.clonalis.com

Standing on the land that has been the home of the O'Conors of Connacht for 1,500 years, this 45-roomed Victorian Italianate mansion may seem a little daunting on arrival, but it's magic - and the hospitable owners, Pyers and Marguerite O'Conor-Nash, enjoy sharing their rich and varied history with guests, who are welcome to browse through their fascinating archive. Amazing heirlooms include a copy of the last Brehon Law judgment (handed down about 1580) and also Carolan's Harp. Everything is on a huge scale: reception rooms are all very spacious, with lovely old furnishings and many interesting historic details, bedrooms have massive four poster and half tester beds and bathrooms to match - and the dining room is particularly impressive, with a richly decorated table to set off

Marguerite's good home cooking. Clonalis House is set amid peaceful parklands and is a good base for visits in counties Roscommon, Galway, Mayo and Sligo. Two attractive self-catering cottages are also offered, in the courtyard; details on application. **Rooms 4** (3 en-suite, 1 with private bathroom, all no smoking). B&B c.€85pps, ss€20. Residents' D Tue-Sat, c. €40 (24 hrs notice required). D not available Sun or Mon. **Directions:** N60, west of Castlerea.

Strokestown Park House & Garden

Strokestown Co Roscommon
Tel: 071 963 3013
Email: info@strokestownpark.ie Web: www.strokestownpark.ie

GARDEN

Restored walled gardens on historic estate

The great south border in the restored six acre walled garden at Strokestown Park is a happy tribute to changed times. Colour keyed, with planting running through the shades of the spectrum from sizzling red hot pokers and blazing ligularia to coolest blue delphiniums, the 18 foot deep bed has put Strokestown on the map as the garden with the longest borders in these islands.

Strokestown's previous claim to record breaking fame was to have the widest street in Ireland built for the 2nd Lord Hartland in an attempt to rival Vienna's Ringstrasse, and to establish the pre-eminence of the Pakenham Mahon family who owned the estate from the 17th century to the 1970s.

In 1979 Westward Motors acquired the estate, conserved the house and contents which had become frozen in the amber of time, and opened it to the public together with a Famine Museum in the former stables. The garden was the final, triumphant phase of restoration, very little was left of the previous Edwardian incarnation but, with the aid of funding from the Great Gardens Restoration Scheme, the garden was reinterpreted with a design by Helen Dillon and Jim Reynolds.

The visit opens with a vista down the garden - seen through decorative gates given to Olive Pakenham as an engagement present in 1914 - to a vista closer folly overlooking a lily pond. Beech hedges were used to create compartments for the different areas of the garden, which include an ABC sculpture walk with appropriate sculptures in leafy niches, a winter garden, a fernery and a winter cutting garden.

A rose garden with cluster flowered reliables like 'Trumpeter 'and' Sexy Rexy' is overlooked by a raised viewing point surrounded by a pergola. Period details like the tennis court and croquet lawn, redolent of the leisured era of the 'big house', have been retained - and the most recent phase of restoration has taken in the vegetable garden and the old glass house, with the additional feature of a Georgian teahouse.

Open daily mid-Mar-end Oct, and for pre-booked groups at other times. Supervised children and dogs on leads welcome; wheelchair friendly. Famine museum; restaurant; house open. Plants for sale. Admission c. €5. **Directions:** *Well signed off N5.*

Ballina Area
COUNTRY HOUSE/ GARDEN

Enniscoe House

Castlehill Crossmolina Ballina Co Mayo
Tel: 096 31112
Email: dj@enniscoe.com Web: www.enniscoe.com

This hospitable Georgian house on the shores of Lough Conn was built by ancestors of the present owner, Susan Kellett, who settled here in the 1660s - and it is a very special place for anglers and other visitors with a natural empathy for the untamed wildness of the area. The house is surrounded by woodlands, where Susan has built an extensive network of paths, and in recent years she has also undertaken major renovations in the gardens, which are part of the Ireland West Garden Trail. The gardens have a long history - having been cared for by several generations of keen gardeners, they fell into decline in the mid 20th century but their star is once more in the ascendant, with one walled garden now authentically restored as an ornamental garden and with many interesting features including a long rockery, while a second now produces organically grown vegetables. Garden plants are offered for sale, and there are tea-rooms opening onto a terrace overlooking the ornamental gardens, also a shop stocking quality "non-tourist" items and collectables And that is far from being the end of the story as converted outbuildings at this remarkable place also offer much of interest, including a genealogy centre (The Mayo North Family History Research Centre, Tel: 096 31809), and a small but expanding rural museum with working blacksmith. The house itself has great charm: with family portraits, antique furniture, crackling log fires, warm hospitality and good home cooking, it makes a lovely place to come back to after a day in the rugged countryside. The traditionally furnished bedrooms are large, very comfortable and, like their en-suite bathrooms, regularly refurbished; spacious reception rooms include a fine drawing room, with a big log fire and plenty of seating, and a more intimate dining room which makes a fine setting for Susan's wholesome 5-course dinners, which make predictably good use of local produce. The gardens are open at all times for residents (without charge), otherwise by appointment. Brown trout fishing on Lough Conn and other trout and salmon fishing nearby; boats, ghillies, tuition and hire of equipment can be arranged. Golf and equestrian nearby. Children welcome; dogs allowed by arrangement. **Rooms 6** (all en-suite, 2 no smoking), B&B about €88 pps, ss c. €12.D daily, 7.30-8.30pm; D, c. €45; non-residents welcome by reservation. Self-catering units also available. Gardens open Apr-Sep by appointment. House closed Nov-early Apr. MasterCard, Visa, Laser. **Directions:** 2 miles south of Crossmolina, on R315.

Cong
HOTEL / RESTAURANT / GARDEN

Ashford Castle
Cong Co Mayo
Tel: 094 954 6003 Fax: 094 954 6260
Email: ashford@ashford.ie Web: www.ashford.ie

Ireland's grandest castle hotel, with a history going back to the early 13th century, Ashford Castle is set in 350 acres of parkland, and anyone who loves beautiful surroundings will be thrilled to stay here - or even simply call in for a meal, or visit the extensive gardens and grounds. Grandeur, formality and tranquillity are the essential characteristics, first seen in the approach through well manicured lawns, in the entrance and formal gardens and, once inside, in a succession of impressive public rooms that illustrate a long and proud history – panelled walls, oil paintings, balustrades, suits of armour and magnificent fireplaces. Accommodation varies considerably due to the size and age of the building, and each room in some way reflects the special qualities of the hotel; the most luxurious are at the top of the castle - many with magnificent views of Lough Corrib, the River Cong and wooded parkland. The hotel's exceptional amenities and sports facilities are detailed in a very handy little pocket book; in it you'll find everything you need to know about the equestrian centre, falconry, hunting, clay target shooting, archery, cycling, pony & trap tours, golf (resident instructor & equipment hire), tennis, lake & river fishing, lake cruising, jogging, guided walking & cycling tours on the estate - and a guide to scenic routes and attractions in Mayo and Galway; for any visitor to the area, this little book is a gem. When dining at the castle, there is a choice between **The Connaught Room** - an exquisite small dining room which is normally reserved for residents - and the much larger **George V Dining Room**. The acclaimed executive head chef, Stefan Matz, oversees the cooking for both restaurants; the house style is broadly classical French, using the best of local ingredients – Atlantic prawns, Galway Bay sole, Cleggan lobster, Connemara lamb, and speciality produce like James McGeough's wonderful cured Connemara lamb (dried lamb), from Oughterard - in sophisticated dishes that will please the most discerning diner.Irish farmhouse cheeses and warm soufflés are among the tempting endings for luxurious meals which are invariably enhanced by meticulous attention to detail. Service, as elsewhere in this legendary hotel, is discreet and extremely professional. **Rooms 83** (6 suites, 5 junior suites, 32 executive, some no smoking). Lift. 24 hour room service. Room rate about €420 (max 2 guests). **Connaught Room Seats 20**. D only, 7-9 daily. **Seats 130**. L daily 12.30-2, D daily 7-9.30. Set L c.€36, Set D c.€80 A la carte D also available. SC15%. *All meals in the castle are by reservation, but Afternoon Tea is served at The Cottage, for day visitors to the grounds. Amex, Diners, MasterCard, Visa, Laser. **Directions:** 30 miles north of Galway, on Lough Corrib

Newport
COUNTRY HOUSE / RESTAURANT

Newport House
Newport Co Mayo
Tel: 098 41222

Email: info@newporthouse.ie Web: www.newporthouse.ie

For two hundred years this distinctively creeper-clad Georgian House overlooking the river and quay, was the home of the O'Donnells, once the Earls of Tir Connell. Today it is one of Ireland's best-loved Irish country houses, and has been especially close to the hearts of fishing people for many years. The day's catch is weighed and displayed in the hall - and the fisherman's bar provides the perfect venue for a reconstruction of the day's sport; but, in the caring hands of the current owners, Kieran and Thelma Thompson, and their outstanding staff, the warm hospitality of this wonderful house is accessible to all its guests – not least in shared enjoyment of the club-fender cosiness of that little back bar. There is a beautiful central hall, sweeping staircase and gracious drawing room, and bedrooms which, like the rest of the house, are furnished in style with antiques and fine paintings. And those who relish the pleasures of really good food and fine wines, will find that the lovely elegant, high-ceilinged dining room makes the perfect backdrop for chef John Gavin's "cooking which reflects the hospitable nature of the house" in fine meals made with home-produced and local foods; home smoked salmon is a speciality and fruit, vegetables and herbs come from a walled kitchen garden that has been worked since 1720 and was established before the house was built, so that fresh produce would be on stream for the owners when they moved in - and, predating the current fashion by several centuries, pure spring water has always been piped into the house for drinking and ice-making. And then there is Kieran's renowned wine list that, for many, adds an extra magic to a meal at Newport: the foundations of this cellar go back many decades to a time when Kieran was himself a guest here; great wines are a passion for him and, while acknowledging that they are irreplaceable, he offers them to guests at far less than their current retail value. **Rooms 18** [2 with private bathrooms (non connecting), 2 with bath & separate shower, 4 ground floor, 1 disabled]. Children welcome. Limited wheelchair access. Pets allowed in some areas. B&B c.€120 , ss €26, no S.C. **Restaurant: Seats 38**. D daily 7-9; Set D c. €59. Toilets wheelchair accessible. Non-residents welcome by reservation. Closed early Oct-mid Mar. Amex, Diners, MasterCard, Visa. **Directions:** In village of Newport.

North West

Ballymote
COUNTRY HOUSE/ ACCOMMODATION

Temple House
Ballymote Co Sligo **Tel: 071 918 3329**
Email: stay@templehouse.ie Web: www.templehouse.ie

One of Ireland's most unspoilt old houses, this is a unique place – a Georgian mansion situated in 1,000 acres of farm and woodland, overlooking the original lakeside castle which was built by the Knights Templar in 1200 A.D. The Percevals have lived here since 1665 and the house was redesigned and refurbished in 1864 – some of the furnishings date back to that major revamp. Roderick and Helena Perceval have now taken over from Roderick's parents, Sandy and Deb but, although there are ongoing improvements, there are no major changes envisaged. The whole of the house has retained its old atmosphere and, in addition to central heating, has log fires to cheer the enormous rooms. Spacious bedrooms are furnished with old family furniture (some also have some modern additions) and bathrooms are gradually being upgraded - not an easy task in a house of this age, but a high pressure water system has now been installed in most of them. Guests have the use of an elegant sitting room with open fires, and evening meals based on produce from the estate and other local suppliers are served (every day except Sunday or Wednesday) in the very beautiful dining room - followed by coffee with home-made fudge in the Morning Room. There is plenty for guests to explore on site, with miles of woodland walks, a lake (with rowing boat - guests may fish for pike), walled gardens (which supply seasonal produce for the kitchen), and formal terraced gardens to stroll around. And a visit to historic **Lissadell House and Gardens** (www.lissadellhouse.com; Tel 071 916350), north of Rosses Point at Ballinfull, would make a great day out; the former home of Countess Marcievicz is now in private ownership and the gardens - including a once-famous alpine garden, and a walled Victorian kitchen garden - are now under restoration and open by appointment. Children welcome. No pets in the house. **Rooms 6** (5 en-suite, 3 shower only, 1 with private bathroom). B&B c.€75pps, ss €25. Residents D about €40, 7.30pm (book by 1pm); licensed. No D Sun or Wed. Closed Feb & Mar. MasterCard, Visa, Laser. **Directions:** Signposted on N17, 7 miles south of N4 junction.

Riverstown
COUNTRY HOUSE

Coopershill House
Riverstown Co Sligo
Tel: 071 916 5108 Fax: 071 916 5466
Email: ohara@coopershill.com Web: www.coopershill.com

Home of the O'Hara family since it was built in 1774, this is one of the most delightful and superbly comfortable Georgian houses in Ireland - a lovely, restful destination for garden lovers, it is at the centre of a 500 acre estate and well placed for exploring this unspoilt area - including historic Lissadell House & Garden (www.lissadellhouse.com; Tel: 071 916350) near Rosses Point, which is within easy range. Peacocks wander elegantly on the croquet lawns (and roost in the splendid trees around the house at night), luxurious rooms are wonderfully comfortable and have phones and tea/coffee making facilities, and the house not only has the original 18th century furniture but also some fascinating features – notably an unusual Victorian free-standing rolltop bath complete with fully integrated cast-iron shower 'cubicle' and original brass rail and fittings, all in full working order. Lindy runs the house and kitchen with the seamless hospitality born of long experience, and creates deliciously wholesome, country house home cooking which is served in their lovely dining room (where the family silver is used with magnificent insouciance – even at breakfast); a neatly maintained vegetable garden supplies the kitchen - and home-reared venison with red wine is a house speciality. A surprisingly extensive wine list offers no less than six house wines - and has many treats in store. Tennis, cycling, fishing, croquet, snooker room. Dogs allowed outside. Children welcome. **Rooms 8** (7 en-suite, 1 with private bathroom, 1 shower only). B&B c. €111pps, ss €19. D daily at 8.30, c. €55 (non residents welcome by reservation). Licensed. Closed end Oct-early April, except for house parties (12-16). Amex, Diners, MasterCard, Visa, Laser. **Directions:** Signposted from N4 at Drumfin crossroads.

Ardara
B&B

The Green Gate
Ardvally Ardara Co Donegal
Tel: 074 954 1546
Web: www.thegreengate-ireland.com

Paul Chatenoud's amazing little B&B is a one-off. Above Adara, up a steep and twisting boreen (follow his unique signing system) that will reward you with a stunning view on arrival, Paul offers simple but comfortable accommodation in his unspoilt traditional cottage and converted outbuildings. It's a far cry from the Parisian bookshop he once ran, but this romantic little place is magic. In the morning (or whenever you wake up - he will be working around his lovely garden and is happy to stop at any time it suits his guests), he cooks up breakfast while you take in the laid-back homeliness of the cosy cottage sitting room. If the morning is fine he may serve breakfast in the garden (just where is that beautiful music coming from?) while he regales you with stories of famous people who have fallen in love with The Green Gate. Be glad you found it, because he's probably right - it may well be "the most beautiful place anywhere in Ireland"; just leave the Merc at home - and come with an open mind. If a return to nature is what you long for, this is the place for it - the perfect anti-dote for perpetually pampered people. **Rooms 4** (all with en-suite bathrooms - full bath). B&B c. €35 pps, ss€10.Open all year. **No Credit Cards. Directions:** One mile from Aradra, on the hill.

Ardara
COUNTRY HOUSE / RESTAURANT

Woodhill House
Ardara Co Donegal
Tel: 074 954 1112 Fax: 074 954 1516
Email: yates@iol.ie Web: www.woodhillhouse.com

Formerly the home of Ireland's last commercial whaling family, John and Nancy Yates' large country house is set in its own grounds overlooking the Donegal Highlands, and the hard restoration work they have put in over more than fifteen years is now bearing fruit. This hospitable house has a full bar and offers accommodation in the main house and nearby converted outbuildings - rooms are all en-suite, but vary greatly in position, size and character so it is worth spending a few minutes discussing your preferences when booking. There's also a restaurant (booking recommended as it's very popular locally) offering quite traditional food based on local ingredients (wild salmon, Donegal mountain lamb), at reasonable prices. While not exactly close by, visits to the premier Donegal gardens could easily be built into a tour and garden lovers will in any case find this a congenial place to stay, as the gradual restoration of the gardens (including a walled kitchen garden) is perhaps Nancy's greatest challenge and it's turning out beautifully, not only on the kitchen garden side but as a pleasure garden too. Renovations, on both the main house and some fine outbuildings, continue on an on-going basis; additional rooms, overlooking the garden, have recently been added, to be followed by some with wheel-chair accessibility. Children welcome. Pets permitted in some areas. **Rooms 9** (6 shower-only). B&B c. €55 pps, ss €25. **Restaurant: Seats 40** (private room, 15). Reservations required. D 7-10 daily, Set D c.€38. Bar open normal hours (no food). Restaurant closed Nov-Mar (except New Year); house closed only 20-27 Dec. Amex, Diners, MasterCard, Visa, Laser. **Directions:** Quarter mile from Ardara village.

Bruckless
COUNTRY HOUSE

Bruckless House

Bruckless Co Donegal **Tel: 074 973 7071**
Email: bruc@iol.ie Web: www.iol.ie/~bruc/bruckless.html

Cliff and Joan Evans' lovely 18th-century house and Connemara pony stud farm is set in 18 acres of woodland and gardens overlooking Bruckless Bay. This serene place is ideal for people who enjoy quiet countryside, and is convenient for visiting Salthill Walled Garden at Mountcharles. It is a delightful place to stay - the gardens are not too formal, but beautifully designed, extensive and well-maintained - they really enhance a visit here, as does the waterside location: guests have direct access to the fore-shore at the bottom of the garden. Family furniture collected through a Hong Kong connection adds an unexpected dimension to elegant reception rooms that have views over the front lawns towards the sea, and the generous, comfortably furnished bedrooms. Accommodation includes two single rooms and there is a shared bathroom - although the house is large, the guest bedrooms are close together, so they are ideal for a family or a group travelling together. Enjoy home-produced eggs at breakfast, which is the only meal served - guests are directed to local restaurants in the evening. Self-catering accommodation is also available all year, in a two-bedroomed gatelodge. **Rooms 4** (2 en suite, all no smoking). B&B c.€60pps, no ss.Weekly rates also offered; sc acc available. Closed Oct-Mar. Amex, MasterCard, Visa. **Directions:** On N56, 12 miles west of Donegal town.

Laghey
COUNTRY HOUSE

Coxtown Manor

Laghey Co Donegal
Tel: 074 973 4575 Fax: 074 973 4576
Email: coxtownmanor@oddpost.com Web: www.coxtownmanor.com

Just a short drive from the county town, this welcoming late Georgian house set in its own parkland is in a lovely, peaceful area close to Donegal Bay with many interesting visits nearby. Belgian proprietor, Edward Dewael - who fell for the property some years ago and is still in the process of upgrading it - personally ensures that everything possible is done to make guests feel at home. A wood-panelled bar with an open fire is well-stocked, notably with Belgian beers and a great selection of digestifs to accompany your after dinner coffee - and it opens into a very pleasant drawing room. Accommodation includes five very large new bedrooms with excellent bathrooms and plenty of room for luggage in a recently converted coach house at the back of the house - yet many guests still prefer the older ones for their character; while not perhaps as luxurious, they are large, comfortable and well-proportioned, and some have countryside views and open fireplaces. But the heart of the house is the elegant and well-appointed period dining room, which is - like the food served here - attractive yet not too formal. Dining is mainly for residents, and menus offer a wide choice of mostly classic dishes with an emphasis on carefully sourced ingredients, notably seafood (scallops from Donegal Bay, clams and mussels from Lissadell, for example), also Thornhill duck and local Charolais beef - a sound foundation for proficient cooking. Breakfast is sure to be a treat too, and will include Fermanagh dry-cured bacon and freshly-laid eggs from Edward's free-range flock of chickens in the field behind the house. Staff are warmly professional, and Coxtown provides a highly enjoyable experience all round. Children welcome. Walking; garden. Pets allowed in some areas. **Rooms 10** (2 junior suites, 9 en-suite, 1 shower only, 1 with private bathroom). B&B c. €99 pps, ss €20. Restaurant (open to non-residents by reservation if there is room): **Seats 25.** D Tue-Sat, c.€46, closed Sun & Mon. Licensed. House closed early Nov-mid Feb. Amex, MasterCard, Visa, Laser. **Directions:** Main sign on N15 between Ballyshannon & Donegal Town.

Letterkenny
HOTEL / RESTAURANT

Castle Grove Country House Hotel
Letterkenny Co Donegal
Tel: 074 915 1118 Fax: 074 915 1118
Email: reservation@castlegrove.com Web: www.castlegrove.com

Parkland designed by "Capability" Brown in the mid 18th-century creates a wonderful setting for Raymond and Mary Sweeney's lovely period house overlooking Lough Swilly; it is, as Mary Sweeney says, 'an oasis of tranquillity', and would make a very comfortable and relaxing destination in itself, as well as an ideal base for visiting nearby gardens including Glenveagh National Park and Ballydaheen gardens. Constant improvement is the policy and recent changes include a new conservatory and the conversion of an adjoining coach house to make seven lovely bedrooms - all carefully designed and furnished with antiques to feel like part of the main house; the original walled garden is also under restoration as part of an on-going development of the gardens which will continue for several years. Mary Sweeney's personal supervision ensures an exceptionally high standard of maintenance and housekeeping, and bedrooms are spacious and elegantly furnished with antiques; bathrooms are gradually being upgraded, where practical, to provide walk-in showers as well as full bath. Good breakfasts include a choice of fish as well as traditional Irish breakfast, home-made breads and preserves; the restaurant is open for dinner every evening and lunch is available by arrangement. Two boats belonging to the house are available for fishing on Lough Swilly. Not suitable for children under 12. No pets. **Rooms 14** (1 suite, 2 junior suites, 2 shower only, 2 disabled, all no-smoking) B&B about €80 pps, no ss. Open all year except Christmas. Amex, Diners, MasterCard, Visa, Laser. **Directions:** R245 off main road to Letterkenny.

227

COUNTY DONEGAL

Glenveagh Castle Gardens

Glenveagh National Park Churchill Nr. **Letterkenny** Co Donegal
Tel: 074 913 7391
Email: glenveagh@duchas.ie

GARDEN

Elaborate series of gardens with tender specimens in a wilderness setting.

The more improbable the location the more exotic a garden seems, like some silken tent pitched in a savage wilderness. There could hardly be more Gothic setting for Glenveagh Castle than the wild vastness of Lough Veagh. The isolated ice age valley is set in 25,000 acres of bare mountain and moorland in a national park, hardly the place you expect to find Chusan palms and tree ferns.

Formerly owned by evicting landlord John Adair, his benevolent American widow Cornelia began to lay out the grounds and plant the gardens after his death in 1885.

After a chequered period when it was occupied by both sides in the Civil War, and owned by a Harvard Professor Kingsley Porter who disappeared mysteriously on Inisbofin Island, Glenveagh was blessed in the ownership of American gas meter heir Henry McIlhenny. A connoisseur and legendary host who

entertained celebrities like Greta Garbo and Grace Kelly at the castle, McIlhenny was also a passionate gardener.

He engaged garden designers Lanning Roper and Jim Russell and, between 1947 and 1983, vistas, stonework statuary and a whole series of interlocking gardens were added to the grounds.

Cars are left behind at the interpretative centre and an eco friendly bus carries passengers along a winding road beside the lake to McIlhenny's dreamlike creation. Behind the castle lies an ornamental potager, with a traditional herbaceous border running through the centre, ranks of vegetables contained by neat box hedges, a dolphin fountain and a Gothic orangerie designed by Philippe Julien. Beside the house there is a small Italian garden, its classical busts and clipped formality in complete contrast to the exotic profusion of the Pleasure Ground, with its swirling masses of damp loving hostas,

astilbes and rodgersia, and exotic shrubs like *Michelia doltsopa* and *R cinnabarinum*. Changes of style and vistas of the dramatic landscape delight the senses. There is a formal flagged terrace known as the Belgian Walk, lined with huge terra cotta pots of azaleas, a dramatic flight of 67 steps climbing the hillside between *R cilliatum*, a hidden rose garden, a Viewing Garden, a Swiss walk through magnificent rhododendrons, and a Himalayan garden - all waiting to be discovered. Throughout the grounds there are all kinds of unusual and

tender specimens, *Eucryphia moorei*, *Styrax japonica* the katsura tree, stately large-leaved rhododendrons like *R falconeri* and *R sinogrande*, and Japanese *Trochodendron aralioides*.

In 1983 Henry McIlhenny gave the castle and gardens to the nation and it is now cared for by the Heritage Service of the Office of Public Works.

Open daily Feb-Nov, 10-6.30. Children welcome; no dogs; partial wheelchair access; restaurant; interpretative centre. Castle also open. (Tea Rooms at the Castle specialise in good home baking).
Directions: *12km from Churchill, on the R251.*

COUNTY DONEGAL

Salthill Walled Garden

Salthill **Mount Charles** Co Donegal
Tel: 074 973 5387
Email: etemple@eircom.net Web: www.donegalgardens.com

GARDEN

New garden with lawns and herbaceous perennials in an old walled garden setting.

When Elizabeth Temple started to reclaim a 200 year old walled garden, she did the logical thing and started gardening near the door. Nothing remained in the walled acre except a greenhouse and some paths, and a new garden - rather than a restored one - evolved.

Now vegetables are grown traditional Donegal style in 12 foot wide ridges around the walls, with the decorative plants in the centre. Planting is designed to give a season long display - starting with daffodils and other spring bulbs, and running through hard working plants like thalictrums, hardy geraniums, lichnis, agapanthus, cardoons, and phlox - and crocosmia wreathe a circular lawn. Old fashioned roses are a feature of the garden and include the single white *R mulliganii*, **'Sanders White Rambler'**, **'Veilchenblau'** and the golden rambler **'Alistair Stella Grey'**. Shrub and mixed borders make up the rest of the design, with hydrangeas blushing in the acid soil, eucryphias and *Viburnum bodnatense* **'Dawn'**.

An unusual feature is a beech room sheltering Zantadeschias and white crinum lilies, and a potting shed adds a picturesque touch. Salthill is gardened organically and Elizabeth finds that feeding roses really well is the best protection against pests. The walled garden creates a microclimate, and gives protection against the winds once used to dry the salt which gives the townland its name.

Open late Apr-early Sep, Mon-Thu, 2-6 also Sat May-June; otherwise groups by arrangement. Supervised children and wheelchairs welcome. No dogs. Occasional plant sales. Admission, c. €5.
Directions: *Take N56 Donegal Town-Mount Charles; continue on bypass until reaching red and white Toyota garage. Turn left; go through two crossroads, then 0.9 miles down hill. Garden is on the left.*

Ballydaheen

Portsalon Letterkenny Co Donegal
Tel: 074 915 9091
Email: mnd8733@eircom.net

GARDEN

A six acre cliff top garden with strong Japanese influence.

The bare windswept cliffs on the western shore of Lough Swilly are the last place that you might expect to find an exotic garden. But thanks to the benign Gulf Stream, a micro climate and shelter belts around the site, Ballydaheen can lay claim too being the most northerly open garden in Ireland.

Twenty years ago only the ruins of a hill farm stood near the path to the geological attraction known as the Seven Arches, where the sea has carved out a series of caverns from the pre-Cambrian quartzite at the foot of the cliffs. David and Mary Hurley began by planting pines and native trees around their new home as protection against salt laden gales. Within their shelter are a series of gardens, the most dramatic being the Japanesey garden laid out around a pool edged with rocks, dwarf conifers and foliage plants with an island complete with a traditional stone snow viewing lantern.

Everything is trim perfection in the meandering layout of paths that lead through a stream garden crossed by a vermilion bridge, and on to a rose garden, laburnum and rhododendron walks, and a vegetable garden. It is the contrast between the manicured grounds and the wild sea and cliffs that make the garden so exhilarating. This six acre garden continues to evolve, special additions include an oriental folly with panoramic views across the Lough. It is also a thoroughly inspiring seaside garden showing just how much can be grown - including tender plants like tree ferns and Australasian species - once shelter has been established.

*Open mid-April to mid May & late May to late Aug, Mon-Sat 10-7; otherwise by appointment. Supervised children welcome; not suitable for wheelchairs. No dogs Admission c. €5. **Directions:** From Portsalon, take the road past the golf club - the garden is just over a mile further on.*

Rathmullan
COUNTRY HOUSE / RESTAURANT / GARDEN

Rathmullan House
Rathmullan Co Donegal
Tel: 074 915 8188
Email: info@rathmullanhouse.com Web: www.rathmullanhouse.com

Set in lovely gardens on the shores of Lough Swilly, this gracious early nineteenth century house is fairly grand with public areas which include three elegant drawing rooms, but it's not too formal - and there's a relaxed cellar bar with a separate entrance, where informal meals are served. Built as a summer house by the Batt banking family of Belfast in the 1800s and run as a country house hotel since 1961 by the Wheeler family, it makes a pleasant base for visiting gardens in the area (Ballydaheen, Glenveagh Castle, Glebe House at Churchill) and the gardens here - which include a productive walled garden - are open to the public all year except Jan/early Feb. A sympathetically designed extension has recently been completed, offering ten very desirable, individually decorated new bedrooms - those in the original house vary in

size, decor, outlook and cost, but all are comfortably furnished in traditional country house style. **The Weeping Elm Restaurant** - famous for its tented ceiling, originally designed by the late Liam McCormick, known for his striking Donegal churches - specialises in using local produce, organic when possible. Cooking here is upbeat traditional and carefully-sourced menus offer a wide choice - including specialities like Fanad Head crab plate, loin of Rathmullan lamb with cauliflower purée and rosemary jus and, perhaps, a compôte of garden fruits with carrageen pudding. The carrageen is equally at home at breakfast too - each morning a tremendous buffet is laid out, offering a huge variety of juices, fruits, cooked ham, smoked salmon and farmhouse cheeses, home-bakes and preserves - plus a menu of hot dishes, cooked to order. Donegal has an other-worldliness that is increasingly hard to capture today and Rathmullan House is remarkable for its laid-back charm and special sense of place. Swimming pool, steam room, tennis. Children welcome. Pets permitted by

arrangement. **Rooms 32** (19 with separate bath & shower, 9 ground floor, 2 for disabled). B&B c.€110 pps, ss €45. **Meals: Weeping Elm Restaurant** D daily; **Cellar Bar:** L & D (daily in Jul-Aug), **Batts Bar** (L daily, all year, also D for residents only). Amex, MasterCard, Visa, Laser. **Directions:** Letterkenny-Ramelton - turn right to Rathmullan at the bridge; through Rathmullan village, turn tight to hotel.

North

The Brown Trout

Coleraine Area
ACCOMMODATION

209 Aghadowey Road Co Londonderry BT51 4AD
Tel: 028 7086 8209
Email: jave@browntroutinn.com Web: www.browntroutinn.com

Golf is one of the major attractions at this lively family-run country inn, but it's a pleasant and hospitable place for anyone to stay - all will soon find friends in the convivial bar, where food is served every day - and outside in a pleasant barbecue too, in fine weather. Accommodation is not especially luxurious, but very comfortable, in good-sized en-suite rooms which are all on the ground floor, arranged around the main courtyard, and have plenty of space for gear. New cottage suites overlooking the golf course (just 100 yards from the main building) are the first of this standard to be completed in Northern Ireland. There's also an evening restaurant up a steep staircase (with chair lift for the less able), overlooking the garden end of the golf course. A dedicated kitchen team produces good home cooking with local fresh ingredients for daytime food (soups, freshly made sandwiches and open sandwiches, baked potatoes, pasta) and evening meals like hot garlic Aghadowey mushrooms or ribeye steak with a Bushmills whiskey sauce. **Rooms 15** (1 disabled, most wheelchair friendly); B&B c. £45 pps, ss £15. Bar meals 12-9 daily (to 10 in summer); Restaurant daily, from 5pm. A la carte. Open all year. Axex, Diners, MasterCard, Visa, Switch. **Directions:** Intersection of A54/B66, 7 miles south of Coleraine.

Greenhill House

Coleraine Area
FARMHOUSE

24 Greenhill Road Coleraine Co Londonderry
Tel: 028 7086 8251
Email: greenhill.house@btinternet.co.uk Web: www.greenhill-house.co.uk

Framed by trees and with lovely country views, the Hegarty family's Georgian farmhouse is at the centre of a large working farm. In true Northern tradition, Elizabeth Hegarty is a great baker and greets guests in the drawing room with an afternoon tea which includes a vast array of home-made teabreads, cakes and biscuits - and home baking is also a highlight of wonderful breakfasts that are based on tasty local produce like bacon, sausages, mushrooms, free range eggs, smoked salmon, strawberries and preserves. There are two large family rooms and, although not luxurious, the thoughtfulness that has gone into

furnishing bedrooms makes them exceptionally comfortable – everything is in just the right place to be convenient - and Elizabeth is constantly maintaining and improving the decor and facilities. Bedrooms now have direct dial telephones, and little touches - like fresh flowers, a fruit basket, After Eights, tea & coffee making facilities, hair dryer, bathrobe, good quality clothes hangers and even a torch - are way above the standard expected of farmhouse accommodation. There's also internet access, a safe, fax machine, iron and trouser press available for guests' use on request. Guests have been welcomed to Greenhill House since 1980 and, wonderfully comforting and hospitable as it is, Elizabeth constantly seeks ways of improvement, big and small: this lovely house and the way it is run demonstrate rural Irish hospitality at its best. *There are plans to convert some of the outhouses, for self-catering accommodation.

23 Mountsandel Road

23 Mountsandel Road **Coleraine** Co Londonderry
Tel: 028 7963 2180

GARDEN

Informal garden with trees, shrubs, old roses, pond and vegetable garden.

After a working lifetime of expertise in the usefulness of bugs it is hardly surprising that Professor Emeritus of Biology, Amyan MacFadyn, has an organic approach. His garden on the heavy clay soil on the banks of the River Bann is a testament to the efficacy of biodiversity (there are masses of frogs and birds to control pests like aphids), and to natural approaches like the use of green manure (comfrey and pink flowered buck wheat.)

This is an informal garden, with lush green lawns and a bog garden awash with primulas, bulbs and roses scrambling up the sheltering trees where the Bann floods occasionally. Higher up, gravel paths wind around beds full of treasures: dioramas, eryngium, choice crocosmias and a productive vegetable garden. MacFadyn's particular love is old roses - especially Noisettes apricot **'Desprez à Fleur Jaune'**, **'Madame Alfred Carrier'** and **'Blush Noisette'** and Bourbons **'Boule de Neige'**, **'Zépherine Drouhin'**, **'Madame Isaac Perrier'** - and he knows their habits (**'Madame Pierre Oger'** is particularly susceptible to black spot). The steep rocky upper part of the garden is curtained in climbing rambling roses, and in autumn roses like *R moyesii* offer a spectacular display of hips.

The Professor is a fund of knowledge about all manner of things: the way parasitic wasps control cabbage white butterflies, for example, and how the *Berberidopsis* growing in his garden provides an economic lifeline for the Chilean rainforest natives who weave baskets from its stems. Their way of life is now under threat by a Japanese multi-nationals intent on buying up the forest for paper production. The odd weed should be disregarded in the face of such wisdom.

Open by appontment, May – Sep. Supervised children; no dogs; not suitable for wheelchairs; plants for sale. **Directions:** *Just across the river from the Court House.*

Blackhill House

5 Crevolea Road Blackhill Nr. **Coleraine** Co Londonderry
Tel: 028 7086 8377

GARDEN

Compartmentalised garden, strong on structure and planting.

In a gardening world in love with cool blues and iced pinks, Mrs Rae McIntyre has a refreshing taste for the hot stuff of the plant world. True to form, her very first successful cutting from which she caught the gardening bug was her favourite scarlet and orange flowered Chilean holly *Desfontania spinosa*. In colour keyed planting schemes, the zingy orange of tiger lilies, apricot hemerocallis, sizzling *Crocosmia* **'Spit Fire'** and red hot pokers blaze around a rectangle of lawn in the largest of a series of compartmentalised gardens. Here a pool surrounded by a collection of iris is the first eye catcher before visitors are drawn around a rectangle of path between shrub and herbaceous borders.

Dwarf species and hybrid rhododendrons - their foliage every bit as fascinating as their blooms - ferns, meconopsis, acers like autumn scarlet *A* **'Osakazuki'** and old roses feature strongly. Exciting things happen, as they do - a stewartia with its golden stamens flowered for the first time in 2004, in August the eucryphias are abuzz with bees, and the display of rhododendrons starts from February onwards. Within the beautifully planted scheme of things, there is a scented winter garden, a peaceful white garden with raised beds around a long pool and an essential seat for contemplation, and a gravelled garden in the former stack yard. After 17 loads of stones were removed, it became a place to grow lavenders, for a yellow and grey border, and for a bed of willows like *Pterocarya fraxinifolia*.

Open all year to groups of less than 10, by appointment. Not suitable for children; partial wheelchair access; no dogs. Admission c. £2.50. **Directions:** *Off the main A29 Coleraine to Garvagh road, 6 miles from Coleraine. House is first on left.*

stock image

Feeney
COUNTRY HOUSE

Drumcovitt

704 Feeney Road Feeney Co Londonderry BT47 4SU
Tel: 028 7778 1224
Email: drumcovitt.feeny@btinternet.com Web: www.drumcovitt.com

Drumcovitt is an intriguing house with an impressive Georgian front dating from 1796 - and, behind it a much older farmhouse, built about 1680. It is a listed building and many of the windows and wonderful interior features have been retained but, however interesting its history, today's creature comforts are very much in evidence - central heating extends throughout the house and an adjacent converted barn, and there are big log fires to relax beside while enjoying a fine collection of books, or making a jigsaw. Well-maintained gardens and grounds surround the house, which is convenient to a number of gardens - and this unspoilt area is also perfect for walking, bird-watching, visiting archaeological sites in the Sperrins and much else besides: golf, the Giants Causeway, Bushmills, Derry city and much of Donegal are within easy striking distance. All three guest rooms in the house are spacious and comfortably furnished although, in true country house fashion, bathrooms are not en-suite: two good modern showers (one overbath) are shared by the three rooms. The Sloan family are solicitous but relaxed hosts, who enjoy sharing their unique home and the area around it with guests; Chris Sloan and his partner Sarah Wallis look after the day to day running of the house, but Chris's mother, Florence, is still involved and cooks for guests. This is a delightful place, but not one to rush through so allow more than one night if you can. Fax, safe and ironing facilities available for guests' use. **Rooms 3** (two with double & single beds, 1 twin, all with phone, tv, tea & coffee trays) Children welcome. B&B c. £30, no ss. D by arrangement. Self catering also available. Open all year except Christmas. Amex, Diners, MasterCard, Visa, Switch. **Directions:** Half a mile east of Feeney village, on B74 off A6.

Londonderry
HOTEL / RESTAURANT

Beech Hill Country House Hotel
32 Ardmore Road Londonderry Co Londonderry
Tel: 028 7134 9279 Fax: 028 7134 5366
Email: info@beech-hill.com Web: www.beech-hill.com

Just south of Londonderry, surrounded by peaceful woodland, waterfalls and gardens, this pleasing house dates from 1729 and retains many of its original details; it will be of special interest to American guests as the US Marines had their headquarters here in World War II and there is an informative small museum of the US Marine Friendship Association in the hotel. Proprietor Patsy O'Kane is an hospitable and caring hostess and her ever-growing collection of antiques adds character to guest accommodation and public areas alike, including a traditional bar and a fine dining restaurant, which is in the former snooker room, now extended into a conservatory overlooking the gardens. Good food has always been a priority at Beech Hill and the restaurant, which is elegantly appointed in traditional style, is a particularly attractive feature; although there are sometimes changes in the kitchen, there is a tradition of using local ingredients to advantage in updated classical French cuisine, which has earned a following - and the wine list

offers a number of famous New World wines with Northern Ireland connections. Beech Hill is well placed for visiting gardens in Londonderry and north Antrim, and the Magilligan Lough Foyle car ferry allows easy access to the Inishowen Pensinsula in County Donegal - and, of course, there is Derry city to explore. Tennis, fitness suite; golf, equestrian, fishing nearby Children welcome. Pets allowed by arrangement. **Rooms 27** (2 suites, 3 junior suites, 10 executive rooms,). B&B about £60pps, ss about £10. SC discretionary. Lift. Open all year except Christmas. **Ardmore Restaurant: Seats 100.** L, c. £18 & D, c.£28 daily. Children welcome. Toilets wheelchair accessible. Reservations advised. Amex, MasterCard, Visa, Switch. **Directions:** Off main Londonderry road, A6.

28 Killyfaddy Road

28 Killyfaddy Road **Magherafelt** Co Londonderry
Tel: 028 7963 2180

GARDEN

Cottage style garden on 1 acre with a vibrant collection of herbaceous plants.

When Mrs Buchanan first started gardening, 32 years ago, she and her husband split the garden between them. Somehow over the years her flowers have overflowed into his vegetable patch and, in the way that gardens do, theirs just grew - taking in a piece of field with gorgeous view of the Sperrins known as the Sunset Strip, plus an extra half acre across the road.

The end result is an appealing cottage garden where grass paths swirl between beds bursting with delectable plants. You never quite know what is going to be round the next corner, perfumed drifts of pink, white and mauve phlox with splashes of *Helianthus* **'Lemon Queen'**, curiosities like a variegated embothrium, a lurking savage beast, or blue tear drop shapes of *Pratea pendunculata* spared by the lawn mower.

Only two rules applied in the making of the garden, there were no straight lines and Mrs Buchanan grew everything she could gets her hands on from seed, mail order and cuttings with such success that she now sells irresistible herbaceous plants propagated from the garden. Some species are special favourites: Salvias like *S. involucrata*, and **'Scarlet King'**, hellebores, lilies, Siberica iris and primulas. "The plants are in charge here", says Mrs Buchanan. There are lots of things to be learned from her garden - how to grow mistletoe, why *Verbena corymbosa* is much more obliging than her fashionable cousin *bonariensis*. There are new features – a pond with bog garden or a woodland area and unusual plants like *Picea abies* **'Nidiformis'** with its tutu skirts, willow gentians, snakes head fritillaries, a cut leaved beech, dangerous but exotic Loasa or turtle headed *Chelone obliqua* - to be discovered at every turn.

Open all year by appointment, under the Ulster Gardens Scheme. Children welcome; not suitable for wheelchairs; no dogs. Teas by arrangement. **Directions:** *From centre of Magherafelt, 2nd turn on left on Moneymore Road.*

Upperlands
COUNTRY HOUSE

Ardtara Country House

8 Gorteade Road Upperlands Co Londonderry
Tel: 028 7964 4490 Fax: 028 7964 5080
Email: valerie_ferson@ardtara.com Web: www.ardtara.com

This former home to the Clark linen milling family is now an attractive, elegantly decorated Victorian country house with a genuinely hospitable atmosphere - and it is well placed for visiting gardens in County Antrim as well as Londonderry. Well-proportioned rooms have antique furnishings and fresh flowers, and all the large, luxuriously furnished bedrooms enjoy views of the gardens and surrounding countryside and have king size beds, original fireplaces and TV and DVDs, while bathrooms combine practicality with period details, some including free-standing baths and fireplaces. A pleasant bar overlooks the gardens at the side of the house - a relaxing place to enjoy an aperitif before dinner: good food has always been important at Ardtara and the dining room, which was previously a snooker room and still has the full Victorian skylight and original hunting frieze, makes an unusual setting for fine dining. Head chef, Olivier Boudon, has experience in countries as diverse as China and Poland, so you may expect some unusual influences in the cooking and presentation (including a number of 'gala servings' such as serving caviar on ice), although the main influence is classical French. Breakfast will be another high point, so allow time to enjoy it. Woodland walks. Tennis. Pets allowed by arrangement. **Rooms 8** (3 suites). B&B £75pps, ss £10. **Restaurant: Seats 65** (private room 30); reservations required; non residents welcome. D daily c. £35, L Sun only, c. £20. Licensed. Toilets wheelchair accessible. Open all year. Amex, MasterCard, Visa, Switch. **Directions:** M2 from Belfast ,to A6. A29 to Maghera, then B75 to Kilrea.

Maherintemple

51 Churchfield Road Ballycastle Co Antrim
Tel 028 2076 2234

GARDEN

Old world walled garden with rill, bog garden and great plants.

The hidden worlds of walled gardens have a magic of their own and this one is no exception. Part of the charm is the diverted stream running through a rill round three sides of the garden (with pools and basins for filling watering cans) before falling into a lush bog garden. It's partly the romantic atmosphere of the Victorian garden with bricked lined walls, ripening fruit, paths of river stones velvety with moss and the glimpses of Knocklayd hill through the surrounding trees. But not least is Mrs Casement's love of her choice collection of plants built up and cherished in the light loamy soil over a 30 year period.

The tour begins with a flourish, down an aisle like path between an interesting congregation of plants: salvia patens, agastache, herbaceous clematis, pulsatillas to name but a few. A turn in the path brings a change of mood, a rock garden shelters tender shrubs and plants and slopes down to the basin of the bog garden. Once a pond this is now filled with swathes of primula, astilbes iris, zantadescia and mimulus. Himalayan primulas have colonised beside the rill as it runs around the garden past treasures in the most sheltered corners: crinum lilies, *Buddleja colvelei* grown from a rooted cutting, fiscularia and immaculate beds of asparagus purple beans and other decorative vegetable. A green gothic door leads into a second garden with lawns and a woodland garden. This place was used to grow vegetables for evacuated orphans during the war and had not been kept up for years, so its present incarnation is a wonderful achievement.

Open by appointment, May-Aug. Children welcome; no dogs; partial wheelchair access; plant sales.
Directions: *Turn left off the Glenshesk Road out of Ballycastle, Maherintemple is 1.5 miles on left.*

Ballycastle Area
COUNTRY HOUSE

Whitepark House

150 Whitepark Road Ballintoy Ballycastle Co Antrim
Tel: 028 207 31482
Email: bob@whiteparkhouse.com Web: www.whiteparkhouse.com

A warm welcome from chatty and well-informed hosts Bob and Siobhán Isles awaits visitors to this pretty old house, which enjoys stunning views of Whitepark Bay and is set in lovely, well-maintained gardens - with a path down to the beach just across the road. The three bedrooms have only one bathroom between them but Bob and Siobhán are considering adding en-suite bathrooms along with other necessary changes planned shortly; meanwhile, this is a house of great charm and character, and guests do not find it too difficult to forfeit a little convenience for the pleasure of being here. Bedrooms all have distinctive colour themes and lots of exotic touches to give each its special personality, and there is a lovely feeling of being surrounded by a well-loved garden. There's also a very comfortable and homely sitting room looking onto the garden, with couches, easy chairs and an open fire to relax beside - and, as elsewhere in the house, much to occupy the interested guest. Bob likes to see guests well prepared for the day ahead and, as a vegetarian, he's well placed to make a great vegetarian breakfast in addition to the traditional Ulster Fry. Well placed for visits to many of Antrim's finest gardens, including Benvarden, Magherintemple and 2 Old Galgorm Road, which are all nearby. **Rooms 3** (one bathroom for all; no smoking). B&B from £30 pps, ss£5. 5% surcharge on cc payments. MasterCard, Visa. **Directions:** On Antrim coast road A2, between Giants Causeway and Ballintoy; on east side of Whitepark Bay.

2 Old Galgorm Road

2 Old Galgorm Road **Ballymena** Co Antrim
Tel: 028 2564 1459

GARDEN

Large town garden with herbaceous boder, alpine sinks and water garden.

The gradualist approach has a lot of advantages when taking on a large garden and that is exactly the way the Glynns went about transforming their two and a half acres after they moved into their Victorian home 27 years ago.

Each year they set themselves a new project, uncovering a hidden rockery beside a pond, turning a small walled garden into a raised terrace with a herbaceous border down one side and raised beds on the other. The entrance gate was changed and an area known as The Point planted with dwarf conifers and rhododendrons, including the Glynns' favourite yellow flowered rhododendrons like **'Yellow Crest'** and the dwarf larch *Larix kaempiferi* **'Nana'**.

"In a garden this size I try to get something flowering every day of the year," says Mrs Glynn. The result is a very rewarding garden with subtle changes of mood and an enviable collection of plants. Snowdrops – there are over 200 varieties of snowdrop including autumn flowering *Galanthus regina-olgae* - are among favourites which include witch hazels, alpines cosseted in over 30 troughs, erythroniums and hellebores like *H x* **'Eric Smithii'** planted along the area known as Paddy's Path after the donor of some of the many ferns in this shady area. The bog garden where gunnera, Himalayan primula and cardiocrinum lilies flourish, contrasts with the woodland areas planted with rhododendrons, spring bulbs and *Meconopis* **'Slieve Donard'** and the rockery area graced with *Hydrangea sargentii* and *villosa*.

Open May-Sep by appointment; supervised children pemitted; dogs on leads allowed; not suitable for wheelchairs. Teas by arrangement, c. £2.50. **Directions:** *At the junction of the Old and New Galgorm Roads, on the A42 Ballymena Portglenone Road.*

Benvarden

Ballymoney Co Antrim
Tel: 028 2074 1331
Email: Benvarden@onetel.net.uk Web: www.benvarden.com

GARDEN

Beautifully reinterpreted old walled garden.

Two of the more colourful associations with Benvarden concern a previous owner known as 'Half Hanged McNaughton' and the lions roaring from the far side of the River Bush.

None of this disturbs the serenity of the two acre walled garden there. While the walls are thought to be 300 years old, the garden within them has been beautifully reinterpreted over the last 40 years by Hugh and Valerie Montgomery.

A series of separate areas add up to a memorable whole - who could resist a Blue Moon Garden, or the parterre with box-edged beds filled with lavender laid out around a silver pear? Or fail to walk around the walls covered with espalier fruit trees roses or the climbing hydrangea *H petiolaris* where waves of *Alchemilla mollis* spill over beds bursting with Solomon's seal, hostas, delphiniums, campanulas and primulas?

The particular star in this garden is the sunburst rose garden with hybrid tea roses planted in blocks of colour around an Italianate fountain. Exuberant old fashioned roses fountain over arches down the central gravelled walk and there is a model vegetable garden with a restored bothy. Beyond the walled garden there is a walk via a pond backed by shrubs and on to the river which is spanned by a graceful iron bridge. As for the lions and McNaughton you will have to go to Benvarden to find out more.

Open May by appointment; Jun-Aug, Tue-Sun & bank hols, 11.30-5. Supervised children welcome; suitable for wheelchairs. **Directions:** *From Ballymoney take the Portrush road for Ballybogy; turn right onto B67 for Ballycastle; the entrance is two miles on the right.*

Ballymoney
RESTAURANT WITH ROOMS

Harmony Hill Country House

Balnamore Ballymoney Co Antrim
Tel: 028 2766 3459 Fax: 028 2766 3740
Email: webmaster@harmonyhill.net Web: www.harmonyhill.net

Trish and Richard Wilson's unusual restaurant is peacefully situated in a 5-acre woodland garden, with a mill race bordering and lots of birdlife in the old mill building. The house itself is something of an enigma, single storey, with an interesting and rather grand eighteenth century section - including a beautiful light-filled drawing room, and broad raised verandah outside it - on the left as you go in, and, at the end of a mysterious plant-filled passage towards the back of the house, there is quite a substantial restaurant which, again, divides into two areas of very different character. One section is divided into booths, providing a homely spot for solitary guests dining in the company of a good book, or for times when the restaurant is not busy enough to use all the scrubbed pine tables; the other section is more open, with traditional dining tables, but the whole set-up is very appealing. Open fires play a major part in the life of this house - there's a big fire in the drawing room and one in the restaurant too - the logistics of running so many fires must be quite a challenge, but they give the house great atmosphere. And the menu is also most unusual: instead of simply naming the dishes, they are presented as little recipes, hence 'Soused Trout: Gently poach the freshest trout fillets in white wine vinegar & court bouillon peppered with star anise & pickling spice, chill well then serve with a light salad of mixed leaves, radish and quail's eggs'. Ingenious. Accommodation (predictably unusual) is also offered. **Seats 50.** D Wed-Sat, 6.30-9.30; L Sun only, 12.30-2. Closed Mon-Tue & 25-26 Dec. (B&B c. £36pps). MasterCard, Visa, Switch. **Directions:** Off A26, 1.5 miles outside Ballymoney.

Belfast
GUESTHOUSE

Ravenhill House

690 Ravenhill Road Belfast Co Antrim BT6 0BZ
Tel: 028 9020 7444
Email: info@ravenhillhouse.com Web: www.ravenhillhouse.com

Although it is close to a busy road, the Nicholson family home should appeal to garden lovers wishing to stay in Belfast, as this late Victorian redbrick house has some sense of seclusion, with mature trees, private parking and a quiet tree-lined street alongside. A comfortable ground floor lounge has an open fireplace, a big sofa, lots of books and a PC for guests who want to use the Internet (at a modest charge). Bedrooms, which are a mixture of single, twin and double rooms, are comfortably furnished with style - beds and other furniture have been specially commissioned from an Islandmagee craftsman; all are en-suite, with tea/coffee making facilities and TV. Breakfast is the only meal served (the Nicholsons will direct you to the best choice for dinner, or consult our website www.ireland-guide.com) and it is sure to be the highlight of a visit here: served in a bay-windowed dining room with white-damasked tables, the breakfast buffet is displayed on the sideboard in a collection of Nicholas Mosse serving bowls - a feel for craft objects that is reflected elsewhere in the house. A printed breakfast menu shows a commitment to using local produce of quality and includes a vegetarian cooked breakfast; the Nicholsons source with care and make everything they can on the premises, including marmalade and wheaten bread for breakfasts. All these good things, plus a particularly helpful attitude to guests, make this an excellent, reasonably priced city base. **Rooms 5** (all en-suite, 3 shower only; all no smoking). B&B c. £32.50pps, ss £12.50. Open all year. MasterCard, Visa, Switch. **Directions:** Follow signs for A24 to Newcastle. 2 miles from city centre, located on corner of Ravenhill Road and Rosetta Park, close to the junction with Ormeau Road (A24).

Glenmount

34 Dunleady Road Dundonald **Belfast** Co Antrim
Tel: 028 9048 6324

GARDEN

A child friendly hillside garden with mixed planting of shrubs herbaceous plants and herbs.

If you have never sniffed Balm of Gillead, or teed off around a child-friendly garden with a miniature golf course where the holes have names like Lake OKeechokee, then you might be entertained by horti-culturist Nick Burrow's whimsical one acre garden. Laid out with grass paths falling like streams around island beds behind a 230 year old farmhouse with a spectacular views across Strangford Lough, the 10year old garden is full of original ideas - in fact there is nothing quite like it.

stock image

There's a circle of variegated hollies with an oak being trained as a parasol over the top, a carrot compound which completely defeats carrot flies, raised salad beds with crops like Tahtsol and coriander, a berry garden with Tayberries and their cousins Tammel berries, autumn strawberries in a strawberry house, golden escallonia clipped into a river, a climbing frame like a Giant's Causeway of logs - and a great deal more besides.

Each area of the garden is hidden from sight around beds and bends, and in the top section there is a great place to sit and admire the view amid colourful plants like watsonias *Geranium procurrens*, *Stachys macrantha*, *Ligularia* **'The Rocket'**. And on the way out there is a treat in the form of a small nursery with unusual plants propagated by Nick.

Open by appointment, May-Sep. Entry c. £3. Children welcome; no dogs; not suitable for wheelchairs; plants for sale; teas by arrangement. **Directions:** *Turn off the Dundonald to Newtownards Road, turn left up the hill at Lidl store, number 34 is at the top of the hill.*

Redcot

35 Kings Road **Belfast** Co Antrim
Tel: 028 9079 6614

GARDEN

Large town garden with herbaceous and grass borders, woodland and wild garden

This two and a half acre garden in suburban Knock is as unexpected as it is full of surprises. In its hidden heart the woodland glade is a Robinsonian paradise where plants from all over the world romp in happy abandon under a sheltered canopy of trees.

The garden is situated on sandy soil, once part of an ice age lake bed. Little was left of the original Victorian garden surrounding the 1888 house which has been in the same family for generations together with a persistent gardening gene inherited by Mr Knox Gass and active for his 30 years of gardening there.

The front garden, screened by century old trees and planted with Loderi rhododendrons, a handsome cedar, cherries and bulbs, acts as a peaceful introduction. A pergola clad in *Wisteria* **'Caroline'** leads on to an enclosed garden with a circular bed filled with covetable plants like *Verbena bonariensis*, *Geranium maderense*, a banana tree and a small formal area with a chorus of paeony trees, before opening onto a spectacular double border, one side planted with handsome perennials like *Helianthus* **'Limelight'** thalictrum, *Potentilla* **'Molten Fire'** and herbaceous clematis, the colours shading from hot to cool. The other is planted with grasses from miscanthus to chionochloa to *Stipa giganta* and the structural forms of yucca .

The steep banks, with logs steps, and the floor of the dell are full of interest, with a fernery, naturalised lilies and phlox, a river of primulas, a meconopsis bed and unusual shrubs like pseudopanax, *Mukdenia rossii* and tree ferns which look spectacular viewed from above a spot where a waterfall is planned. A lawn surrounded by mixed borders and a terrace with a most tempting array of plants for sale, propagated from the garden and from exotic seeds, completes the picture.

Open May-Sep, by appointment. Children welcome; no dogs; partial wheelchair access; plants for sale.
Directions: *From the Upper Newtownards Road turn right into Knock Road, Kings Road is 2nd right.*

Bushmills
HOTEL / RESTAURANT

Bushmills Inn
9 Dunluce Road Bushmills Co Antrim
Tel: 028 2073 3000
Email: mail@bushmillsinn.com Web: www.bushmillsinn.com

The Bushmills Inn is one of Ireland's best-loved hotels and, although it has grown since its establishment as a 19th-century coaching inn, recent development has been thoughtful: a new wing added some years ago was so skilfully designed that it is hard to work out where the old ends and the new begins. Inside, it's the same story: all the features which made the old Inn special have been carried through and blended with new amenities. The tone is set by the turf fire and country seating in the hall and public rooms – bars, the famous circular library, the restaurant – carry on the same theme. Bedrooms are individually furnished in a comfortable cottage style and even have "antiqued" bathrooms – but it's all very well done and avoids a theme park feel. It would make a comfortable base for visiting the north Antrim gardens - or simply exploring this beautiful coastline and its hinterland; and, the Magilligan-Greencastle ferry day trips can comfortably include a visit to the Inishowen peninsula in Co. Donegal. The inn is known for its wholesome traditional food and makes a good place to plan a break when touring, as it offers both day and evening menus in cosy surroundings. **Rooms 32** (22 in Mill House, 10 in Coaching Inn; 6 superior, 7 shower only, 1 disabled). B&B from c. £79 pps. **Restaurant:** L&D daily (reservations recommended); daytime food available in bar. MasterCard, Visa, Switch. **Directions:** On the A2 Antrim Coast road, in Bushmills village where it crosses the river.

Rowallane Garden

Saintfield **Ballynahinch** Co Down
Tel: 028 9751 0131
Email: rowallane@nationaltrust.org.uk Web: www.ntni.org.uk

GARDEN

Ornamental demesne with wonderful rhododendrons, azaleas and walled garden.

Rowallane is at its most glorious in spring and autumn, thanks to the display of rhododendrons and azaleas and the final blaze of glory of ornamental trees and shrubs, but it is a lovely place at any time of year. The 52 acre demesne near the old linen town of Saintfield was first enhanced by the Rev John Moore, who laid out the pleasure grounds and was responsible for the curious stone cairns like pyramids of Ferrer Rocher. His nephew, Hugh Armytage Moore, planted the collection of rhododendrons, magnolias and flowering shrubs: this is gardening with nature on a grand scale, shrubs and trees - many from China and Chile - are planted in the Robinsonian manner, along informal paths in an area known as the Spring Ground.

Each area in the wild garden is linked by grassy paths and has its own special atmosphere: there is the mysterious Bishop's Rock, and the Hospital, where sick calves were grazed.

The earliest rhododendrons bloom in December and the display of blossom reaches a peak in May with a colour range running from deepest red like *R sanguineum* through purples, blue and yellow, to the creamy bells of *R falconeri*. But there are fascinating trees and shrubs to be seen here at any time, the brilliant autumn colours of prunus, sorbus and acers like *A palmatum* var *heptalobum*, the summer displays of the fluttering bracts of the handerchief tree and the white flowers of stuartia with their golden crowns of stamens. There is a bandstand where The Rev Moore sometimes used to preach to his flock, and also a wild flower meadow and a lake waiting to be discovered. The walled garden with the National Penstemon Collection is worth a visit in its own right (there are over 50 varieties). Beside the arched gateway there is a silver and blue garden and although the grid of paths is formal the planting is eclectic, with a mix of shrubs, trees, bulbs and herbaceous plants. There are unexpected carpets of the autumn crocus, corners where Southern hemisphere plants like agapanthus varieties flourish - and, among the more spectacular sights to be seen, are the summer displays of snowy hoheria flowers, drifts of azure meconopsis in the shady borders and showy magnolias.

There are some cultivars which are special to Rowallane, *Viburnum plicatum* **'Rowallane'** and a primula romantically named **'Rowallane Rose'**. Rowallane is now the headquarters of the National Trust.

*Open all year: mid-April-mid Sep, 10-8; mid Sep-mid Apr, 10-4. Supervised children welcome; partial wheelchair access; no dogs; tea room. **Directions:** Just outside Saintfield on the A7 Belfast to Downpatrick Road.*

Seaforde Gardens

Seaforde **Downpatrick** Co Down
Tel: 028 4481 1225
Email: plants@seafordegardens.com

GARDEN

Atmospheric walled garden with a Eucryphia collection.

In its own way Seaforde has the answer to Japan's cherry blossom viewing season. The garden holds the national collection of eucryphias, known poetically as the 'White Knights of August'. Gleaming with clouds of white blossom crowned with golden stamens and a-buzz with contended bees, the 19 different varieties of Eucryphia, planted in two allées, are a sight to take root in memory.

The gardens date back to the mid18th century and belonged to the original Seaforde House, which was burnt in 1816 and replaced. They have been reclaimed by Patrick Forde and, in place of the labour intensive bedding designs beloved of Victorians, the pleasure grounds now have a hornbeam maze with a rose bower made from the skeleton of a Nissen hut, and a summer house built from central heating pipes. Echiums grow to giant proportions in the shelter of the walls and climbing roses romp through trees and lilies and tender Melianthus major luxuriates amid magnolias, rhododendrons and the willow leaf podocarpus. Other attractions include a nursery with many unusual shrubs (some propagated from Patrick Forde's plant expeditions to the East), a tropical butterfly house, and a woodland walk leading to a pond.

Open daily. Apr-Sep; Mon-Sat 10-5, Sun 1-6. Children welcome; partial wheelchair access; no dogs; plant sales. **Directions:** *Just outside Seaforde on the Belfast-Newcastle Road.*

Guincho

69 Craigdarragh Road Helen's Bay Nr. **Bangor** Co Down
Tel: 028 9048 6324

GARDEN

Informal 12 acre garden with rare shrubs and trees, and stream and woodland area.

On a very grand scale indeed, this 12 acre garden surrounding an unusual Portuguese style house is a place to experience unforgettable sights, scents and sounds. It would be worth a visit for gorgeous hydrangea **'Sea Foam'** alone, glimmering with flowers in dappled shade , to meet the original of the elder S **'Guincho Purple'** or to discover the newly created rock pool fringed with primula.

The garden, with mysterious paths leading off to hidden destinations, was laid out in the 1930s but planted by Mrs Frazer Mackie from 1948 to 1979 with rare trees, plants and shrubs, many of them grown from seed. The area between the house and the road is laid out with shrubberies and island beds of shrubs set in manicured lawns.

In the centre of the garden a huge lake-like lawn is surrounded by acers, magnolias, bamboos, turquoise blue hydrangeas, a huge stand of gunnera under a blue cedar and specimen trees. Paths burrow through glades of rhododendrons and camellias along a hosta walk, or an exotic walk planted with South African plants, including eight different varieties of agapanthus and flowering *Beschorneria yuccoides*. Another leads to to Mrs Mackie's little circular garden with her special treasures S **'Guincho Purple'**, a champion *Pseudopanax crassifolius*, *Hakea saligna* and *Myrtus lechleriana* with its burnished copper juvenile leaves.

In the valley, the stream walk is carpeted with spring bulbs - crocus, chionodoxia, scilla and grape hyacinths - and leads eventually to a waterfall. This area is being replanted sensitively under the supervision of Head Gardener, Nick Burrowes. In true Robinisonian manner the ground in this jungly area is populated by plants from around the world, including carpets of erythroniums (N America) *Dicksonia antartica* (Australasia) *Dacrydium franklinii* (Tasmania), *Gevuina avellana* (Chile), and large leaved rhododendrons like Falconeri, Fortunei and Thompsonii ranges, together with perfumed Loderii hybrids. The garden is now owned by Mr and Mrs Cairns, who kindly continue to open it under the national Trust Gardens open by appointment scheme.

Open May -Sept by appointment. Supervised children; no dogs; partial wheelchair access. Admission c. £3.50 with guided tour. **Directions:** *Off the main Belfast-Bangor Road, take the Craigdarragh Road for Helen's Bay; garden is a quarter of a mile on the left.*

Comber
B&B / GARDEN

Anna's House & Garden

35 Lisbarnett Road Lisbane Comber Co Down
Tel: 028 9754 1566
Email: anna@annashouse.com Web: www.annashouse.com

Anna and Ken Johnson's charming house near Strangford Lough looks over their own ten-acre wildfowl lake to the rolling north Down country-side, and not only does it make a comfortable base for visits to major County Down gardens - three National Trust gardens are nearby, including Mount Stewart - but they have a wonderful garden of their own as well. Developed over thirty years from what was once an open two-acre field, a winding grass footpath now leads visitors through a series of contrasting garden rooms ranging from a productive kitchen garden - handily positioned near the entrance and, like the rest of the garden, worked organi-cally - to other areas with very different characteristics: whispering woodland in one place, vivid flowering shrubs in another, and

then a secret pond... There is a cosy sitting room for guests' use and accommodation is quite simple and cottagey - who could fail to be charmed by real Irish linen on the beds, and uninterrupted rural views, especially when two of these pretty rooms have seating areas and their own balconies? Breakfast - an organic feast with freshly baked breads and scones - is usually the only meal served, but it is sometimes possible to share an evening meal with Anna and Ken. **Rooms 3** (all en-suite, 2 shower only, 1 ground floor / wheelchair acessible, all no smoking). B&B £32.50pps, ss£7.50. MasterCard, Visa. **Directions:** From Lisbane, follow the brown B&B signs.

Holywood
HOTEL / RESTAURANT

Hastings Culloden Hotel

Bangor Road Holywood Co Down
Tel: 028 9042 1066 Fax: 028 9042 6777
Email: res@cull.hastingshotels.com Web: www.hastingshotels.com

Formerly the official palace for the Bishops of Down, Hastings Hotels' flagship property is a fine example of 19th-century Scottish Baronial archi-tecture with plasterwork ceilings, stained glass windows and an imposing staircase - and, as it is set in beautifully maintained gardens and woodland overlooking Belfast Lough and the County Antrim coast-line, many garden lovers will prefer to be based here rather than in the city. Period furniture and fine paintings in spacious high ceilinged rooms give a soothing feeling of exclusivity, and

comfortable drawing rooms overlook the lough. Spacious, lavishly decorated guest rooms include a large proportion of suites and a Presidential Suite, with the best view; all are lavishly furnished and decorated with splendid bathrooms and many pampering details such as bathrobes, a welcoming bowl of fruit, and nice touches like ground coffee and a cafetière on the hospitality tray. Wireless internet access is available in all areas, and there are video/DVD players in suites. The Culloden is a top busi-ness and conference venue, with excellent facilities, including a fine health club; the 'Cultra Inn' - a bar and informal restaurant in the ground - provides an alternative to the discreetly luxurious Mitre Restaurant, which offers fine dining overlooking the lough. Children welcome. No pets. **Rooms 79** (2 suites, 17 junior suites, 22 executive rooms, 2 disabled, 40 no-smoking). Lift. Air conditioning. 24 hr room service B&B c. £100 pps, ss about £60. **Mitre Restaurant:** D daily, L Sun only; reservations required. Toilets wheelchair accessible. Hotel open all year. Amex, Diners, MasterCard, Visa, Switch. **Directions:** 6 miles from Belfast city centre on A2 towards Bangor.

Holywood
COUNTRY HOUSE / RESTAURANT

Rayanne Country House
60 Demesne Road Holywood Co Down
Tel: 028 9042 5859 Fax: 028 9042 5859
Email: rayannehouse@hotmail.com Web: www.rayannehouse.co.uk

Situated in mature gardens close to Redburn Country Park, and with views across Belfast Lough, the McClellands' family-run country house is a tranquil spot. Bedrooms, some with lough views, are individually decorated to a high standard, with phones and television - and little extras like fresh fruit, spring water, sewing kit, stationery and a hospitality tray with bedtime drinks and home-made shortbread as well as the usual tea & coffee facilities. It's a relaxing place, with friendly staff and a great breakfast, offering a wide range, including unusual dishes such as prune soufflé, French toast topped with black and white pudding & served with a spiced apple compôte, and a 'healthy house grill' (with nothing fried). **Restaurant:** Conor McClelland, who returned to take over Rayanne with 15 years as an international chef under his belt, cooks for up to 30 guests in their restaurant D'Vine Dining, which is open to non-residents by reservation. Parking (10). Children welcome. Pets allowed by arrangement. Garden, walking. **Rooms 8** (3 shower only, all no smoking). B&B c. £87.50 double (single c. £67.50). D c.£38, by reservation. Open all year except Christmas. MasterCard, Visa, Switch. **Directions:** Take A2 out of Belfast towards Holywood (6 miles).

Holywood Area
B&B

Beech Hill Country House
23 Ballymoney Road Craigantlet Co Down BT23 4TG
Tel: 028 9042 5892
Email: info@beech-hill.net Web: www.beech-hill.net

Victoria Brann's attractive Georgian style house is set in the peaceful Holywood Hills and is handily

placed in relation to the city, airports and ferry port; Mount Stewart Gardens are just 15 minutes away, and garden visits in Belfast city are easily accessible from here. Beech Hill has great style - and the benefit of an exceptionally hospitable hostess, who does everything possible to ensure that guests have everything they need. Ground floor bedrooms have panoramic views over the North Down countryside and are furnished with antique furniture - and, believe it or not, the beds are made up with fine Irish linen; all also have bathrooms with lots of special little extras. Breakfast is a meal worth allowing time to enjoy - and it is served in a spacious conservatory overlooking a croquet lawn. * Self catering accommodation is also offered at The Colonel's Lodge, in Beech Hill garden (also available for B&B). **Rooms 3** (all en-siuite, 1 shower only; all no smoking). B&B c. £35, ss £15. **Directions:** A2 from Belfast, bypass Holywood; 1.5 miles from bridges at Ulster Folk Museum, turn right up Ballymoney Road, signed Craigantlet - 1.75 miles on left.

Newtownards

Mount Stewart House & Gardens

Newtownards Co Down **Tel: 028 42788387**
Email: mountstewart@nationaltrust.org.uk. Web: www.ntni.org.uk

Superbly designed and planted formal garden, in beguiling woodland and lakeside grounds.

Inspired by Edith, Marchioness of Londonderry, Mount Stewart is surely a contender for the most splendid garden in Ireland. The influential Londonderrys were part of the golden circle of their day and, when Edith came to Mount Stewart in 1919, she set about transforming what she saw as a dark and sad ancestral home into a sumptuous setting for entertaining guests like Winston Churchill and Harold Macmillan.

Within the 80 acre 19th century garden with its lake and specimen trees, a series of intricately designed and brilliantly planted formal gardens were laid out around the house at a time when garden design had reached an exquisite peak.

Offering beautiful contrasts of mood, the gardens move from the geometric parterres of sizzling reds, yellows and oranges on one side of the Italian garden and silvers and mauves on the other, to the cool greens and curvaceous design of the Spanish garden with its circular pool overlooked by a pantiled loggia and screened by arches of clipped leylandii.

There are touches of pure whimsy in the Dodo Terrace, where stone carvings represent the animal characters given by Edith to members of her Ark Club such as: Winston the Warlock and Harold the Humming Bird. The silver and white planting in the circular Mairi Garden, named for Edith's youngest daughter echoes the rhyme "Silver bells and cockle shells", in this case with campanulas, agapanthus, stachys and Perovskia 'Blue Spire'. Gertrude Jekyll contributed the design for the earliest garden in the series, known as the Sunken Garden, and planted it with a wonderful combination of blue, purple, yellow and orange.

A 'Red Hand of Ulster' in the Shamrock Garden side by side with an Irish harp is surrounded by yew hedges clipped into the shape of all manner of creatures from deer to devils. Beyond this area the garden merges into informality, towards the Lily Wood where tender trees and shrubs prosper in the micro climate of the Ards Peninsula. There are unforgettable displays to be see, not only of lilies but of colonies of Himalayan poppies. The paths winding around the lake offer a dreamlike view of the hill topped by Tir Na n'Og, the Londonderry's private burial ground, which is planted with exotic shrubs - some of them fruit of plant hunting expeditions subscribed to by Lady Edith.

Elsewhere in the 78 acres of grounds are the Coronation Walk, rhododendron glades with of the aristocracy of the rhododendron family *R. sinograde* and *falconeri* and many others, and the Jubilee Walk planted in 1935 for George V's Jubilee. Not to be missed is the Temple of the Winds, designed by James 'Athenian' Stewart in 1780; based on the Tower of Andronicus Cyrrestes in Athens, it looks out over Strangford Lough. The garden merits a full day visit and the Londonderry ancestral home is also open to the public. The estate is now in the hands of the National Trust and the gardens are splendidly kept up by head gardener Nigel Marshall and his team.

Lakeside garden open daily; formal garden Apr-Oct daily. Supervised children welcome; wheelchair access, no dogs; tea room and shop. Admission c.£4.20 **Directions:** *On Eastside of Strangford Lough on Belfast-Portaferry Road.*

Useful Contacts...

We strongly recommend that you check the opening times and other data supplied in this guide when planning your itinerary, by contacting individual gardens using the contact details supplied in each entry.

Other references and contacts which may be useful include:

Failte Ireland & Northern Ireland Tourism (and their respective local information offices) provide up to date information on gardens open to the public.

Houses, Castles & Gardens of Ireland (listing published annually):
Tel 01 288 9114
Email: info@castlesgardensireland.com

The Irish Garden (Tel 01 286 2649;
Email: editor@theirishgarden.ie)
This monthly magazine is always a useful reference, especially in May, when they publish their comprehensive annual 'Gardens Open' guide.

GARDEN TRAILS / LOCAL GROUPS:

Co Carlow:
▸ Carlow Garden Trail
(email: info@carlowtourism.com)

Co Cork:
▸ Cork Open Gardens (leaflet from Neil Williams, Tel 021 4613379)
▸ West Cork Garden Trail (June; www.westcorkgardentrail.com; leaflets from Failte Ireland)

▸ Blackwater Valley Garden Trail
(info: Tel 025 82222)

Co Galway:
▸ Connemara Garden Trail (leaflets from Breandan Ó Scannaill Tel: 095 21148; Email:thepapershop@anu.ie
▸ Ireland West Garden Trail (leaflet/map from Ireland West Tourism, Forster Street, Galway. Email: info@irelandwest.ie; www.irelandwest.ie)

Co Limerick
▸ Limerick Garden Trail
(www.limerickgardentrail.com)

Co Tipperary
▸ South Tipperary Garden Trail (July; leaflet from Mildred Stokes, Tel: 052 33155)

Co Waterford
▸ Private Gardens of South East Festival (June; brochure from Margaret Power
Tel 051 832081)

Co Wicklow
▸ Wicklow Gardens Festival (May-Aug; full guide from Wicklow County Tourism, St Mantan's House, Kilmantin Hill, Wicklow Town. Tel: 0404 20070; Email: wctr@iol.ie ; Web:www.visitwicklow.ie)

Further Recommendations

Additional recommendations for places to stay and eat (including a number of daytime cafés and restaurants) which you may find useful on your travels, are listed by county below. For full details, and for information on new discoveries which we may have added to our database, visit our website
www.ireland-guide.com

DUBLIN CITY & COUNTY
▸ Chapter One Restaurant (fine dining), 18/19 Parnell Square, **Dublin 1**
Tel: 01 873 2266
▸ Avoca Café, Suffolk St., **Dublin 2**
Tel: 01 672 6019
▸ Dunne & Crescenzi, South Frederick Street (& branches) **Dublin 2** Tel 01 677 3815
▸ Eden (contemporary restaurant), Meeting House Square Temple Bar **Dublin 2**
Tel 01 670 5372

▸ Kilkenny Restaurant & Café, Nassau Street, **Dublin 2** Tel: 01 677 7075
▸ L'Ecrivain (fine dining restaurant with terrace) Lower Baggot Street, **Dublin 2**
Tel: 01 661 1919
▸ One Pico Restaurant (fine dining), Molesworth Place, **Dublin 2** Tel: 01 676 0300
▸ Queen of Tarts (traditional tea rooms near Dublin Castle) Cork Hill Dame Street **Dublin 2**
Tel: 01 6707499

- Thornton's Restaurant (innovative fine dining) Top Floor Fitzwilliam Hotel, St Stephen's Green **Dublin 2** Tel 01 478 70008
- Andersons Food Hall & Café (deli & wine bar/café near Botanic Gardens), The Rise, Glasnevin, **Dublin 9** Tel: 01 837 8394
- Cavistons Seafood Restaurant (lunch) Glasthule Road, **Dun Laoghaire** Tel 01 280 9245
- King Sitric Fish Restaurant & Accommodation, East Pier, **Howth** Tel: 01 832 5235
- Gardenworks (garden centre/café), **Malahide** (near Malahide Castle) Tel 01 845 0110
- Red Bank House & Restaurant, (restaurant with rooms) Church Street, **Skerries** Tel: 01 849 1005
- Stoop Your Head (harbourside seafood restaurant/bar), **Skerries** Tel: 01 849 1144

CO CARLOW
- The Forge Restaurant (café/crafts), **Ballon** Tel: 059 915 9939
- The Lord Bagenal Inn, **Leighlinbridge** Tel 059 972 1668
- Rathwood Café (garden centre café), **Tullow** Tel: 0503 56285

CO CAVAN
- Planet Earth (bakery/wholefood shop & café), **Bailieborough** Tel: 042 966 5490
- MacNean House & Bistro (restaurant with rooms), **Blacklion** Tel: 071 985 3404
- The Olde Post Inn (restaurant with rooms), **Cloverhill** Tel: 047 55555
- Cinnamon Stick Café, **Virginia** Tel: 049 8548692

CORK CITY
- Café Paradiso (restaurant with rooms) **Western Road** Tel: 021 427 4943
- Crawford Gallery Café (lunch), **Emmet Place** Tel: 021 427 4415
- Farmgate Café, **English Market** Tel 021 427 8134
- Idaho.Café, (daytime café), **Caroline Street**, Tel: 021 427 6376
- Isaacs Restaurant, 48 **MacCurtain Street**, Tel: 021 450 3805
- Ivory Tower (innovative cooking) **Princes Street** Tel: 021 427 4665
- Jacques Restaurant, **Phoenix Street** Tel: 021 427 7387
- Proby's Bistro, **Crosses Green** Tel: 021 431 6531

CO CORK
- Annie's Restaurant, **Ballydehob** Tel: 028 37292
- Bushe's Bar (pub/B&B), **Baltimore** Tel: 028 20125
- Mary Ann's Bar & Restaurant (seafood), **Castletownshend** Tel: 028 36146
- Harts Coffee Shop (home baking),

Ashe Street, **Clonakilty** Tel: 023 35583
- Hayes' Bar, Pub, The Square, **Glandore** Tel: 028 33214
- Island Cottage Restaurant (classical cooking), **Heir Island** Tel: 028 38102
- Toddies Restaurant (L&D in summer, outdoor tables), **Kinsale** Tel: 021 477 7769
- All Things Nice (deli/café), Main Street, **Leap**, Tel: 028 34772
- The Bosun (pub/restaurant), **Monkstown** Tel: 021 484 2172
- O'Callaghan-Walshe, (seafood restaurant), The Square, **Rosscarbery** Tel: 023 48125
- T J Newman's, (café/pub), **Schull** Tel: 028 27776
- Kalbo's Bistro, (café/restaurant), North Street, **Skibbereen** Tel: 028 21515
- Aherne's Seafood Restaurant & Accommodation, North Main Street, **Youghal**, Tel: 024 9242

CO DONEGAL
- Aroma Coffee Shop, Craft Village, **Donegal Town** Tel 073 2322
- Glenveagh Castle Tea Rooms, **Glenveagh National Park** Tel 074 9137090
- Kealys Seafood Bar, Bar/Restaurant, **Greencastle** Tel: 074 93 81010
- Ardeen, **Ramelton** Tel: 074 915 1243
- Frewin, **Ramelton** Tel: 074 915 1246
- Fort Royal Hotel, Hotel/Restaurant, **Rathmullan** Tel: 074 91 58100

GALWAY CITY
- Devondell, B&B, Lr. Salthill, **Galway** Tel: 091 528 306
- Goya's, (daytime bakery/café), Kirwans Lane, **Galway** Tel: 091 567010
- The Malt House Restaurant, High Street, **Galway** Tel: 091 567866
- Revive Coffee & Sandwich Bar, Eyre Street, **Galway** Tel: 091 533779

CO GALWAY
- Dolphin Beach Country House, Lr Sky Road, **Clifden** Tel: 095 21204
- Mitchell's Restaurant, Market Street, **Clifden** Tel: 095 21867
- Two Dog Café, Church Hill, **Clifden** Tel: 095 22186
- Blackberry Café & Coffee Shop, **Leenane** Tel: 095 42240
- Delphi Lodge, Country House, **Leenane** Tel: 095 42222
- Pangur Bán (restaurant in traditional cottage) **Letterfrack** Tel 095 41243
- Moycullen House, Restaurant with Rooms, **Moycullen** Tel: 091 555 621
- Lough Inagh Lodge Hotel, **Recess** Tel: 095 3470
- Corrib Wave, (waterside guesthouse), Portcarron, **Oughterard** Tel: 091 552 147

CO KERRY

- O'Neills at The Point, (bar/seafood beside ferry) Renard Point, **Cahirciveen** Tel: 066 947 2165
- QCs Seafood Bar & Restaurant, **Caherciveen** Tel 066 2244
- Derrynane Hotel, **Caherdaniel** Tel: 066 947 5136
- Iskeroon, Country House, **Caherdaniel** Tel: 066 947 5119
- Chart House (restaurant), The Mall, **Dingle** Tel: 066 915 2255
- Gorman's Clifftop House, Restaurant/Guesthouse, **Ballydavid**, **Dingle** Peninsula Tel: 066 915 5162
- Lord Baker's Restaurant & Bar, **Dingle** Tel: 066 915 1277
- Milltown House (waterside guesthouse), **Dingle** Tel 066 915 1372
- Out of the Blue (harbourside fish restaurant), **Dingle** Tel: 066 915 0811
- Jam (café, deli & picnics), Henry St, **Kenmare** Tel: 064 41591 & High St **Killarney** Tel: 064 31441
- The Lime Tree Restaurant, Shelburne Street, **Kenmare** Tel: 064 41225
- Mentons @ The Plaza, Restaurant, Killarney Plaza Hotel, **Killarney** Tel: 064 21150
- Mulcahys Restaurant, Henry Street, **Kenmare** Tel: 064 42383
- Packie's, Restaurant, Henry Street, **Kenmare** Tel: 064 41508
- Purple Heather, (daytime bar/restaurant), Henry Street, **Kenmare** Tel: 064 41016
- Beaufort Bar & Restaurant, bar/restaurant, Beaufort, **Killarney** Tel: 064 44032
- Killarney Park Hotel (hotel, restaurant/bar meals), **Killarney** Tel 064 35555
- Knightstown Coffee Shop, Café, **Valentia Island** Tel: 066 9476887/ 087 783 7544
- Nick's Seafood Restaurant & Piano Bar, Restaurant, **Killorglin** Tel: 066 976 1219
- Avoca Handweavers, Café, **Moll's Gap** Tel: 064 34720

CO KILKENNY

- Waterside, Restaurant/Guesthouse, The Quay, **Graiguenamanagh** Tel: 059 97 24246
- Lacken House, Restaurant with Rooms, Dublin Road, **Kilkenny** Tel: 056 776 1085
- Hudsons (restaurant), **Thomastown** Tel: 056 779 3900

CO LAOIS

- Preston House, Restaurant with Rooms, Main Street, **Abbeyleix** Tel: 0502 31432
- Ivyleigh House, Guesthouse, Bank Place, Church Street, **Portlaoise** Tel: 0502 22081
- The Kitchen & Foodhall, (restaurant/deli) Hynds Square, **Portlaoise** Tel: 0502 62061

CO LIMERICK

- Dunraven Arms Hotel, (hotel/restaurant), **Adare** Tel: 061 396 633

- O'Shaughnessy's (historic pub, garden), **Glin** Tel 068 34115
- Flemingstown House (farmhouse accommodation), **Kilmallock** Tel 063 98093

CO LONGFORD

- Aubergine Gallery Café (restaurant), **Longford** Tel: 043 48633

CO LOUTH

- Georgina's Bakehouse (tearooms/café), Castle Hill, **Carlingford** Tel: 042 937 3346
- Ghan House (restaurant//country house), **Carlingford** Tel: 042 937 3682
- Forge Gallery Restaurant, **Collon** Tel 041 982 6272
- Boyne Valley Hotel & Country Club, **Drogheda** Tel: 041 983 7737
- Ballymascanlon House Hotel, **Dundalk** Tel: 042 935 8200
- Fitzpatrick's Bar & Restaurant, Jenkinstown, **Dundalk** Tel: 042 937 6193

CO MAYO

- The Beehive (café/craft shop), Keel, **Achill Island** Tel 098 43134
- Gaughans, (pub/bar meals), O'Rahilly Street, **Ballina** Tel: 096 70096
- Mary's Bakery & Tea Rooms, **Ballycastle** Tel 096 43361
- Café Rua (café), New Antrim Street, **Castlebar** Tel: 094 902 3376
- Rosturk Woods (waterside B&B/self catering), **Mulrany** Tel: 098 36264
- Ardmore House (hotel/seafood restaurant), The Quay, **Westport** Tel: 098 25994
- The Creel (café/restaurant) The Quay, **Westport** Tel: 098 26174

CO MEATH

- Gardenworks (garden centre/café), **Clonee** Tel 01 825 5375
- The Spire Restaurant, **Duleek** Tel: 041 982 3000
- Bellinter House, (hotel/country house), **Navan** Tel: 01 677 4845
- The Ground Floor Restaurant, Bective Square, **Kells** Tel: 046 924 9688
- Vanilla Pod Restaurant, Headfort Arms Hotel, **Kells** Tel: 046 924 0063
- The Loft Restaurant, Trimgate Street, **Navan** Tel: 046 906 6185

CO OFFALY

- Thatch Bar & Restaurant (restaurant/pub), Crinkle, **Birr** Tel: 0509 20682
- Glendine Bistro, B&B/Restaurant, **Kinnitty** Tel: 0509 37973
- The Wolftrap (bar/restaurant), William Street, **Tullamore** Tel: 0506 23374

CO SLIGO

- Atrium Restaurant (café), The Niland Model Arts Centre, **Sligo** Tel: 071 914 1418

CO TIPPERARY
- Café Hans, Café, Moore Lane, **Cashel**
  Tel: 062 63660
- Chez Hans, (atmospheric restaurant), Moore
  Lane, **Cashel** Tel: 062 61177
- Kilmaneen Farmhouse, Ardfinnan, Newcastle,
  Clonmel Tel: 052 36231
- Coolbawn Quay (waterside hotel/restaurant),
  Coolbawn, **Nenagh** Tel:067 28158
- Country Choice Delicatessen & Coffee Bar,
  Kenyon Street, **Nenagh** Tel: 067 32596
- Fiacrí Country House Restaurant & Cookery
  School, **Roscrea Area** Tel: 0505 43017
- The Tower (bar/restaurant/B&B), Church
  Street, **Roscrea** Tel: 0505 21774

CO WATERFORD
- White Horses (café/restaurant), **Ardmore**
  Tel: 024 94040
- Powersfield House (guesthouse), Ballinamuck
  West, **Dungarvan** Tel: 058 45594
- The Tannery (restaurant with rooms), Quay
  Street, **Dungarvan** Tel: 058 45420
- Faithlegg House Hotel, **Faithlegg**
  Tel: 051 382000
- Ballyrafter Country House Hotel, **Lismore**
  Tel: 058 54002
- Barça Wine Bar & Restaurant, Main Street,
  Lismore Tel: 058 53810
- Diamond Hill Country House, Guesthouse,
  Slieverue, **Waterford** Tel: 051 832855

CO WESTMEATH
- Left Bank Bistro, Fry Place, **Athlone**
  Tel: 090 649 4446
- Wineport Lodge (waterside restaurant/accom-
  modation) **Athlone** Tel: 090 6439010
- Belfry Restaurant (fine dining),
  Ballynegall, **Mullingar** Tel: 044 42488
- Gallery 29, (bakery/café, Oliver Plunkett St.,
  Mullingar Tel: 044 49449
- Ilia A Coffee Experience, (café/deli), Oliver
  Plunkett Street, **Mullingar** Tel: 044 40300

CO WEXFORD
- Aldridge Lodge (restaurat with rooms),
  Duncannon Tel: 051 389116
- Sqigl Restaurant & Roches Bar, Quay Road,
  Duncannon Tel: 051 389188
- Monfin House, (country house accommoda-
  tion), St Johns, **Enniscorthy** Tel: 054 38582
- Ferrycarrig Hotel (hotel & restaurants),
  Ferrycarrig Bridge Tel: 053 20999
- La Dolce Vita (Italian deli/daytime restaurant)
  Trimmers Lane **Wexford** Tel 053 70806

CO WICKLOW
- Avoca Handweavers (shop & café/ restaurant;
  also at Avoca & Powerscourt), **Kilmacanogue**
  Tel 01 286 7466
- Marc Michel Organic Life Café (organic shop
  & light meals), **Kilpedder** Tel 01 2011882
- Marriott Druids Glen Hotel,
  Newtownmountkennedy Tel: 01 287 0800

NORTHERN IRELAND
BELFAST/ANTRIM
- James Street South, 21 James Street South,
  Belfast Tel: 028 9043 4310
- Restaurant Michael Deane (fine dining) /
  Deanes Brasserie, Howard Street, **Belfast**
  Tel: 028 9033 1134
- Roscoff Brasserie, Linenhall Street, **Belfast**
  Tel: 028 9031 1150
- Lynden Heights, (restaurant), **Ballygally**
  Tel: 028 2858 3560
- Marlagh Lodge, Country House, **Ballymena**
  Tel: 028 2563 1505
- Londonderry Arms Hotel, **Carnlough**
  Tel: 028 2888 5255

CO DOWN
- The Old Inn, Hotel, 11-15 Main Street,
  Crawfordsburn Tel: 028 9185 3255
- Buck's Head Inn (restaurant), Main Street,
  Dundrum Tel: 028 4375 1868
- Carriage House (accommodation), Main
  Street, **Dundrum** Tel: 028 4375 1635
- Picnic (deli/café), **Killyleagh**
  Tel: 028 4482 8525
- Paul Arthurs (restaurant with rooms), Main
  Street, **Kircubbin** Tel: 028 4273 8192
- Edenvale House (country house/B&B),
  Portaferry, **Newtownards**
  Tel: 028 9181 4881
- Portaferry Hotel (hotel & restaurant),
  Portaferry Tel 028 427 28231
- Burrendale Hotel & Country Club,
  Castlewellan Road, **Newcastle**
  Tel: 028 4372 2599
- Sea Salt Bistro (café/restaurant), Central
  Promenade, **Newcastle** Tel: 028 437 25027
- The Cuan (pub/guesthouse), **Strangford
  Village** Tel: 028 4488 1222

CO. LONDONDERRY
- Inn at Castledawson (restaurant/bar/ accom-
  modation) Main Street, **Castledawson**
  Tel 028 7946 9777
- Lime Tree Restaurant, Catherine Street,
  Limavady Tel: 028 7776 4300
- Browns Restaurant (bar /brasserie/restaurant),
  Bonds Hill, **Londonderry**
  Tel: 028 7134 5180
- Cromore Halt Inn (restaurant/guesthouse),
  Station Road, **Portstewart**
  Tel: 028 7083 6888

INDEX

2 Old Galgorm Road, Ballymena 243
21 Library Road, Shankhill 32
23 Mountsandel Road, Coleraine 235
28 Killyfaddy Road, Magherafelt 239
Aberdeen Lodge, Dublin 4 11
Adare Manor Hotel, Adare 190
Addison Lodge, Dublin 9 16
Airfield Gardens, Dublin 14 17
Altamont, Tullow 109
Andersons Food Hall & Café, Dublin 9 16
The Angler's Return, Roundstone 214
Anna Nolan's Garden, Cabinteely 27
Anna's House & Garden, Comber 252
Annes Grove Garden, Castletownroche 142
Ardcarraig, Bushy Park 201
Ardgillan Castle & Demesne, Balbriggan 24
Ardmore House, Kinnitty 56
Ard-na-Sidhe Hotel, Caragh Lake 177
Ardtara Country House, Upperlands 240
Ashford Castle, Cong 218
Ashley Park House, Nenagh 118
Aultareagh Cottage Garden, Dunmanaway 153
Ballaghtobin, Callan 112
Ballindoolin House & Garden, Carbury 62
Ballinkeele House, Enniscorthy 95
Ballinlough Castle, Clonmellon 50
Ballon Garden, Ballon 103
Ballydaheen, Letterkenny 231
Ballyduff House, Thomastown 114
Ballykealey Manor Hotel, Ballon 104
Ballyknocken House, Ashford 69
Ballymakeigh House, Youghal 176
Ballymaloe Cookery School Gardens 172
Ballymaloe House, Shanagarry 173
The Ballymore Inn, Ballymore Eustace 68
Ballynahinch Castle Hotel, Recess 212
Ballyvolane House, Fermoy 157
Barberstown Castle, Straffan 66
Barraderry Country House, Kiltegan 83
Barrowville Town House, Carlow 105
Bassetts at Woodstock, Inistioge 112
The Bay Garden, Enniscorthy 97

Beaufield Mews Restaurant
    & Gardens, Stillorgan 34
Beaulieu House & Garden, Drogheda 41
Beech Hill Country House Hotel, L'Derry 238
Beech Hill Country House, Holywood 253
Belcamp Hutchinson, Malahide Area 31
Belvedere House, Gardens
    & Park, Mullingar 51
Benvarden, Ballymoney 244
Birr Castle Demesne, Birr 53
Blackhill House, Coleraine 236
Blairs Cove House, Durrus 154
Blanchville House, Maddoxtown 114
Bow Hall, Castletownshend 144
Brigit's Garden & Café, Rosscahill 211
BrookLodge Hotel, Macreddin 84
The Brown Trout, L'Derry 234
Bruckless House, Bruckless 225
Burren Perfumery Tea Rooms, Carron 195
Burton Hall Gardens, Dublin 18 21
Bushe's Bar, Baltimore 136
Bushmills Inn, Bushmills 248
Butler House, Kilkenny 113
Café Paradiso, Cork City 147
Cahernane House Hotel, Killarney 183
Cappoquin House Gardens, Cappoquin 124
Captains House, Dingle 179
Carrabawn Guesthouse, Adare 190
Carraig Abhainn Gardens, Durrus 155
Carrig Country House, Caragh Lake 178
Carysfort Lodge, Blackrock 26
Cashel House Hotel & Gardens, Cashel 203
Cashel Palace Hotel, Cashel 118
Casino House, Coolmain Bay 164
The Castle Country House, Dungarvan 126
Castle Durrow, Durrow 58
Castle Grove Country House Hotel,
    Letterkenny 227
Castle Leslie, Glasslough 46
Castlecoote House & Gardens, Castlecoote 215
Cedar Lodge, Midleton 169
The Chantry Restaurant
    & Scenic Gardens, Bunclody 92

Chestnut Lodge, Bray 74
Churchtown House, Rosslare 100
Clonalis House, Castlerea 215
Clone House, Aughrim 72
The Coach House, Glandore 159
Cois Cuain Gardens, Bantry 137
Coolclogher House, Killarney 186
Coopershill House, Riverstown 223
Coursetown Country House, Athy 61
Coxtown Manor, Laghey 226
Creagh House, Doneraile 152
Currarevagh House, Oughterard 209
Derreen Garden, Killarney 184
The Dillon Garden, Dublin 6 14
Dromoland Castle Hotel,
   Newmarket-on-Fergus 198
Drumcovitt, Feeney 237
Dunbrody Abbey Tea Rooms, New Ross 92
Dunbrody House Hotel, Arthurstown 90
Enniscoe House & Gardens, Ballina 217
Fairbrook House Gardens & Museum of
   Figurative Art, Kilmeaden 128
Farmgate Café, Cork City 147
Farmgate, Midleton 171
Farran House, Farran 151
Fernhill Garden, Dublin 18 22
Flemings Restaurant, Cork City 148
Fota Arboretum & Gardens, Carrigtwohill 141
Four Seasons Hotel, Dublin 4 12
Foxmount Country House, Waterford 132
Gash Gardens, Portlaoise 60
Glanleam House
   & Subtropical Garden, Valentia Is. 188
Glasha, Ballymacarbry 123
Glebe Country House, Ballinadee 165
Glebe Gardens, Baltimore 134
The Glen Country House, Kilbrittain 164
Glendale Gardens, Dublin 14 20
The Glendine Bistro, Kinnitty 56
Glendine Country House, New Ross 91
Glenmount, Belfast 246
Glenveagh Castle Gardens, nr Lettterkenny 228
Glin Castle & Pleasure Grounds, Glin 192
Good Things Café, Durrus 154
Graigueconna, Bray 75
Grangecon Café, Blessington 72

Grasse Cottage, Dún Laoghaire 28
Great Southern Hotel, Killarney 185
Great Southern Hotel, Parknasilla, Sneem 187
The Green Gate, Ardara 224
Greenhill House, Coleraine 234
Gregans Castle Hotel, Ballyvaughan 194
Grove Gardens, Kells 37
Guincho, Helen's Bay 251
Hanora's Cottage, Ballymacarbry 122
Hardymount, Tullow 111
Harmony Hill Country House, Ballymoney 245
Harrington Hall, Dublin 2 8
Hastings Culloden Hotel, Holywood 252
Hayfield Manor Hotel, Cork City 149
Heywood Gardens, Ballinakill 57
Hilton Park, Clones 45
Hotel Dunloe Castle & Gardens, Killarney 186
Hunter's Hotel, Rathnew 86
Hunting Brook Gardens, Blessington 73
Illnacullin, Glengarriff 162
June Blake's Garden
   & Nursery, Blessington 73
Kilfane Glen & Waterfall, Thomastown 115
Kilgraney House, Bagenalstown 101
Kilkenny Design Centre, Kilkenny 113
Killeen House, Bushy Park 202
Killurney Garden, Clonmel 119
Killyon House, Navan 39
Kilmokea Country Manor
   & Gardens, Campile 93
Kilravock Garden, Durrus 156
Kilruddery House & Gardens, Bray 76
Knockabbey Castle & Gardens, Tallanstown 43
Knockree, Dublin 18 23
Kylemore Abbey
   & Victorian Walled Garden 207
Lakemount Gardens, Glanmire 160
Lakeview Gardens, Mullagh 47
Larchwood House Restaurant
   & Garden, Bantry 138
Lennon's Café Bar, Carlow 106
Lismore Castle Gardens, Lismore 130
Lisnavagh Gardens, Rathvilly 107
Lissadell House & Gardens 222
Lissanroe Garden, Skibbereen 175
Lisselan Gardens, Clonakilty 145

Listoke Gardens, Drogheda 42
Lodge Park Walled Gardens, Straffan 67
Longueville House & Gardens, Mallow 167
Lorum Old Rectory, Bagenalstown 102
Loughcrew Historic Garden, Oldcastle 40
Lovetts Restaurant & Brasserie, Cork City 150
Maherintemple, Ballycastle 241
Man of Aran, Inis Mór 200
Marlfield House, Gorey 98
Martinstown House, The Curragh 64
The Maryborough House Hotel, Cork City 150
The Merrion Hotel, Dublin 2 9
Mir, Kilquade 81
Mobarnane House, Fethard 121
Mornington House, Multyfarnham 52
Mount Congreve, Kilmeaden 129
Mount Juliet Conrad, Thomastown 116
Mount Stewart House
　& Gardens, Newtownards 254
Mount Usher, Ashford 70
Moyglare Manor, Maynooth 65
Mulberry's Restaurant, Leighlinbridge 106
Mulvarra House, St. Mullins 108
The Mustard Seed
　at Echo Lodge, Ballingarry 191
Muxnaw Lodge, Kenmare 182
National Botanic Gardens, Dublin 9 16
National Garden Exhibition Centre,
　Kilquade 82
Newport House, Newport 220
Number 31, Dublin 2 8
Nuremore Hotel, Carrickmacross 44
O'Shaughnessy's Pub, Glin 193
Otto's Creative Catering (O.C.C.),
　Butlerstown 140
Packie's, Kenmare 182
Park Hotel Kenmare, Kenmare 180
Plattenstown House, Arklow 69
Powerscourt Gardens, Enniskerry 78
Powerscourt Terrace Café, Enniskerry 80
Primrose Hill, Lucan 29
The Purple Heather, Kenmare 182
Radisson SAS St. Helen's Hotel, Dublin 4 13
Ram House, Gorey 99
Rathmichael Lodge, Shankhill 33
Rathmullan House, Rathmullan 232

Rathsallagh House, Dunlavin 77
Ravenhill House, Belfast 245
Rayanne Country House, Holywood 253
Redcot, Belfast 247
Renvyle House Hotel, Renvyle 213
Restaurant Patrick Guilbaud, Dublin 2 10
Richmond House, Cappoquin 125
Rock Cottage, Schull 174
Rockfield House, Drumconrath 36
Rolf's Restaurant & Winebar, Baltimore 135
Rosleague Manor Hotel, Letterfrack 208
Ross Lake House Hotel, Oughterard 210
Roundwood House, Mountrath 59
Roundwood Inn, Roundwood 88
Rowallane Garden, Ballynahinch 249
Salthill Walled Gardens, Mount Charles 230
Salville House, Enniscorthy 96
Saratoga Lodge, Templemore 121
Seaforde Gardens, Downpatrick 250
Seamist House, Clifden 206
Seaview House Hotel, Bantry 139
Sheedy's Country House Hotel,
　Lisdoonvarna 197
Sheen Falls Lodge, Kenmare 181
Shelburne Lodge, Kenmare 182
Sherwood Park House, Ballon 104
Sion Hill House & Gardens, Ferrybank 127
Slipway, Baltimore 136
The Station House Hotel, Kilmessan 38
The Step House, Borris 105
Strokestown Park House & Garden,
　Strokestown 216
Tahilla Cove Country House, Sneem 187
The Talbot Botanic Gardens, Malahide 30
Temple House, Ballymote 222
Tinakilly Country House Hotel, Rathnew 87
Tullynally Castle & Gardens, Castlepollard 49
Vandeleur Walled Garden, Kilrush 196
Viewmont House, Longford 48
Walton Court, Oysterhaven 166
Warble Bank, Newtownmountkennedy 85
Waterford Castle Hotel, Waterford 132
Whitepark House, Ballycastle 242
Williamstown Garden, Carbury 63
Woodhill House, Ardara 224
Zetland Country House, Cashel Bay 205

Georgina Campbell's Ireland...

...the Guide

The comprehensive guide to great food and gorgeous
places to stay throughout Ireland - simply indispensable!

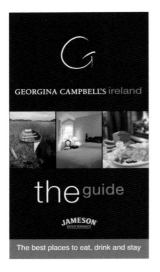

512 page, colour features

€20 US$20 Stg£14.99

ISBN 1-903164-12-5

"Ireland's premier guide"
The London Guardian

"encyclopaedic"
Tom Doorley, The Irish Times

"This is the business"
Cara Magazine

"By far the most reliable"
Food & Wine Magazine

...Best of the Best

A highly selective, full colour guide
to the very best of Irish hospitality,
north and south

256 page, full colour -
€20 US$20 Stg£14.99

ISBN 1-903164-21-4

**"This simple and user-friendly guide
is crammed full of colour photographs
and useful titbits; a discerning guide
to the very best of Irish hospitality."**
Dubliner Magazine

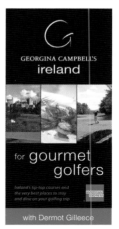

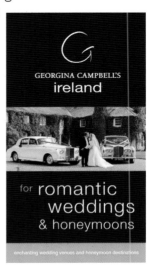

www.ireland-guide.com

Georgina Campbell's www.ireland-guide.com is a rapidly growing online guide to quality Irish hospitality based on the critically acclaimed series of published guides "Georgina Campbell's Ireland."

It currently includes:

▸ Hospitality – independently assessed descriptions to the best of Irish hospitality divided into three main areas – Eat, Drink & Stay.

▸ Establishments – can be found through searches by location, price bands, cuisine type and/or facilities/activities provided and many more criteria. We cover a broad range of hospitality including hotels, restaurants, pubs, castles, cafes, guesthouses, B&Bs etc.

▸ Travel Ireland – information on all regions and the 32 counties of Ireland, activities throughout the country and travel features. There are also sample itineraries and useful links to help users to plan their Irish holiday. They can also book ferry tickets and hire cars through our travel partners.

▸ Award Winners – An area that outlines all of our award winners over the years highlighting the very best of Irish hospitality

▸ Shopping – ireland-guide.com Book Shop, users can purchase all of Georgina Campbell's guide books and cook books online.

▸ www.golf.ireland-guide.com - this new sub-site to Irish golf and hospitality is the most comprehensive and user friendly site for the discerning traveller planning a golfing trip (holiday or weekend break) in Ireland. Ireland's best golf courses are linked to the finest hospitality in their locality.